1

away from home"!

That is the situation that I found myself in after working at home for twenty-odd years. Yes, I had been away a few days here, a week there, but things were all about to change. Circumstances were about to take me further a-field, out of commuting distance, off to other countries, away from family and friends, **away from a much loved Montrose Football Club**.

Departing into the unknown I had a wife who could not see me off from the railway station- we had never been parted- two boys who acted as though they weren't really bothered, but I could see the look on their faces. **It was a shock to the system, but a bigger shock was yet to come.**

Have you ever tried to support your team away from home!

Season 2005 – 2006 & the story of supporting Montrose FC
while being - Drawn AWAY from HOME

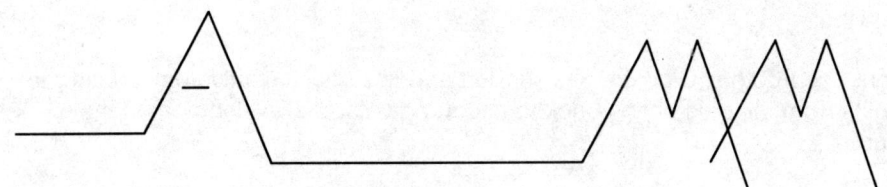

In Memory

David Stott, supporter (sadly missed).

Allan Kennedy, player and striker (he gave the supporters a season to remember).

Willie Johnston, Honorary President of the Club, who died during the writing of this book. A loyal servant of Montrose F.C.

To

Janet, for the faith and support given when I found myself in an untenable position and for holding things together while I am working away from home.

Gareth, for his weekly Montrose F.C. updates as co-author, sceptic and – "who undoubtedly is the worst referee".

Bryce, for his frequent visits to the Netherlands, giving much needed enthusiasm, spontaneity, ideas and ultimately publishing advice.

For

Montrose Football Club, to give support and financial incentive by donating all profits from the sale of this book to encourage Youth Development at the Club.

Finally

To all who buy this book, in anticipation, THANK YOU!

Forward

'Why? Because we only sing when we're winning! Maybe it was when I was last home before the 2004 season ended, standing by the "knoll" looking across Links Park down the tunnel waiting for the teams to emerge headed by "Spec Saver's" man of the day, the referee. The Proclaimer's blast out over the tannoy, I'm Gonna Be (I would walk five hundred miles), how many fans or supporters would walk, some before the game ended, some muttering never to come back. "The Complainer's".

If only people would support the team and back the Board. Henry Hall is the best manager we have had since the days of John Holt when Montrose last gained promotion. New ideas are needed to raise revenue and this can only be done if people give the team the support required through good times and bad. Leaving Links Park that day I thought, it certainly is a challenge!

I 'm no mastermind, and I've never attempted to write a book before but for several years now I have worked away from home. I have suffered the frustrations of not knowing, and not being part of, community life. This book is for Montrose Football Club, something for the community and something to do just to keep a lonesome sanity.

In writing "Drawn Away from Home", I have tried to capture my feelings and frustrations, and experiences which I have encountered as a professional engineer, a father, and that of a rose tinted supporter who dreams of better days and a season to remember!

A.M.Miller

Acknowledgements

- Montrose Football Club
- Ian Paterson Photography (Club Photographer)

- The Press
    - Montrose Review
    - The Courier & DC Thomson
    - Press and Journal
    - Daily Record, Freelance Journalists

- Gable End Grafitti

- Montrose Dynamo

- Mo Mo SuperMo

- Pie and Bovril

- Internet Web Site inclusions

Copyright Notice -

First published 2006
By Lulu Publishing Limited
www.lulu.com

copyright © A.M.Miller

Chapter and Verse

Brief Overview of Montrose and the Football Club

The town -
It is said, "Here's the Basin, there's Montrose, shut your een and haud your nose". A seaport and market town surrounded by water on three sides with the Basin providing a sanctuary for nature and a pungent smell.
Population eleven thousand and six-hundred, with locals referred to as "Gable Endies", a legacy from the town's eighteenth century architectural styles when merchants built their houses with the gable end to the street.

The Club –
It was my seventh birthday, I walked out onto Links Park hand held by club captain Dave Paterson, it was against Stenhousemuir, we won and I was mascot for the day. Memories of what seemed a long time ago, but the club has been there for much longer than I can remember.

Founded in 1879, winners of the Qualifying Cup and admitted to League Division Two in season 1929. Securing a mid-table position in their first season, Montrose's league status was interrupted by the Second World War in season 1939-40 with only four games having been played. When the leagues were resurrected in 1945-46, there was no place for Montrose in 'B' Division. After spending a few seasons in 'C' Division Montrose were finally accepted into 'B' Division in season 1955-56 and have been a fixture of the Scottish League scene ever since. League structures have changed over the years, Clubs have had up and down seasons, some have grown and some seek to avoid going into administration.

Honours have been few, season 1984-85 saw Montrose as Second Division champions and they were also runners-up in 1990-91. Promotion from Division Three was also achieved during season 1994-95 but there has been little to cheer about for ten years now, honours are thin, only games are remembered, one offs.

The team is managed by Henry Hall, who some may remember in his playing days with Dundee United and St Johnstone before he went into coaching and management. Kerrigan, Webster and cult hero of the "knoll", Barry Donnachie, are not household names. It is only when you support a diddy team that these names may mean something and from there, a love grows!

G.B.Miller

Preface

"It's a funny old game", quoted Jimmy Greaves and I am not talking about football. One day everything is fine the next you find yourself "drawn away from home"!

That is the situation that I found myself in after working at home for twenty-odd years. Yes, I had been away a few days here, a week there but things were all about to change. Circumstances were about to take me further a-field, out of commuting distance, off to other countries, away form family and friends, away from a much loved Montrose Football Club.

I have always had a passion for the game of football and have been a firm believer in supporting my local side, through thick and thin, good times and bad. You might say who would support East Stirlingshire, a team that has languished in the depths of Division Three for so many seasons. Well I can – it was my local team. Before moving to Montrose some seventeen years ago, I was a "Portonian", a native of Grangemouth. So yes, I am another incomer!

My work targets the bio-pharmaceutical industry and in particular project control and management. I am now officially termed self-employed, no work, no money. So basically contractors are never sick, they can't afford to be. You have to go where people require your expertise and knowledge. I vividly remember my first venture into the unknown and believe me it is an unknown out there. There are so many different cultures and languages, laws and rules, speed limits and road signs. Departing into the unknown I had a wife who could not see me off from the railway station, we had never really been apart, two boys who acted as they weren't really bothered, but I could see the look on their faces. It was a shock to the system, but a bigger shock was yet to come. **Have you ever tried to support your team away from home!**

The story begins here…

Chapter 1

Drawn Away from Home

Season 2004/2005 has ended, respite for the players, but not for the supporter. The media wheels still turn, albeit slowly, season 2005/2006 beckons. Rumours are rife, body language had told the story of the expectations of some players who were out of contract. Wood, Sharp and Smart looked to be on their way to other clubs, the manager Henry Hall has a new team to build and quick.

But first, where am I?

Same work, different city.I find myself in the Netherlands (not Holland! The Dutch don't like it being called Holland) in the City of Breda, boasting one hundred and sixty thousand of a population. The city architecture is similar to the gable ends of Montrose and it is surrounded by canal waterways. The Grote Markt, the central point signified by the Cathedral and square, hosts many cafés, bars and restaurants. I am accommodated in Baronie, a quiet, residential area of Breda not far from my work kennel. Luckily I have the use of a bicycle, Dutch transport for all, priority over pedestrians and cars, and very economical. NAC Breda is the local top-flight football side and they play in the Dutch First Division and have just signed Pierre Van Hooijdonk, the ex Celtic player, for next seasons campaign. The expectations are high!

When I arrived, I found that the majority of Dutch residents could speak some English and that the initial learning curve would not be as steep as I first envisaged or have experienced with language problems in the past. How do you explain that you want to buy a tin opener to a Kazak? In this case I eventually gave up after being offered toasters, food mixers and a cheese grater. In these situations you find that you have to make the best of things and be able to laugh. Laughter is a great safety valve as you can find yourself very much on your own without conversation and without a link to necessities of life – WHAT WAS THE MONTROSE SCORE? It can be so frustrating, you wish you were there, you look at the clock, in your mind you kick-off, then it's half time and then the mental arithmetic kicks in – if we win today we will be second. It's true, don't count your chickens before they hatch, it's a lesson learned.

Have you ever tried to support your team away from home?!!! Let me get my frustrations out one by one. Many places where I have worked have internet- great to have the access-only to find that the IT department have applied the letter of the law and made the company a secure site. This happened to me some time ago while in Ireland of all places, www.montrosefc.co.uk , access denied, sport is a non-work related topic. Everybody talks about sport at work, that's why we go to work! Companies are paranoid, productivity means more to them than a happy workforce. Imagine the time I could waste, if I not only surfed the net but also smoked and had a weak bladder. We are professional beings, we can surf and smoke during lunch, a time that is often taken up by meetings.

Aragghh! – Then there are the web sites themselves!
A) They are not kept up to date.
B) The servers are down or url page cannot be found.
C) You get three lines which constitute a full and detailed match report, apparently, which also turns out to be woefully incorrect. Then low and behold you realise that Henry Hall has played the match with ten men and three substitutes, this is reflected in the reported team lines. Frustration, frustration, frustration! Thankfully we now have www.gableendgraffiti.co.uk a well informed, regularly updated, frank and forthright blog! posted by 'Steeplejack' another 'incomer'. The newspapers are no better. In USA Today (equivalent to the Scottish Sun but without 'Page 3') you might just be lucky to see printed the English Premier results- they may unexpectedly appear in Tuesday's edition.

Concerning location, Montrose is in the unfortunate or fortunate position whatever way you look at it, always above Arbroath on the map. The town is in the county of Angus but borders the Grampian region. The local newspapers for this area are, *The Courier*, a Dundee paper which is printed by DC Thomson, and there is also the Aberdeen based paper, *The Press and Journal*. Both papers apparently serve to report on the local football teams in their area. However, coverage once again of the lower divisions suffers, and other than a Saturday and a Monday edition there is little to focus on. So can you just imagine asking for a Courier or a Press and Journal newspaper abroad? Even our English neighbours would give me a strange look and think: "What is he on"? A few times, more by luck, I was actually able to pick up a "Sunday Mail" in Ireland (The South). I had gone for petrol one Sunday and it was early morning, well nine am. - that's early for a Sunday. The garage was just opening and the attendant was cutting the string that binds the newspapers and there on the top was the *Sunday Mail*, a big red beacon of hope for lower league match reports. I picked up the paper (it was one euro), the attendant smiled, and said "We only get three of these". Well after that there was no longer any extra hours in bed on a Sunday.

The paper had been printed in Northern Ireland, obviously for the Glasgow Rangers contingent but a few had found their way across the border to appease the Celtic masses. In the Netherlands the prices of alleged home based newspapers (usually only printed across the border in Belgium) vary vastly. They sell for between two and three euros (two pounds ten pence). Sunday papers are more expensive, that is if you can obtain one, as the shops are closed except on *Koopzondag*, the first Sunday of each month, when the Dutch shop till they drop. I find that usually the train station, albeit later in the day, has a selection of two: *The Telegraph* and *The Times*. Such choice! The news may be up market, but there is no mention of Montrose F.C. Such is the way when you support a supposed 'diddy' team.

In this day of satellite technology you would think that you would be able to tune into most television programmes no matter the time delay. Saturday night in Atyrau, Kazakhstan, for me, was viewing an English premiership game. Atyrau had clear blue skies, there wasn't what we would call a cloud, but always at the critical second, the signal would go down, or someone staying in the building (nine storey 'oil money built' apartments) would go up to the roof, and adjust the communal satellite dish receiver. This usually resulted in no television for the remainder of the weekend. During my work in Ireland, I had the UK channels BBC 1 and 2. On a Saturday I would return from work to watch *Final Score* (on the spot reports). The vide-printer brings in the goals when they happen, and the final score as the games draw to an end, proceeded by the round up, division by division, of the latest score. What more can someone ask for? An ideal programme for armchair fans and for those of us (there are many) working away from the action.

Well, let me tell you what can go wrong and what is wrong. The programme comes on with a great flourish and the obligatory English Premiership latest score and scorers are pushed to the fore. There is a panel at the side of the screen that continuously rotates, updating you with the four English Divisions and then on to the Conference Division and then the Scottish Divisions. This is where I blow a gasket, they only have the Scottish Premier and First Division – oh to be promoted by two divisions! So I wait watching the vide-printer intensely, hoping that Montrose will score so that I can see the current score, or the full time result. Two options. The result was no late goals for the Mo, and yes, you've guessed it, the full time score was missed on the vide-printer as a live report was broadcast from some premiership ground, reporting on a nil-nil draw. Still, the full-time classified results will be on at five minutes to five, so parked in the chair, I go through the agony of the four English Divisions and the Conference League. At last: Scottish Football. The voice announces "The Scottish Premier League" and then Division One. I hear the voice say Arbroath nil (they are at home this day), there is silence, a Chick Young look-alike appears with the full round-up of football in Northern Ireland. They have only switched to BBC Northern Ireland before the end of the transmission! I really despair at times! So it's then down to the shopping centre and the television shop to stare through the window at Sky Sports Soccer Saturday with the legendary Jeff Stirling for the round up. Talk about the wee boy at the sweetie shop window!

Usually the radio is a non-starter anywhere, but there have been a few faint signals of Radio Scotland on the car radio here in Breda. It was enough for me to invest in a DAB radio, by far a stronger transmitted signal, I should be all set now. Unknown to me there is no DAB signal in Holland. There I have said it. Holland, Holland, Holland! Scuppered yet again. So as you can see it is very difficult to support your team when you are away from home, especially if they are in the lower divisions and hence the need for Montrose to attain promotion this season. But first, the manager, Henry Hall, has to build a team and I have a project in conceptual design phase to progress, the similarities are startling.

Project work is like a season. A timeline has a start date and a completion date. Between these two points a game is played both tactically and politically, for what ever reason, but is usually financially motivated. I have always seen my job as being the same as that of a football manager, receiving plaudits when the project is going well but criticised when things are falling apart. You are always looking for a positive result, motivating others to achieve it, and, in the end, left managing the resources available within a restricted budget that someone else has set for you.

If it all sounds too familiar, it is because it is not too different from Henry Hall's impending season of 2005 – 2006. Through the years I have accepted the fact that you are only as good as your last job, or in Henry's case: season. We do not all have crystal balls, we must stay focused and target our dreams by achieving our goals – that's what gives job satisfaction and is the reason why we play this game, so join the club!

When starting any project, if you spend time on the front-end preparation, no matter how arduous a task is, you will then reap the benefits later when it really matters. Too often people take the easy approach, thinking that they have all the time in the world, only to find that it catches up with them. Pre-season is important for the following reasons: the making of signings; resurrection of fitness levels and trying out new playing formations; preparing for when it matters; and the day the team has to stand up to be counted. If you fail to plan – you plan to fail. An old cliché, but sadly one that is true, and one that we fall foul of time and time again, thinking that it will just automatically happen. For Henry, he must eye promotion. What manager wouldn't? But like myself, the quest is to win, and more importantly, fulfil the challenge that has been set!

'Conceptual design' is an engineering term used for initial options available in a proposed build, deciding things like steel or concrete structure: a glazed or cladding façade? It is a basis to build a project on, or in this case: a team. Some additions could eventually turn out to be a wish list. Wishing for a goalkeeper, a defender, and prolific goal-scorer is every manager's dream. I wish!

Indicative costs are formulated, estimates are proposed, and budgets are initiated in order to proceed with design studies or, in Henry's case, a budget to sign players. This, for the manager, dictates what he can't afford and what he can, leaving him to trim his cloth to suit, sometimes to the detriment of team balance.

Henry has been left with a first team squad that could compete in a five-a-side league. Having been accused of leaving signings too late last season by some supporters, the manger and coach have the concept of design to rebuild the team for next season, bearing in mind that pre-season is only around the corner and that training will start on June 21st. The board are supportive and a budget for next season is given. With the team from last season reduced to Elliot Smith and Neil Stephen, it is important that Montrose move quickly to either re-sign those out of contract or start negotiations with players from opposing clubs or those who have been released by their clubs. It looked a daunting task, Henry was already resigned to losing 'striker' Martin Wood and goal-scoring midfielder Craig Smart, but was hopeful that left-winger Graeme Sharp might stay at the club. Proven goal-scorers all three, with Craig Smart the club's leading scorer for the season just gone. A void has to be filled, but you can't rush these things unless, that is, you have been in talks before the season has ended. Speculation prior to the last game of the season was that Wood and Sharp would be joining Peterhead who were promoted to division two as runners up. Smart on the other hand was reported to be in talks with Raith, Cowdenbeath and East Fife. How true this was, no one knew, but the body-language was all too telling.

Re-signings of previous squad players take place. *Junior Hall* (Euan) is first. Presumably this was discussed at the tea-table. Others follow: Webster, Dodds, and defender Stuart Ferguson put pen to paper. The latter faces an operation, on a cruciate ligament injury to his knee that will keep him out of action until December. Six players signed, and one walking wounded!

At last, on June 10th, there is a flurry of newspaper articles and commotion on various web sites - Montrose adds four new faces. After some speculation, defender Paul Doyle, who was on loan from Clyde last term, signs on a permanent basis, after having an excellent season at Links Park. Paul only just failed to pip Neil Stephen for player of the year when on loan. His release from Clyde is Montrose's gain. The other three additions are new to the club: Willie Martin, a striker from Elgin City (top scorer with 10 goals last season), is a player who gives 120% effort, digs deep and will chase lost causes. He is a very welcome addition to the side and will give a bit of height to the front line. Midfielders Martyn Fotheringham and Andy Cargill also sign. Fotheringham arrives from first division side St. Johnstone after being given a free transfer by Saint's new manager Owen Coyle, after only viewing him in one reserve match. Martyn was on loan to near neighbour Brechin last season, and is a very exciting and intriguing prospect for the Montrose fans for the season ahead. Cargill has played for fellow Angus clubs, Forfar and Arbroath, and was recently released from Ayr United. He is a versatile player with a physical presence who has a lot of experience which I hope he can pass on to the younger team members. So far, so good!

Just so fans don't forget about the game, the Bells Cup first round draw is published on Friday May 27th. Montrose are again drawn away from home, this time it is in a different direction, to Dingwall, and the farthest north league club, First Division Ross County. I am sure Alex Smith, Ross County's manager will be happy with the draw, or will he?

First reaction is that it is a good draw financially as the ties are being played on the 30th July and are sure to draw a crowd of three thousand plus. It's the first game of the season-who knows we might just knock-out last years runners-up and proceed to the next round. Then again, we might pick up injuries with the game being so tough and also early in the season. The league is more important and a good start is imperative.

Footballers have short careers. Football managers, you would think, would be longer, but in this world of success it can be the sword that strikes when results are not going the way the board would like. Sadly for Alex Smith, his term in office at Ross County came to an abrupt end on returning from holiday. If we only back-track to April 23rd. we find Smith accepting and signing a new one-year contract. He stated that he saw it as a great compliment from the club to be able to potentially target and appoint a successor such as Paul Lambert, initially as a player coach when he leaves Celtic in the summer. June 10th, Smith receives MBE in the Queens Birthday Honour's List. Later that day, Ross County severed Smith's contract and an end of an era at Dingwall. John Robertson, the ex- Inverness Caley Thistle and short lived Hearts boss, has since been appointed. It reminds me of my own situation and the lyric "What a difference a day makes, just 24 little hours".

Pre-season games are lined up in the form of a strong Aberdeen side, near neighbours Forfar, and two games against Highland league opposition Deveronvale and Duncan Shearer's Buckie Thistle. All games are at Links Park, but to that in a later chapter, Montrose still doesn't have enough bodies to form a team.

More negotiations seem to be taking place, wish lists are coming into effect, and web site message board contributors/supporters are making suggestions, spreading more rumours, unable to detect fact from fiction. I am glad that Henry Hall is his own man, after all, the buck stops with him and only him. If he had to manage a team picked by the supporters this would surely fail. I have seen it so often where a client insists upon a certain person to lead a project. Nine times out of ten, said person is out of their depth and displays a lack of competence.

Rumours, rumours and more rumours, but nothing concrete. How big a squad do we really need, Henry will know the answer to this question. You can do the sums, eleven for a team plus five on the bench plus twenty percent for injury and suspension. Socks and shoes off and that comes to twenty. Will the budget support this number? Only time will confirm this projection. Last Season I felt that due to injury and some suspensions- not many as Montrose did have a good record of discipline, on the field- players were asked to play out of position to cover the spaces vacated by the suspended. It is important to have a squad that has depth and the options and versatility to cover. Montrose full-back, Barry Donnachie, picked up a few bookings last season. He is a talented player who tackles hard and is good on the overlap. Most bookings he incurred were for chuntering on at the referee and linesmen – aptly sponsored by Spec Savers. Henry's teaching skills are to the fore, usually in the first half when he is able to keep his pupil in check down the dug-out side. The problem comes in the second half when Barry is playing parallel to the "knoll" a mound on the north touchline, a soap-box for hecklers, where, egged on by the support, he inevitably delivers a speech worthy of a booking and the linesman's raised flag. One game that I did witness last season was against Stenhousemuir, along with a bird's eye view of the sending off of Craig Smart. Professional players must respect one another and play the game to the rules. The sending off was only worthy of a booking, if that, and the antics of the opposing player was worthy of an Oscar!

Names of possible signings start to emerge from the "Chinese Whispers" and further intuition is required to work out some of the other clues that are revealed. For instance, word is, Montrose are interested in a goalkeeper who has been released from a top five premier league club. Scanning last years team squads, Hibernian have released an Aberdeen born goalkeeper, so the rumours start. One player that Montrose do have interest in, is local lad, Greg Henslee. Arbroath are reputed to be looking for £15,000 for his services. Peterhead are interested in the player, but are only willing to part with £4,000 and have yet to offer Montrose money for signing Wood and Sharp, payment which seems to be in limbo. Another case of don't count your chickens. Henslee would be a great signing for the club. Although he plays midfield for Arbroath, I would tend to play him as the ultimate striker. I remember him as a lad playing with the Montrose Cub Pack, and one game in particular. Montrose Cubs were playing Forfar on a Saturday morning, the game was just into the second half and it was the time when Montrose F.C. were managed by Jim Leishman. A car drew up close to the park down at Broomfield and out jumped a director from the club. The car engine was left running, he had been sent down to see if there were any local possibilities that Leishman should watch. Within three minutes he turned on his heels stating nothing here then, and drove off. Not only was Greg Henslee playing that day but also Kevin Webster a player who has been with Montrose for a few seasons. At least four other players that day have since played in the junior ranks. I thought it was an opportunity missed as his striking power was tremendous for his age.

The defence is short of cover but there are players who are versatile enough to step into the breach. Another defender would not go a-miss, but who knows what is in Henry's mind.

If it ain't broke, why fix it! May 28th the Scottish Football League announced at their A.G.M. that a play-off system would be introduced for the coming season. Next season's Third Division winners will automatically go up to Division Two. The teams aspiring to second, third and fourth spots will play-off with the ninth placed side of Division Two. All I can say is that Montrose must firmly make the number one spot theirs as it is the only way to guarantee promotion!

Pre-season training begins, first training session at Caird Park in Dundee. Henry Hall has succeeded in signing five of last season's squad on one year deals. The five players include, club captain Steve Kerrigan, goalkeeper Michael Hankinson, defender Barry Donnachie and strikers Calum 'Laurencekirk Assasin' Watson and ex Dundee and Arbroath striker Duncan Mclean. All put pen to paper, giving Henry a squad of 17 signed players but he also confirms that he is looking for another three players. Marc Connelly, who seemingly has scored over one hundred goals in the Dundee Sunday leagues in consecutive seasons is offered pre-season training with the squad with a view to sign if he makes the grade. Jim Butter has also signed or has he? That's the trouble with working away, you sometimes surmise, but at thirty-nine I think Jim Butter's goalkeeping skills will be reserved for the bench and the coaching of young Michael Hankinson and possibly A.N.Other!

2005-2006 Fixtures are out! I troll though the dates to see if I will be able to catch any of the games prior to Christmas. I see two possibilities, funnily enough, our home derby game against local side Arbroath on August 27th and our away game on November 5th. Yes it's Arbroath again but at Gayfield (look out your winter woollies). The rest of the games which coincide with my infrequent visits are out, as I have other things to tend too, things that get neglected, notably family. Montrose kick-off their league campaign at Elgin on August 6th a day for supporters to play dodge the caravan on their journey to Borough Briggs. I also notice that there are two clear Saturdays early on in the season, September 3rd. and October 8th. It would be good to arrange a friendly game possibly against Brechin to enable the team to gel and gain consistency in their play. There is also a mid-week game against Albion Rovers pencilled in for October 25th. Other free dates could be 10th.December and 7th. January if we fail to get past the first round of the Scottish Cup on the 19th of November. One more fact which alarmed me a bit, is that prior to Christmas, Montrose have only eight home games and will have played ten away. It is not good for the coffers or for hospitality. Let's hope that the two home games at New Year bring in a good crowd of travelling supporters from East Fife and locals from Arbroath.

Further news in today's "Courier", Montrose look ready to step in for Greg Henslee. That is good news! His move to Peterhead is now at an impasse in negotiations and he soon could become a Montrose player. Henry has also stated that now that he has seventeen players on the books, he would be looking for another three players to finalise the squad. Previous calculations of a squad of twenty were in the right ball-park- time will tell who the three additions might be. Greg Henslee looks like being one and you still can't rule out the return of Wood and Sharp as Peterhead have still to come up with a suitable offer. I personally would prefer the addition of a goalkeeper and possibly the return of Sharp. Also in the running is Stephen "Chippy" Fraser, an on loan player from the latter part of last season, but having since been released by St. Johnstone.

June 18th., the Intertoto Cup first round ties started today, unbelievable when you think that Montrose have yet to start training for the new season. Clubs that tend to participate in the pointless yet potentially money spinning exercise usually have poor seasons.

By the end of June the full squad should be in place, but pre-season training sessions started on Tuesday June 21st, a six week run into the first competitive game at Dingwall. Montrose are training Tuesday, Thursday and Saturday, in order to build up fitness. Three weeks into the regime comes the first friendly match on July 12[th,] against Aberdeen. I hope that players do not pick-up injuries in these games, but it also vitally important to attain match fitness for the long arduous season ahead. Four days later, Forfar are visitors and three days after that, Highland league side Deveronvale serve as opposition. Three games in one week, followed by a fixture against another Highland league outfit, Buckie Thistle, the following Saturday and one week away from the trip to Ross County and John Robertson's baptism at Victoria Park.

If you fail to plan, you plan to fail – it's a tight schedule. The season seems to start earlier each year. When I was a lad (a long time ago) the season started mid August with the League Cup, eight sections of four teams and a ninth with the remaining five sides. You may say an uneven number but East Stirlingshire had moved to Clydebank thus attaining the name ES Clydebank with the Steadman brothers. Finally after some supporter intervention the courts rule the return of East Stirlingshire to Falkirk but Clydebank remained in the league- thus thirty-seven sides. I remember the return to Firs Park; a pipe band led the march from the supporters club in Grahams Road into Firs Street. The park had been closed for some time, members opened the turnstiles only for the support to find the terraces knee high in grass and weeds and a football pitch of dandelions. Alloa supporters that night must have thought Recreation Park was a mansion!

The League Cup at that time was based on league play with the section winners and runners up going through to a knock-out stage. There was a lot to be said for this type of tournament, as you were paired with at least one "Premier Club" and this was a good early season money spinner for clubs in lower divisions. I wish the Scottish League would re-think and return the tournament to this strategy, if only to give a life-line to clubs in the lower divisions. Another case of "If it ain't broke why fix it"! This constant tinkering of rules and regulations is always to benefit the bigger clubs who only have their own interests at heart.

June 28th, A press release and another signing. I was a bit surprised as I thought this will be the signing of Henslee but the papers revealed in the morning that the signing is a goalkeeper, twenty year old Andrew Reid, released by Scottish Premier League club, Hibernian. Not a lot is known about the young Aberdeen lad, except that he was a Scottish schoolboy internationalist and had served a three year apprenticeship with Nottingham Forest. He also had a spell with Motherwell before joining the Hi-bee's. It's good to see that Montrose can attract a player from a Premier League club, the lure of regular competitive first team football being the obvious attraction. I am sure his full time training status at Hibs will stand him in good stead and that he will be given his chance during pre-season games to claim or at least challenge for the number one spot. Midfielder Stephen Fraser also puts pen to paper. This was one of the possibilities that I had mentioned but was unsure of but obviously Henry Hall saw enough during his loan spell last season to sign him permanently.

So the squad is now nineteen, one spot to fill (according to Henry or my arithmetical genius of 17 + 2 = 19), I REALLY HOPE IT'S HENNER!

Tonight, Woensdag (Wednesday), I watch a Dutch football programme which is looking at training methods and team building which they applied to a youth league team. At the beginning of the programme emphasis was on the importance of keeping shape and formation, moving forward as a team. This was eventually put in to play with each player linked by a tape around their waist which had to be kept taut. They organised a day's team building taking the young lads into a studio to cut a demo recording disc. Who were the leaders and who was game enough to front the microphone? Next day the lads were informed that a few five-a-side matches had been arranged. They were taken to a warehouse, and in rode the Harley Davison brigade. The biggest bikers you have seen, tattoos and all. The games were rough, boys became men, and Dutch courage was required by the young lads. It was nice to see at the end, the team, not the manager voting for their choice of captain and the armband being placed on the chosen one. There are no English sub-titles, you only pick up a word here or there and you rely on the picture telling the story. Just another hazard of being drawn away from home!

I receive a call, "Did you see the "Courier"?" How could I, I am away from home! "Oh sorry, it was sometime last week." "When?" "I really can't remember, maybe it was today." When women read the paper it's usually "Hatches, Matches and Dispatches". They read the paper from front to back but sometimes they get the news back to front. The number of times I have received false scores, hopes built up only to find out days later that the score was in reverse. So what should I know? The paper said that Arbroath's manager (Harry Cairney) was hopeful of re-signing Greg Henslee as Peterhead had failed to make a fresh bid for the player. Hopes are dashed!

Waiting for news of the signing is like waiting for concrete to dry or cure before you can polish and harden the top surface. I remember it was my turn to be the late man, the janitor for those contractors working late. The concrete was laid at noon, it was Ireland, it was damp, that's why Ireland is the "Emerald Isle" and so green. They even have green post boxes. What is wrong with fire engine red! Anyway, the day ended at six o' clock, three left on-site, should be finished by eight or nine. It rained, it stopped, and it rained again. Nine became ten, midnight struck, then one and two. Hope diminished- there was no way the concrete could be polished. It was a long day, and night, with early morning hours, three hours sleep, and another day ahead. So another day and another dollar! Have Peterhead settled the bill for Wood and Sharp?

O ye of little faith, HENNER HAS SIGNED! The waiting is over, another day and another signing, the seventh of the season. Who says? Well it's on the message board and a reliable web site. It must be, it's got to be, but in the morning there is nothing in the brief sport crumbs that are posted on the Courier and P&J web pages. It's a definite maybe, SORTED!

There now is a new squad with a new dawn and the prospect of a great season. The Board should be commended for the support that they have given Henry Hall to secure this squad of players.

It's the end of the month (June) and it's monthly report time - a pain, a lot of effort, who reads them? Dam few! They are also out of date, as it is nearly the end of the following month before they are issued. What is the point! Spreadsheets with financial terms such as committed expenditure, spend to date, yield (let's hope for Montrose that it's promotion), needs for contingency or management reserve. It asks the question, will further funds be made available if required later in the season? Tables and more tables, looking for progress – design 100%, procurement 100% (seven players, what a coup!), pre-season 20%, execution – NIL! A manager sticks his head around the office door-way, will you remember to include the change summary in this months report. Yes, Henry, the table reads –

Players - IN	Players - OUT	On the MOVE
Paul Doyle – ex Clyde	Darren Spink	Ross Graham to East Fife
Andy Cargill – ex Ayr	Matt Slater	Craig Smart to East Fife
Martyn Fortheringham	Daryn Smith	Graham Sharp to

– ex SJ		Peterhead
Willie Martin – ex Elgin		Martin Wood to Peterhead
Andrew Reid – ex Hibernian		
Stephen Fraser – ex SJ		
Greg Henslee – ex Arbroath		

Henry Hall has used his budget well and shown great stealth in pursuing his players of choice and in time for the new season. On paper he has delivered a talented squad. On the pitch, only time will tell, but today we look forward as a milestone has been achieved.

The 'Pie and Bovril' message board tom- toms rumble and posts of a two-horse race appear, along with the names of Montrose and Stenhousemuir. Last season the league was over by Christmas. There was only going to be one winner (Gretna) and Peterhead were close on their heels. The remaining teams were all taking points off each other and were evenly matched. The message boards predicted a competitive league next year and everyone had the same consensus of opinion. Signings seem to have changed opinions, it's too early to tell, not a game has been played, and friendlies are not due to kick-off until July 6th. Why the panic? I for one don't want a re-run of last season or for it to be finished early on, a possible reason for the Scottish League committee introducing the play-off system for this season.

The following day, Saturday brings further details on the Greg Henslee signing, it is confirmed on the Arbroath web site and is in the Courier. I'm home next week and there will be more news in the Montrose Review, maybe things will be a bit clearer.

The weekend is over and it is Monday once more, there are some new posts on the message board of the club's unofficial web site. Clarification is given on the Greg Henslee signing, as the club gratefully acknowledge the Gable Endies' Supporter's Trust and the role they played in brokering the deal. Trust the trust! The manager also hints at more signings in the coming weeks, maybe a few trialists will get a run out during the pre-season friendlies and stake a claim in the squad. Wait, hold the press! More signings, what happened to the squad of twenty? The Courier quoted, Hall, who now has 17 players on his books, said, "I am looking for another three players." That was reported on June 23rd. Since then three players have signed, goalkeeper Reid, Fraser and Henslee. On the club web, Henry states, "There are eighteen players in the squad now, but I still feel that there are a couple of

areas where we can improve, and we will look to see who's available."
Eighteen, I look at the player's link, it has been updated and eighteen players
are listed but no mention of Stephen Fraser. There are three goalkeepers,
Butter, Hankinson and Reid. Has Jim Butter put pen to paper? The remaining
fifteen are made up of six defenders, six midfielders, and three forwards,
making the squad of eighteen. Now I am totally confused, don't know what to
believe, including what has been reported. Third division sides do not get
enough media coverage and there is often a distinct lack of interest by the
press. Reports are brief and relegated to the columns hosting the football
snips. It's sad to say, but the Old Firm rule the roost, the Aberdeens and other
premier clubs fall in behind in the pecking order. Beyond that, the English
premiership teams are even now hoarding the space set a side in the
columns of the Scottish dailies. So what chance has Montrose F.C., for a turn
in the media spotlight!

'Whilst working in Waterford, community television was popular and
even here in Breda they have their own local station. They may only transmit
for a few hours a day, but they interview and cover what is happening in the
community and of local interest. It really puts towns on the map.

Season tickets are on sale and prices have risen. The Scottish League
had increased Division Three gate prices to £9. For the few games that I will
see this coming season I will pay gate prices but truly hope that supporters
will invest in a season ticket. It's money up front for the club, It's interest in the
bank. I often think that sponsorship is the way forward but looking at the club
programme last season I was disappointed to see many players un-
sponsored. If businesses and shops in Montrose would only sponsor a player
it would help to generate much needed funds and also in return bring some
added retail back into the town on a Saturday. As I am self-employed I feel
my statement is a bit like the pot calling the kettle black. So this season I will
invest in the sponsorship of a player, after all it's the price of season ticket
and the price of my absence. I will set it up on my visit home prior to the
Aberdeen pre-season friendly. It will also give me someone to follow at a
distance through the season, but who?

The deed is done and I decided to sponsor Andy Reid the goalkeeper and by chance had a few words with him on Saturday, as Gareth bought his season ticket at club vice-chairman Robert Ritchie's shop. At first sight Reid is a big lad, fairly tall and stands well, he tells me he is playing the first half of the Aberdeen game. It's good to see that he is getting a chance to claim the number one spot as I hope I am not sponsoring the bench for the season. I wish him good luck for the Aberdeen game before I depart out onto Murray Street and into the sunshine.

The Challenge Cup first round ties were drawn July 19th and Montrose secure a home draw against First Division opponents Clyde. It is several years since the two clubs have met. If I remember rightly, Montrose were managerless (before the appointment of Dave Smith from Whitehill Welfare) and Clyde had the one and only Charlie Nicholas playing who was at that time coming to the end of his career.

Clyde has undergone vast changes in personnel due to financial difficulties that beset the club. Manager Billy Reid has left the club to takeover the managerial seat at Hamilton Academicals. Several players have followed their manager's example in signing for clubs who can pay a full-time wage. Ex – Tottenham and Glasgow Rangers player Graham Roberts has filled the manager's seat and taken over at the helm. His young signings to date have been done in a trendy and media friendly "pop-idol" way. These trials led to a recruitment of players mainly freed from premier league youth and reserve sides, for example Scotland under 21 striker Tam Brighton released by Rangers.

It's an interesting tie and Montrose could cause an upset. Having home advantage is a bonus and this is definitely a game that Montrose can win.

Other games of note include the battle of the Campbell brothers, Ian and Dick, whose respective sides Brechin and Partick Thistle meet at Glebe Park, Cowdenbeath is at home to St.Johnstone and Forfar have home advantage against Ross County which could provide further upsets for First Division clubs. Both Dundee and St Mirren slipped the net to obtain byes. The ties are to be played August 9/10th.

Montrose are now well into pre-season and the supporters are back at Links Park. By the time the Challenge Cup was drawn, some games had taken place and players were playing for a place in the team!

Chapter 2

Pre-season (In the beginning)

Having now the concept of a team, the pre-season friendlies will hopefully blend and produce the best starting eleven for the new season. I find myself project-wise moving from conceptual design to pulling all the elements together and to making an execution plan for the upcoming project. I travel to see design consultants in Rotterdam and pass the stadium that is home to the fallen giants of Dutch football – Feyenoord; and visit Nijmegen where club side NEC play. The Netherlands is flat. There is no other word to explain it. It is easy to navigate and get around, after all you can only get lost. I find the Dutch very enthusiastic about sports and especially *voetbal*. Their game is well managed and a good youth structure is in place. I sometimes think back to Ivo den Biemen, over from Holland to study at Aberdeen University. He also played for Montrose, after being spotted playing for the University side. There are a lot of young Ivo's, the level of skill is excellent, but many will remain in the local Dutch junior leagues and fade into obscurity, undiscovered. Ivo took his chance with Montrose and was later transferred to Dundee. He also had spells with Falkirk and Dunfermline. He has now returned to Holland but is not in the Brabant telephone book!

On publication of the fixtures there is work to do, sponsorship deals and packages, match ball sponsors and hospitality, buses to organise and kit to arrange, plus hopefully a team photograph. To be top notch you have to at least look the part. Montrose for the coming season will be keeping the same home and away strips which is a bonus. It is one of the better strips and is well liked by the supporters. The home strip is a royal blue v-neck top with blue shorts and blue socks. Just what every wee boy should want on Christmas Day. Sadly it's not the case. They would rather sport the blue of Glasgow Rangers or a green Celtic jersey, there's nothing like supporting your local team. I feel sad when I see buses leaving or going through the town loaded with supporters travelling to the giants of the premier league. Gate prices are higher and a home game is still an away game when you consider the travelling they have to do. Then there is the cost of programmes, the grease laden and tongue burning Scottish pies (makes a Saturday a Saturday), not to mention liquid refreshments in a cup with added un-dissolved sediment. It's lost revenue for the small local clubs. The club's away strip is a lemon yellow. I don't know when or where the introduction of the colour yellow came in. Montrose's colours were always blue, white and red. If anything I would have thought that black would have been introduced as this was their colours back in 1879 when the club was founded. Blue,

Black and White. Inter Milan, Club Brugge and Chelsea and many more champions but not Montrose, but why not?

Traffic lights, red, amber and green, fluorescent colours to signify danger, we've had them all. Yes, goalkeepers need to be seen but why can't we just have the normal red, green or yellow jersey? Fashion parade over lads, comb your hair for the team photograph. Yet another hairstyle for Kerr Dodds. Henry, just brush yours to the side!

To be successful like any business, financial support is upper-most in the Board's mind. Resources that are available to them are limited. The town of Montrose has a population of eleven thousand and six hundred. Crowds in past seasons have been a fluctuating three to five hundred, depending on a winning streak. Help from sponsorship is required, but unlike major cities, industry in Montrose had been on the slide, the latest being employees of pharmaceutical giants GSK, who were facing final closure of the plant at the end of 2006. A major sponsor for a third division side, someone who is local and who has a passion for the club is a rare beast and only a lottery winning supporter would be able to give a sizeable injection of money. English Premiership giants tour countries such as China, Japan and Singapore. A short sharp hit, a few days out of a pre-season, expanding their fan base and massive financial gains for seasons to come selling their merchandise, but Montrose do not have this luxury open to them. Sadly in this world, only money breeds money. So survival will be down to many small investments, 50-50 draws and donations of money raised at club events. In Breda, NAC have an open-day, meeting the manager, players and backroom staff. It's a day to promote and sell the club. On sale are season tickets, strips and hospitality of varying levels. It's a family day, it brings Dad (and in some cases Mum) along with their kids and it also has potential to bring people through the gates.

It is a three day event, with two games on Friday night, an open day on Saturday hosting a supporter's knock-out tournament and the finals of the round robin on the Sunday. A weekend ticket costs fifteen euro, around ten pounds but it rustles up support and generates cash. Montrose tried a type of promotional day back in Jim Leishman's first season. I think it worked as it is the first time that I have seen so many kids wearing a Montrose football kit, veering away from Rangers and Celtic outfits of heroes that they may never see up close. It's time to try something again, possibly with the four Angus teams.

Presently at the club, shirts are supplied by Dutch sports manufacturer Vandenel, but are difficult to obtain as the club shop seems to be limited in the quantities they can stock. This is something that needs to be resolved to be able to entice youngsters, new stock brings new support.

I find myself this weekend ferreting around Breda, trying to organise myself for the start of the new season. I have found an "Internet Café", four euros for two hours, I could log into Radio Scotland, maybe listen to Tam Cowan and "Off the Ball", then again is Tam Cowan worth two euros? Sky Sport's would be an option, I would be able to listen to a Scottish Premier game and look at the Division Three team lines, the delayed scorers and see if Barry Donnachie's name appears with a yellow card with the words un-sporting behaviour. I walk to the TV rental emporium, that's right, just as we have the Co-op (The Emporium) in Montrose, Breda has the TV rental. I enquire in my best Scottish the possibility of a Sky Sports installation – silence – I explain that I do not speak Dutch – Ah! You are German – No, "spreke de engels" – Why didn't you say, I am fluent! Again no joy, I got the impression that you would have to own a pub to get Sky. It is possibly something worth investigating. I wander around and find O'Mearas, an Irish bar, who have Sky and cover the English Premiership games and of course their love for Celtic. The place was quiet but I spoke to the bar attendant, he was from Cork, he introduced me to a customer who I thought was one of the locals, he turned out be Albanian. He had very little English, a bit more Dutch, but we could understand each other perfectly. Football really is a universal language.

I continue on my travels trying to seek out some refuge for the season. Firstly I come across a café, a bit smoke-filled but at least there is sport on the various screens. I decide that it could be a possibility, I look to see that its name is FLY'N'HY. The penny drops. I look around to see if there are people watching as I hastily retreat. Cannabis cafes abound in the Netherlands. I later find another called "Purple Rain" and wonder if Montrose will be "FLY-N-HY" or will it be "Purple Rain" for the fans, their enthusiasm drenched. Only time will tell.

Some supporters say that pre-season games are meaningless but it gives the manager a chance to experiment and find his strongest eleven. I remember being sent to Larbert High School playing fields for a County trial. There were four of us selected to go, we arrived late, the trial had started, I was told that we would play the second half. We did, I was a goalkeeper and was put on to play at right back, none of us played in our normal positions or at all well, but then again maybe Henry was just experimenting. Yes, that's right, the same Henry Hall, some thirty five years ago.

Before friendlies, I remember the days of closed doors, sometimes being allowed in to watch the games and sometimes climbing the wall just to get a glimpse. Usually the first time you saw the new squad of players was at a "Sports Day", held for the supporters with no admission fee charged. There would be sprint competitions, league clubs represented by team players, five-a- side competitions between all the local sides and the day ended with a Blues versus Whites match, first against second string and a wind up of the younger players by their senior counterparts. It was an enjoyable family day; youngsters would pick up autographs and brush shoulders with their heroes.

It will take a few games for players to get to know each other and for telepathy to kick-in, but this process must be in place in four games. It is a lot to ask from the players. Henry Hall has always coached the side to play a passing game instead of the usual route, one punt up the park and heads down tactic that is adopted by most Division Three sides. I hope that Montrose will continue to play the passing game and think that this time they have that little bit extra strength in the middle of the field and strikers who are prepared to shoot from all angles without walking the ball into the net. Too many times last season the build-up play was excellent but that extra touch or reluctance to shoot spoiled many enterprising moves. Also for a team to win promotion, not only do you have to score goals but also keep clean sheets. Last season our goal difference read minus six. If you take Gretna and Peterhead out the equation from last year only Queen's Park and Stenhousemuir returned a plus one and zero balance. Looking at league positions, Montrose recorded fifth place, Queen's fourth and Stenhousemuir, seventh. With the exception of Gretna and Peterhead the remaining league sides were all of the same standard and level. Most teams lacked consistency, with injuries, suspensions and depth of squad bringing winning runs to an end. They could not compete with the likes of big spending Gretna or to a lesser extent, the lure of better wages offered by Peterhead. It will be interesting to see just how these two teams adapt to Division Two football, this coming season. Gretna no doubt will be pushing for promotion yet again but will not have it so easy as last season with teams like Morton and Partick pushing them all the way. I can see and predict that Peterhead will be the team that will finish ninth with the life-line of a play-off to keep Division Two status.

July 12th dawns (Dons). A strong Aberdeen side are due at Links Park this evening, with a seven forty-five kick-off. A good crowd is expected as when this opening fixture celebrated the one hundred and twenty fifth anniversary season 2004-05 there was an attendance in excess of two thousand. Leading 1-0 at half time, Montrose stumbled to a 4-1 defeat. This is not an excuse, but the team was drastically re-shuffled for the second half, fresh legs getting a run out as you would expect. It will be a different game tonight, I think it will be a lot closer; last season was a bit of a leaning curve and lessons were learned. The papers confirm today, prior to the game, that Montrose have seventeen players and three goalkeepers. At last it is confirmed, Jim Butter has signed.

I am home, but have to leave this morning to go to Amsterdam, so yet again I will miss tonight's match. Never mind, fortunately over the years, it's been a case of teach your children.

When working away from home, you have to have a source, a mole or a son who has your same passion and love of Montrose. We bring our children up, giving them knowledge and values, but at times we laden them with a heavy burden. We drag them around the terraces, we make them suffer humiliating defeats and occasionally the joy of winning, but at the end of the day they are their father's clone. Gareth is a regular at games and keeps me up to date by email, text or sometimes telephone.

The telephone can be a life saver when you are in other countries, it can also be a pain. People do not realise that when working abroad, you can be in another day when they are going about their morning routine. It kills me when the phone goes off through the night, you think the worst, a chill runs down your back, you answer, only to find out that it is your mother (no concept of time difference) saying you took a long time to answer. I was in my bed Mum, oh is there something wrong, are you not feeling well? No Mum, I'm fine, well what are you doing in your bed. Mum, its two o'clock in the morning. I'll just let you get back to sleep then. When in Waterford, Ireland, my telephone number was one digit off the local taxi firm, early Sunday morning calls were a common occurrence usually from a caller with a drink-impediment. Where exchanges do not have the most up to date technology or is of Russian origin, the telephone would ring but no one was there. It worries you as it is important that your family has contact. So you call them, only to get an answering machine. It crack's me up! So tomorrow I await a welcome phone call from Gareth and a report on the first friendly game.

July 12th. - ABERDEEN report and teams –
Why wait until tomorrow, eleven pm Dutch time, my mobile phone rings, the voice reports beaten two nil, but there was optimism. Andy Reid looked sound, Fotheringham sprayed passes across the field of play and linked up well with the runners, Willie Martin chased lost causes and never gave up. Henner had a good couple of chances, was strong in the tackle and added a new dimension to the left flank. A fair first showing for the new lads

of Links Park. Eagerly I slept on it, awaiting the web reports of the Courier and Press and Journal the following morning.

It's started already and it is only the first game of a pre-season and you don't know what to believe. Do reporters go home after the first twenty minutes of a match? Some reporters even have photographers with them and still mange to get it wrong! Let me start with the attendance last night at Link's Park. One report quotes one hundred and ninety two the other one thousand, nine hundred and forty-two. It's a big discrepancy. The game started at seven forty-five, did the reporter think it was a seven thirty kick-off, did he leave thinking it was a reserve game or did the picture that his photographer took of the Aberdeen support behind the goal not tell him. Reporting of the Montrose team and substitutions is no better. Reid played the full game according to one of the reports; Dodds was substituted by Cargill at half-time yet played the second period in defence for Paul Doyle. The goal times in the reports, are printed as 57, and 59 minutes or was it 59 and 61, yet another difference of facts.

The headline captions are a giveaway, you can tell what paper is what – the Courier report with a Montrose bias, Aberdeen capitalise on defensive lapses and Warsaw pact debut goal boosts Piotr's chances of a Don's deal, for the Aberdeen news readers.

So, to last night's match report. Montrose lined up for their first pre-season with Reid in goal, a back four of Donnachie, Doyle, Stephen and Smith. The starting midfield included Dodds, Hall, Fotheringham and Henslee, the two strikers being Willie Martin and Watson. Hankinson, Cargill, McLean and Smart (a trialist) made the substitutes bench. Only four players on the bench? Is it true, or is it another discrepancy? No it is true, as confirmed by my mole. Steve Kerrigan is absent due to holidays and Webster has reported ill. Hopefully they will be back for Saturday's game against Forfar.

Jimmy Calderwood's Aberdeen side had two trialists, Polish striker Piotr Wlodarczyk and defender Henry McStay from Halifax (ex-Leeds youth). They lined up with almost a squad of full-timers. Scottish Internationalist, Esson is in goal, protected by McNaughton, Considine, Winter, McStay and Byrne. Nicholson, Clark and Smith supply the midfield with Stewart partnering Wlodarczyk upfront. On the sub's bench are wingback Muirhead, midfielder Dempsey, Adams and young Kyle McAulay. Goalkeeping sub is David Preece.

According to reports, Montrose held Aberdeen comfortably in the first half with Henry Hall the happier manager. Henry played five of his new signings in the first half and brought on Cargill at half time with Hankinson replacing Reid in goal and McLean taking over from Watson who had a good first half. Henry further changed the side in seventy minutes swapping Martin for trialist Smart.

The game started off briskly and at pace, Watson had an early chance, but pulled his shot wide of the goal. Aberdeen attacked and their trialist, Wlodarczyk broke through challenge after challenge by the Montrose defence only to lose control allowing Reid to clear. Minutes later, Aberdeen cleared their lines from a Henslee header which was goal bound. Aberdeen were good on the break and were seemingly very positive when going forward, but Montrose were coping with any threat on goal.

The second half resumed, changes had been made, Dodds assuming the role of sweeper. Eventually the goals came, two in two minutes, at least we agree on that. Montrose lost the ball at the edge of the box, picked up by Dempsey who held the ball up before shooting home. The second goal was a cut-back from Chris Clark to Aberdeen's trialist Wlodarczyk who dallied with the ball before shooting home from close range. The game at 2-0 was not over as Henslee twice caused problems to the Aberdeen defence who breathed a sigh of relief once they had cleared their lines. At the other end of the park, Hankinson pulled of a competent save from Dempsey as the game drew to a close. Aberdeen now head to the Netherlands for a pre-season tour at the end of the week. Will they play NAC Breda?

From the reviews and resources that were accessible it seems a promising start, and the good money spinning crowd of 1942 will help boost the coffers. Notable mentions go to Neil Stephen at centre half. Fotheringham, Martin and Henslee also put in a good shift for Montrose. Hall stated prior to the game that his team choice was compromised by injury and fitness. Andy Cargill has been out a long time with injury and will take time to obtain match fitness. Paul Doyle is not one hundred percent from an injury sustained last season and Stuart Ferguson has undergone a knee operation. On top of that, Kerrigan as stated previously is on holiday. Hall further states that he needs to sign at least another two players before the start of the season.

The trialist, A.N.Other or was it NEWMAN, seemingly had a nice touch on the ball and was Craig Smart of Spartans (a mate of Elliott Smith). If I remember correctly, he caused Arbroath an embarrassment in the Scottish Cup when they were eliminated (or annihilated) a few seasons back. He may be a good fringe player or one for the bench. I hope he gets the chance to partake in future friendlies so a better assessment can be made and a possible offer tabled.

I look up the MFC web site to find it has been updated with a match report and that Stephen "Chippy" Fraser signed before last nights game. More previous reporting inaccuracies as he had signed prior to Henner. Just what do you actually believe, newspapers are wrong, web sites are inaccurate and no two sources agree. It can really wear you down.

I read that Dick Campbell, manager of Partick Thistle has stated that he will never take a team on a pre-season tour to Highland League clubs again. Partick were beaten by Buckie Thistle 3-2. Humiliation, to say the least, but Campbell's grudge was a tackle which occurred in the first minute of a game which was no tepid affair. The tackle was enough for the Partick player to be stretchered off the park and if that wasn't enough he looks as if he will miss the beginning of the season. It is one of the dangers of pre-season- Stuart Ferguson can testify to that after last season when he sustained an injury to his coccyx which put him out for half the season. This must have been a severe blow to somebody who had been ever present in previous seasons, but accidents do happen. My main fear is that we play Buckie after another Highland League hurdle, Deveronvale, in pre-season games to come. Let's hope we don't sustain any injuries as you want to start the season strong and with a full squad. After all we want five on the bench!

The Dutch pre-season has started, NAC Breda are playing a Zundert select on Saturday July 16th. Zundert is a small town located between Breda and the Belgian border. It is reported that Pierre van Hooijdonk is ready to make his debut. The well travelled striker was signed from Fenerbache, but his playing career spans from RBC in Rosendaal, joining NAC in 1991 before moving to Glasgow Celtic. Since then he has spent time at Nottingham forest, Vitesse, Benfica, and Feyenoord. It was noted that Tony Vidmar (ex Glasgow Rangers) has signed for NAC Breda. The newspaper article states in the signings, Tony Vidmar, van het Schotse (from the Scots).

Saturday looms or Loons as Forfaar are the visitors to Links Park. You might think, oh! a spelling error. Aye, on yer bike! The Dutch language has many words with the double a vowel just as "loon" has a double "o". Jan van Loon (he must be from Forfar), is the local agent for the "tweewielers", bicycles for the inhabitants of Breda. His sign displays the Forfar colours of sky-blue and navy, below he advertises a clearance sale. Bicycles come in all shapes and sizes and the Dutch seem to have re-modelled this mode of transport to meet their needs. Many a time since coming here I have turned in total amazement to see a mother, and four of her off-spring transported on one bike. One child was sitting in front of a shield by the handle-bars; two were sitting in seats behind the mother and an additional one wheel cycle where an older child sat pivoted from the rear seat of the main bicycle. On another occasion in Tilburg, I went to cross the cycle lane only to be met by a wheelchair moving at speed and yes, propelled by a bicycle. At night, it is strange to watch the hoards returning from work, a bit like the charge of the light brigade, many have pillion passengers riding side saddle, their work colleague peddling like mad. It amazes me that no one is injured, as many bikes have no brakes and only by furiously peddling backwards are they able to stop.

Breda's only Forfar supporter and "Tweewieler" retailer

Pedestrians beware!

Sometimes you think you've seen it all, but today takes the biscuit. I was in town when I heard the sound of bicycle bells ringing loudly and more than one. On turning around I witnessed a wedding procession and yes, you've guessed it, they were on bikes. Not only were the bride and groom in a buggy propelled by a cycle but the best-man, bridesmaids and ushers followed by guests (some side-saddle) in their wedding attire were all peddling "tweewielers" with white balloons tied on at the back. It's a case of you are invited to the wedding but bring your own bike! I suppose it saved on the expense of hiring wedding cars.

Second division Forfar are now managed by Brian Fairley who moved from Dumbarton after Ray Stewart resigned following Fofar's five – one defeat at home by Montrose in the first round tie of last year's Scottish Cup. Fairley is a new broom and had released several players at the end of the season looking to build his style of side. Forfar lined up against Brechin on Thursday night and were beaten two goals to one by the First Division team. Today's game at Links Park will be a stuffy, physical affair by all accounts as Fairley's tactics will be to hold the play and hit on the break. "Angus Derbys", are never timid affairs and there is no love lost between the two teams. Henry Hall states that he will give a game to every player that is available as they work towards fitness and match sharpness. Currently Hall is running the rule over his pool of players before adding any further new faces. Steve Kerrigan is on holiday and Webster may make his first appearance if he recovers sufficiently from a throat infection. Goalkeeper, Jim Butter has a hamstring injury and is yet to feature.

July 16th - FORFAR report and teams –

The six pm (Dutch time) bulletin is received; I ask what speed did you drive home at as the game has just ended? Breathless he relays that it was one all! Montrose scored first from a penalty. Forfar are a physical side. Euan Hall had a really good game today; he was playing on the right in front of Barry Donnachie. The call was ended with "I really wish some of the Montrose crowd would start supporting the team instead of getting onto Euan and his dad Henry." Sad to say but these critics would do better to stay away.

Montrose once again lined up with Reid in goal, and the same back four of Donnachie, Doyle, Stephen and Smith from the Aberdeen game. Changes were made to midfield and in the striking starting roles. The midfield read Hall, Fotheringham, Cargill, and Henslee with Martin and McLean filling the strike partnership.   Forfar fielded four trialists, as manager Fairley too is looking to add to his squad. It was Forfar who had the first clear chance as they hit the woodwork twice in a two-minute spell with a shot coming off the post and a dipping volley striking the bar. Montrose however rallied and took the lead in 40 minutes from the penalty spot. Forfar's David Lowing impeded Duncan McLean, pulling at the forward. The referee subsequently awarded the penalty which Willie Martin converted with style. Montrose went in at the interval leading 1-0.

Substitutions were carried out at half-time, Hankinson once again replacing Reid in goal, trialist Smart replacing Cargill in midfield and Willie Martin making way for Calum Watson upfront. The second half commenced, and it was Forfar who in 64 minutes once again struck the woodwork with a long range effort. This should have served as a warning to the Montrose defence. Shortly afterwards, it was Fotheringham's turn to strike the woodwork just before Forfar's equalising goal in 71 minutes. The goal scored by Paul Shields was from a Sellar's knock-down from the head. Montrose's goal survived intact in stoppage time when a Shield's header went wide of the near post.

During the second half, Webster replaced Doyle. On this substitution, Montrose changed their line up bringing Elliot Smith inside to Doyle's centre-half position and pulled Henslee back to the left back spot. Webster sat on the left side of midfield. Henry's action of playing Henslee at left back incurred the wrath of a certain part of the crowd. It's the same few so called supporters, they only sing when they are winning and even then they are not happy and will find something to complain about. If they disagree fine but still support the team and don't take it out on junior Hall. After all, you are adults and old enough to know better. The season hasn't started but the terrace critics terrace have!

Montrose completed the match with ten men after Duncan McLean limped off the park after a heavy challenge from his opposing marker. Surprisingly enough there were no bookings and sometimes I think that some players realise that they will get away scot-free for their actions as it is only a friendly. To add to Henry's injury worries, Kerr Dodds picked up a calf strain whist warming up prior to the match. This reduced the bench once more to four available players. I take it that absentee Stephen Fraser will be given a run against Deveronvale once he proves his fitness.

Highlights of the game would be Euan Hall's performance, another clean first half sheet for goalkeeper Andrew Reid and the return of Webster. Barry Donnachie at full back was also back to his chuntering best as he developed his rapport with the linesman. Hall stated that Montrose lost their rhythm in the second period after having a promising first half but must now start to build on performance before the Ross County Bells Cup match.

Two games down and two games to go. The construction of the team is taking place already. Clean-sheet Andrew Reid is in front of three goal Hankinson. The back four of Donnachie, Doyle, Stephen and Elliot Smith look to be fairly settled. I would think that the next two games will secure the strike force front pairing. Personally I would like to see Henslee pushed forward to form a strike partnership with Martin. The midfield is a case of who do you leave out. Kerrigan has yet to play but I would hope he would fill the inside left position of midfield standing alongside Fotheringham. On the flanks I would go for Webster on the right and it's a three way split on the left between Cargill, Fraser and Dodds. Henry Hall will see it differently but he should be pleased with things so far and with a bit of luck the niggling injuries sustained by some of the players will clear.

Aberdeen are in the Netherlands for an eight game tour. They kick-off against SVZ Wierden, where ever that is. Surely I should be able to see one of their games, the Netherlands isn't that big. An hour, east, west and north and you have covered the country's edges, but once again the P&J has only printed the first tour match. Just typical!

Pre-season for Deveronvale so far has been at home against Partick Thistle and Peterhead respectively, tonight they play Montrose in their first away game. Deveronvale have a few ex-Montrose players on their books. Two strikers, Mike McKenzie and Jamie Watt, were at the club in the John Sheran managerial days. McKenzie was a particular favourite of the fans and can be remembered for his Scottish Cup goals, eliminating Arbroath in a replay. In the past two seasons Deveronvale have been Highland League title contenders, so tonight's game should be a good test, but one would expect goals. This game and the Buckie match should be treated as confidence boosting games, especially for the strike force. We must score goals!

July 19th - DEVERONVALE report and teams –
Another phone call from the mole, a message left with my wife as I am out at a business dinner. Messages are relayed as before but questions are not asked. What was the team, who was playing and who scored? When I return I am told that Willie Martin scored a hat-trick and that Montrose had won 3-2. I think that was the score anyway, and I think it's been a close game but in the morning I find out differently. More crossed wires and even when viewing the Montrose FC official web site they have a Jim Martin down as a goalkeeping substitute. Willie Martin's hat-trick must have been a shock to the writer!

Hall fielded a side similar to Saturday's line-up. Once again Reid started in goal, Donnachie, Doyle, Stephen and Smith filled the defensive roles. Two trialists were introduced to the side, one in midfield along with Webster, Fortheringham and Henslee. Upfront Watson was paired with trialist "B". One of the trialists is Craig Smart who plays in his third consecutive game. The other trialist is a mystery. Some think it may be ex-Saint, Ross Forsyth but it could also be Graham Fyfe, an ex Celtic youth player, who has spent time "down there" (England) and was also with Raith Rovers for a spell. Euan Hall, Cargill, Martin and Mclean warmed the bench. Steve Kerrigan, returned from holiday, also secured a bench spot. Jim Butter replaced Hankinson as substitute goalkeeper.

Deveronvale have three ex- Montrose players in their team. An injury to Paul Doyle on the ten minute mark necessitated changes in defence. Hall senior opted to introduce striker Willie Martin (a justified move as Montrose were one down), with Elliot Smith moving inside to takeover from the injured Doyle. Once again Henslee move into the left full back spot till the half-time whistle when the man of mystery (trialist "B") filled the role for the second period of the game.

Deveronvale opened the scoring in eleven minutes through Ross McWilliam who eluded the Montrose defence to slide the ball home. Montrose were sluggish to re-act and could have been further behind to a much improved Deveronvale. It was once again an ex Montrose player who set-up Smith whose drive was well saved by goalkeeper Reid. In twenty two minutes Montrose equalised with the first of what was to be a Willie Martin hat-trick.

The goal came from a Martyn Fotheringham corner with Martin heading into the corner of the net. Goal number two from Martin put Montrose in front after good work by Watson allowing Martin to drill the ball home into an empty net. Going in at the interval with a 2-1 lead, Montrose had the better of the first half.

The second half saw Montrose make a few further changes with Hall replacing trialist "A" and Watson making way for Cargill. Jim Butter made his first start taking over in goal from Andy Reid. The second period also produced a change of formation to a 4-2-3-1 system of play. What ever happened to the days of two full-backs, three half-backs and five forwards?

Eight minutes into the second half, Deveronvale equalised when a free kick was headed past Butter in the Montrose goal by Smith (Mark)- not an own goal from Elliot. Martin headed home to complete his hat-trick in sixty-six minutes again from a Fotheringham pin-point cross. Kerrigan replaced Fotheringham in midfield, making a welcome return after sustaining injury against Elgin last season. Webster wrapped things up for Montrose in seventy-nine minutes shooting high into the net after a fine run down the wing before cutting in and finishing in style.

Henry Hall must be encouraged by this 4 – 2 confidence building win, especially hitting the net four times. Willie Martin's hat-trick of goals, two coming from his head must go down as a highlight as headed goals have been few and far between. Mention must also go to Martyn Fotheringham whose pin-point accuracy when crossing supplied the goals for Martin. Reid's first half performance and superiority between the sticks showed once again his skill in marshalling his defence. It was also good to see Webster on the score sheet. Trialist "B" also caught the eye of the support and may get another chance to prove himself against Buckie. On the down side it is worrying that Doyle was replaced again due to recurring injury and would be a big miss for the start of the season. He would relish the opportunity to play against former employers Clyde in the Challenge Cup. Let's hope that Doyle recovers in time and is able play from the start at County's Victoria Park.

Buckie are fresh from Wednesday's game against Elgin City. Elgin are opposition for the first league fixture for the Montrose team. Injuries affect the Montrose team selection with Martin added to the ever growing list and could be rested. Doyle is out for a couple of weeks and Dodds has a calf strain. Strikers Watson and Mclean are also carrying knocks. Glandular fever victim, Stephen Fraser has recovered but may not play a full game. Hall states that a couple of new faces are required to be added to the squad as injuries mount. Things must be bad as the club have also advertised for a match day physiotherapist and a doctor on call. Why weren't these in place during pre-season?

July 23rd – BUCKIE THISTLE report and teams –
The phone call was late in coming and it was partly my fault as I had a different mobile with me, the other had been left in the car. I had gone to Gent (Belgium) for the day which ended in an overnight stay and another culture lesson. They have urinals positioned in their squares for all to see and when you do get a proper toilet you also have women queuing up behind you to use the porcelain artifacts while you are busy preserving your modesty at the wall taking aim. Its quiet off-putting!

I also feel like the oldest student at the music festival. We had gone to see a young band and they were good, but I was feeling my age having celebrated my birthday a few days earlier on Belgian Independence Day, hence the festival and hence also feeling honoured.

It is Sunday before I find out the score and that Montrose were beaten 2-1. It wasn't much of a game he relents, Montrose had a make-shift team in place and injuries are mounting. Just what I wanted to hear, and to compound things Willie Martin is unavailable for the Ross County and Elgin City games due to suspension incurred while at his previous club. Not good news!

Montrose entertained Buckie at home, who by all accounts were a big commanding team with a physical presence. Not taking anything away from Buckie, they have had a good pre-season having beaten Dick Campbell's Partick, Ross County, Elgin and now the scalp of Montrose.

Montrose started off with Reid once again in goal, with Donnachie, Stephen Fraser, Neil Stephen and Smith providing defensive cover. Henry played a midfield five of Webster, Hall, Kerrigan, Fotheringham and Henslee. The lone ranger up-front counting the crowd was Calum Watson. The bench displayed five, two being keepers, reflecting the injury crisis at Links Park.

Buckie produced the best efforts in a half that they dominated. Andy Reid denied the Buckie forward line by producing saves when it mattered. Webster came to the rescue by heading clear at the back post as Buckie kept up the pressure. Efforts from Stephen, a header and a Fotheringham free-kick was all Montrose could muster as they headed for the tunnel at the half-time whistle. 0-0 at half-time and at this point I think manager Hall called a halt to pre-season with the second-half period being a matter of playing out time.

Second –half substitutions from the bench saw Butter replacing Reid, Watson making way for Martin and Cargill coming off the bench into midfield for Kerrigan who reverted to the centre of defence with Stephen being taken off to be wrapped in cotton-wool. Further injuries could not be encountered and I see this as a precautionary measure. Further changes during the second period play saw the removal of Fraser for trialist Smart with Smith then playing as centre-half and Henslee moving into the full-back berth, a move which caused Henry once again to incur the wrath of a certain faction of "supporters" in disguise.

Emerging for the second-half, Montrose played what was to be their best spell in the game. Buckie keeper Main brilliantly saved from Watson, a Donnachie grounder was blocked and Henslee hit the post from a Kerrigan head-flick. The Buckie goal was under siege, but as often happens, Montrose were caught on the break with the defence failing to clear and a shot from the Buckie winger being driven past Butter. With 67 minutes on the clock, it took Montrose three minutes to equalise. A fierce drive from substitute Craig Smart was blocked but not held by the Buckie keeper and Henslee had the simplest of tasks to convert the rebound. Henner has broken his "duck"! Two minutes later Fotheringham rattled the Buckie cross-bar with a shot as Montrose pressed for the winning goal but it was Buckie who came out on top. In 85 minutes a shot which deflected off Kerrigan lopped over Butter to silence the Montrose support as it entered the net. The remaining five minutes saw a Willie Martin header going past and Webster and Henslee trying their luck at goal. The game ended in defeat.

Hall stated that too many players in the second half had been asked to play out of their normal positions and that fitness was less than 100 %. Fotheringham struck the Buckie woodwork for a third time in the game, obviously not his day on this occasion, but it soon will click for him and everything will be rosy! Hall can take heart from another clean-sheet from Andy Reid and a sound performance from defender Stephen. Fotheringham once again showed his skills in midfield and Hall also produced a steady performance despite some supporters who seem to have it in for him. I for one don't like this crowd reaction which is a repeat of the Forfar nonsense. If they are not happy, I would say to this element of support, don't bother coming to the game. Kerrigan sustained a hefty second-half challenge; I hope he isn't added to the injury list that already includes Doyle, Dodds and McLean. This injury list and the fitness of Fraser and Cargill plus Martin's impending suspensions, could impact on next Saturday's match big time and chances of a result at Victoria Park. Montrose have seven healing days, not that it will help Martin's plight!

Pre-season Round-up

Date	Pre Season		Opposition	Result	Mo Scorer's
12/7/05	Montrose	v	Aberdeen	0 - 2	
16/7/05	Montrose	v	Forfar Athletic	1 - 1	Martin (pen)
19/7/05	Montrose	v	Deveronvale	4 - 2	Martin (3) Webster
23/7/05	Montrose	v	Buckie Thistle	1 - 2	Henslee

Summary – Goals for, 6, goals against, 7. Not a good statistic for the beginning of the season but on the positive side, young Andy Reid has kept three clean-sheets in four starts and has only conceded one goal. Hankinson and Butter have lost three goals a-piece in two starts. On a points basis Montrose would have scored four out of the twelve points up for grabs, again not good reading but the games are used for playing different tactical formations and partnerships, so you can't really judge team performance. First impressions are that goals will come from midfield this coming season with Webster and Henslee already having opened their account. It will only be a matter of time before Fotheringham is also on the score sheet having struck the woodwork on several occasions. Kerrigan again this season looks to be the ball winner with the remaining midfield trio servicing the strikers. In the striking role Willie Martin has impressed and was rewarded for his efforts with a welcome hat-trick. The recognised defence line-up of Donnachie, Doyle, Stephen and Smith has looked good and had only lost one goal when going in at half-time. Henry's second period changes which had some players filling out of position places have conceded 6 goals, but make-shift defences do leak.

Tactical playing formations of 4-4-2, 4-2-3-1 and 4-5-1 have been experimented with. I think against most sides Montrose will play 4-4-2 but against County on Saturday it could be a 4-5-1 that will be in place.

For me the side should read, Reid in goal with a defence of Donnachie, Doyle (providing he is fit), Stephen and Smith. In midfield, places go to Webster, Fotheringham, Kerrigan and Henslee with Watson and Martin forming the striking partnership upfront. Cover on the bench, Hankinson, Hall, Fraser, McLean and utility player Dodds and Cargill. This season Montrose will rely on the full depth of their squad and will need to call on fringe players such as trialist Smart who is yet to sign, and eventually Ferguson, on recovery from his long term injury, but that will not be until December at earliest. There is no further mention of Graham Fyfe or Marc Connelly, reported to have been offered training facilities during pre-season.

Hall had stated that he was looking to add two additional players to the squad but that he was in no rush and would take his time in the matter. I think that time is running out as injuries have take their toll. Henry is currently negotiating with a Scottish Premier League club to secure a central defender on loan. He hopes to have the new face in place for the Ross County game. I suspect that the second player that Henry has in mind for signing could be trialist, Craig Smart. It's a pity that another striker could not be signed but I reckon that Greg Henslee would possibly be pushed into a striking role as there is a surplus of midfield maestros. There is no Reserve League this season, and players who warm the bench could spend a season there with little chance of a game. This is not a good situation to be in as players will get itchy feet, lose interest and more importantly fitness. Montrose also have three goalkeepers, one may be off-loaded as finances are limited.

We are one week away from the Bell's Cup tie and excitement mounts. The first game that I can remember as child is being taken to Falkirk to an end of season game against Airdrie. It was a draw, Airdrie were fighting relegation and struggling for survival at that time in Division One. I had a taste for the game and the following season I remember going to see a League Cup game, again involving Falkirk who played Motherwell. Motherwell won 6-0. It was in the days of Bobby Roberts and Ian St John. I also remember Dundee's league winning side and a capacity crowd at Brockville, where Falkirk played. (It has since been replaced by a supermarket) I was behind the goal; I can still see Alan Gilzean rising to head home. Alan's son Ian Gilzean followed in his father's footsteps as a striker but due to injury he has since followed a coaching role with Montrose and is Henry Hall's assistant. Memories, it is like getting your first football strip. It was my birthday; I received a Heart of Midlothian strip. It was nothing fancy by today's standards, a maroon v-neck top edged with white, white shorts and woollen white socks with two maroon bands. It was something that I treasured but sadly no longer have. We collect various things from our childhood, hanging on to memories. I hear my wife saying, "Put that out!" I reply by saying "This is worth money, it is something special, and it's an heirloom." It is also something to hand down to my son as it had been to me by an uncle. It may not be much, two football programmes, Dundee's pre-season tour of Southern Rhodesia in 1953 under manager Bob Smith. A massive step for any Scottish club to take in these days, they also wore probably the first tartan strip which was commissioned for the tour. The second programme is of that classic entertaining European Cup final between Real Madrid and Eintract Frankfurt held at Hampden Park, Glasgow and home of Queen's Park. The final boasted ten goals, with Real winning 7-3. Forty-five years on and it is only a memory.

Chapter 3

It's not what you know, but who you know!!!!!

It's imminent!

I don't now how many times I have been assured by companies delivering equipment that dates will be met only to find that the supplier's optimism beats any football supporter's dreams. Well the season is now imminent, and squads have been assembled, friendlies are over, managers now put their future on the line.

Many a time it's not what you know but who you know- it's called getting a break or being in the right place at the right time. Movements are monitored through the course of the year, projects come to fruition and teams are formed. Managers know who they want, previous connections, reliability, and people will speak for you and you find that suddenly the game is on!

For Montrose F.C., this may be the season, but heart of hearts tell me that we may slip into that runners-up spot which is no longer there and be set for the dreaded play-offs. Ending up second you could be ten points clear of third or fourth place and finally be pipped by a team who have had a dismal season in the second division but manage to survive by playing two or three play-off matches. Don't get me started!

Montrose-not the only team to strengthen their squad-must stay focused and strive for a good start, notching up points that will keep them in with the leading pack. But what will they be up against.

Albion Rovers – a change of management, great start last year under Kevin 'crunchie' McAllister, but this was short lived, Kevin finally receiving his P60 from the board. Interim manager, Jimmy Lindsay, has handed over the reigns to Jim Chapman who captained Rovers' Division Two title winning side and had previous managerial experience with the Hibernian Ladies side. Chapman has a re-building job on his hands as Rovers' entire squad was released at the end of last season. As Albion assemble a new squad they bring in players who have had previous league experience and also from the junior ranks. Looking at the signings it will take time for the side to blend and I think that the wooden spoon is heading to Cliftonhill.

Arbroath – Signings have included Forfar trio Jay Stein, Davidson and striker King and Roddy Black and Chris Jackson from Brechin. Manager Harry Cairney has added some more new faces to his squad in what is his first managerial season at Arbroath. Montrose relish the return of the Smokies' derby games, as last year our derby was against Gretna, the end of the earth. I look forward to January 2nd. I would see Arbroath tucked in behind Montrose in the table, and potential opposition for Montrose in the play-offs.

Berwick – A change of management with John Coughlin taking over from TV pundit Sandy Clark and in the course of time making a few signings. Craig Coyle, goalkeeper, has signed from Arbroath, the dangerous midfielder Chris McGroaty and ex-Saint Jordan Tait have all signed at the club. Tait has since left after a dispute with the manager. Berwick I think are looking for promotion but I would say that this will be a season of surprise and consolidation and they will end up mid-table in the quest for promotion.

Cowdenbeath - Soon to lose their manager Dave Baikie. A few good signings, with John Cusick moving from Arbroath, and defender McBride from Albion Rovers. The "Blue Brazil "are a tough side but they have the best youth policy going. They are a strong and resilient side, Graham Irons will be in contention for the vacated manager's job, but if Director Gordon McDougall had a conscience then he would ask John Brownlie to return to the club.

East Fife – Two signings from Montrose, Graham and Smart, Brian Fairbairn and his tan are off to Raith Rovers. Additions of striker John Bradford from Albion Rovers and defender Campbell from neighbours Cowdenbeath supplement the existing squad. Manager Moffat has a good squad but a change in long ball tactics would not go a-miss, and a mid table position seems all that will be achieved this season as East Fife do not have the killer touch.

East Stirling – Another season and hopefully an increase in fortunes for wooden spoon specialists, East Stirling. Man of many clubs, Ally Graham, and Ian Diack form the strike partnership of a club in financial strife. Newspaper coverage will be down this season as Daily Record 'reporter' Gordon Parks has moved to Clyde. I would predict that this season East Stirling will be promoted from the wooden spoon position as manager Denis Newall's previous season's experiences start to take effect.

Elgin – Our League baptism opponents are managed by ex- Aberdeen, Rangers, Leeds and Montrose player/coach David Robertson. Montrose has a good record against Elgin having won six and drawn two. Will this be the season for Elgin to break their duck? I hope not. Robertson has made good purchases, signing striker Martin Johnston from Cove Rangers and midfielders Booth and Easton from Forfar and Stenhousemuir respectively. Elgin, a side of youth and experience, are a bit *"Jekyll and Hyde"* and on their day are a difficult side to beat but discipline can let them down. This season will be no different for the Moray team.

Queen's Park – What a surprise, no signings but a few departures to other clubs. Frankie Carroll has signed for Stenny, Danny Ferry for Dumbarton and midfielder Bonnar is off to Albion Rovers. Not good news for their fans. I read from a supporter "Will we ever score?!" Queen's Park has always been a difficult side to break down. They are well organised and never give much away and this season under Billy Stark will be no different from the past. It is goal difference that counts on many occasions and this could be the edge which secures Queen's a spot in the play-offs.

Stenhousemuir – Favourites to win the league and promotion, Stenny supporters will no doubt be confident. Montrose found it difficult to compete last season against Des McKeown's side. The signing of Frankie Carroll from Queen's Park, striker Colin Cramb from Accies and midfielders McAlpine, Mercer and forward Marc McKenzie from Albion Rovers will make it a difficult three points for most clubs. In addition to these signings I reckon goalkeeper Willie McCulloch is the best in the division, on last years showing anyway. Let's hope that my sponsored player Andy Reid can emulate McCulloch's heroics in goal. Stenhousemuir are a hard side to break down; they tend to play a 3-5-2 formation which holds play in the middle of the park. Montrose will find it difficult against this side and may have to change formation to 4-5-1 to match the midfield. In these games the difference will be the strength of the referee who will keep control of play. I think Stenhousemuir will be the team to beat for the number one spot.

There is no Reserve League this season, many players will move to the juniors, be it permanently or on delayed forms. The differential in wages between the Third Division and top junior clubs is diminishing. Soon junior standards will sadly over take this division and clubs will either take the Third Lanark route of extinction or head to the junior leagues as Clydebank were sadly forced to do.

Many signings by managers are a result of contacts, previous connections and good will. It's not what you know but who you know that paves the way for your next move. It is no different in the world of self-employment, being in the right place at the right time, having someone speaking for you and putting your name in the shop window for the position.

The BBC has a crystal ball and foresees Stenhousemuir as league champions, with Berwick, Montrose and Arbroath taking the play-off spots. The remainder of clubs secure league positions from Elgin in fifth place followed by East Fife, Albion Rovers, Cowdenbeath and Queen's Park. East Stirling are destined for the wooden spoon again.

The great psychic "William Hill" has already predicted the final League positions and status at the season end. Their crystal ball has Arbroath as title champions with Montrose, Berwick and Cowdenbeath playing for the scraps of promotion. The remainder of the league reads in sixth place Queen's Park, then Stenhousemuir, Elgin, East Fife, Albion Rovers and lowly East Stirling.

Everyone likes to see their team do well, everyone dreams of promotion, but there can only be one winner. So hopeful for the season, I would predict second spot just losing out to Stenhousemuir. Third place going to local rivals Arbroath and fourth spot between Dave Baikie's Cowdenbeath and the amateurs from Glasgow, Queen's Park. The wooden spoon this season I would think would go to Albion Rovers with East Stirling raising their game and attaining second bottom spot. East Fife-their fans deserve it-will be on the fringe of the playoffs with Elgin and Berwick scrambling for the seventh and eighth spots respectively. We all have our own thoughts; it will be interesting to see at the end of the season whose hopes have been realised and whose dreams have been shattered.

I remember a number of years ago walking from Links Park with David Stott; Partick Thistle had won the League and their fans were jubilant. Montrose favourite Colin McGlashan had scored for Partick and Montrose were relegated from the Division. Some fans start chatting as we walked along Union Terrace. Suddenly David said," Well done lads, you were the better team, you deserve to be promoted." He ended by saying "Safe journey home." Humility in defeat costs nothing, kindness is a courtesy and it was also a lesson learned by me as he only ever gave encouragement while supporting Montrose. How many supporters can live up to these qualities on a Saturday at the Links Park ground? After all it only took to the second pre-season match for the terrace legions to moan!

I also remember a well thought of manager at ICI, who was an avid Rangers supporter, being tapped on the shoulder whilst sitting in the stand at Falkirk and told to sit down. He took no notice until the voice said I will speak to you on Monday. It turned out to be his work's manager. Emotions and behaviours get out of control both off and on the field, the team with the best discipline record and support will win through in the end. Give the team support and encouragement this season and not just when we are winning!

A work colleague Eddie has a saying and that is "We see them come and we see them go", referring to other contractors who don't last the life cycle of the project or are found out to be unfit for the job. It applies to football managers too as some appointments are short lived; even experienced managers feel the edge of the sword as their position is terminated. Alex Smith of Ross County is witness to that. Casting my eye over those in charge in next season's campaign, I see that Albion Rovers have finally appointed a new manager, past player and SFA Football Development Coordinator for South Lanarkshire and previously Hibs ladies manager, Jim Chapman. Little is known of him but hopefully he will be given a chance and that his position will be intact at the end of the season. Arbroath, Cowdenbeath and Berwick have installed new blood at the helm prior to the season's end with Harry Cairney failing to keep near neighbours Arbroath in Division Two. Stenhousemuir have dispensed with the services of assistant Tony Smith, side-kick to Des McKeown. Experienced John *Cowboy* McCormack was appointed as McKeown's number two. On paper this looked to be a very good appointment, McKeown on the other hand may just have had to look over his shoulder, but before the season starts McCormack takes the helm at junior outfit Bellshill. A new appointment is made with Paul Smith the former Berwick manager filling in as McKeown's assistant. Lowly East Stirling under manager Denis Newall (new to the League) started to put together some results and lost out a few times in some close encounters. I would hope his experiences of last season bode well and that he is able to build, bearing in mind the limited resources that he has at his disposal. All in all, I don't see many changes in the managerial hot seats of Division Three; one casualty may be East Fife's Jim Moffat, an ex-goalkeeper at Montrose. Things did not go as expected last season for Fife fans after being relegated the previous season. The pressure is not only on the team but also the Board after they refused a substantial amount of money from their "Supporters Trust" to bring in new players. Word is that the first home game at New Bayview may be boycotted by them due to this refusal. I admire Elgin's manager David Robertson for his youth policy, which after two seasons is starting to pay off. The few experienced signings that he has captured over the summer should give the fans something to talk about. I hope the board have the patience for Robertson's five year plan. That leaves our very own Henry Hall and the gentlemen of football "Queen's Park". Surely they would not sack Billy Stark a player of past notable achievement? Stark on the other hand may move to greater things but the grass is not always greener on the other side.

So to Henry Hall and I should also mention Ian Gilzean – what chances of survival in this cut-throat business of football? The Management and coaching team are made up of manager,

Henry Hall, coach Ian Gilzean and Jim Butter is listed as goalkeeping coach. Hall succeeded John Sheran, after his resignation midway through season 2003-2004. Last year was Henry's first full term in charge and he moulded a side that played a passing game, sometimes taking a touch too many, but progress had been made. Hall and his assistant Gilzean have structured a side that defensively were difficult to beat and well organised. Every team member had a job to do whether it was at a corner or free-kick and this discipline was reflected through the side as Henry bellowed from the dug-out at those who did not carryout his instructions. There was no teacher's pet, only detention later in the dressing room.

Scoring goals and a reluctance to shoot, was one of last season's problems, as some players thought the passing game was that you had to walk the ball into the net. Hall has made every effort to address the situation by signing quality team players who are more direct and have a nose for goal.

The present management team at Montrose is one of the best since the days of John Holt. They deserve to be given a chance and the backing of the support for the future and hopefully for seasons to come.

The "Montrose Review" had a factual supplement in this week's print of the upcoming and potentially exciting season. I would hope that the Review will continue to sustain this quality of reporting, as for many Mo fans the Review is the main outlet for all Montrose FC related news. There is a team photograph that makes you realise just how small the squad is and that there are no youngsters present. The picture is a sign that there is no reserve league, and a possible bleak future, for youth and junior football.

Eighty points! Dick Campbell left neighbours Brechin as manager to join Partick Thistle, Brechin gained promotion last season under Dick's twin brother Ian, gaining eighty points. This seems to be the magic number, a measure of what is needed if we are to win promotion this time round. A stiff task, but not impossible, twenty points a quarter or seven points to lose every nine games. The latter is possible, but unthinkable. A good start for me (the ex-pat supporter) would be eighteen points in the first nine games-66%- while the team blends. Pick up points away from home and keep in with the pack, by gauging the other teams, their strengths and their weaknesses. Starting the next batch of games which takes us from October 22nd to Boxing Day, we need to step-up the pace and target twenty-one points out of the possible twenty-seven. The Scottish Cup starts, it breaks up this period with the possibility of two ties or more if replays are required. I remember last season and the first round tie away to Forfar, probably the best performance of the season, which I missed as usual. I was home, and driving up from Edinburgh,

I was to meet Gareth at the game. Approaching Dundee, the mobile sounded only for him to tell me that the game was off due to a frozen pitch.

Montrose football Club - Season 2005 - 06

Top row from left, Neil Stephen, Stephen Fraser, Jim Butter, Andy Reid, Michael Harkinson, Steve Kerrigan, Paul Doyle
Middle row from left, Calum Watson, Kerr Dodds, Duncan McLean, Greig Henslee, Willie Martin, Euan Hall
Front row from left, Barry Donachie, Elliot Smith, Stuart Ferguson, Henry Hall (Manager), Ian Gilzean (coach), Martyn Fotheringham, Andy Cargill, Kevin Webster

Manager Henry Hall

The game at Station Park was rescheduled for the following Saturday in which Montrose recorded an outstanding 5-1 victory and of course I would be away from home then.

The *"Festive Period"* - two games at home. East Fife before the *"Bells"*, and Arbroath, *"For whom the Bell Tolls"* after. We enter the most difficult period, six points is a must from these two games. This is the period when bookings turn into suspensions and routine can be wrecked by a big money making tie in the Scottish Cup third round. We should be so lucky! In the end if we are fortunate enough to be in the round, the money from a sizeable tie would help the bank balance for next season. A lot of *"what ifs"*, a lot of hope, in a season which has not yet begun! Another twenty-one points the target for a period in which the full depth of the squad will be required, a bit of good fortune on the injury front and possibly a local hero scoring decisive goals that will see Montrose lead the division. Fantasy runs through my mind but I don't dwell on it and move on to the next dream, the fourth quarter. There's a make or break twenty points to capture. It may be a good omen, Queen's Park at Hampden on April 8th.

I remember the days of Doug Rougvie and a trip to a crucial game at Hampden. A game Montrose won 3-0 before gaining promotion in the last game of the season at Palmerston, where Queen of the South play. Happy times, but short lived as we slithered back down a division as the counter landed on the slippery snake of relegation. We need to climb the ladder again! Five home games, four away, a good run in of Elgin and Albion Rovers, and East Fife at home on the last day of the season. This is where the nerves will start to jangle, thoughts of going into the play-off situation, a support that will be with you but a support that will be on your back. Please Henry, no play-offs.

Dreams, nightmares and how many times have I woken up at four in the morning after three weeks into a job asking myself "What am I doing here"! Ask anyone who is self employed and they will tell you the same, but the phase passes and things settle down usually a few days later. My dream, I can see clearly, Montrose sitting eighth in the league, please don't tease! Albion Rovers are top of the league, aye right! Arbroath and Berwick come next. I look again and I wake from my slumbers, it's the start of a new season.

POS		P	W	L	D	F	A	GD	PTS
1	Albion Rovers	0	0	0	0	0	0	0	0
2	Arbroath	0	0	0	0	0	0	0	0
3	Berwick	0	0	0	0	0	0	0	0
4	Cowdenbeath	0	0	0	0	0	0	0	0

5	East Fife	0	0	0	0	0	0	0	0
6	East Stirling	0	0	0	0	0	0	0	0
7	Elgin	0	0	0	0	0	0	0	0
8	Montrose	0	0	0	0	0	0	0	0
9	Queen's Park	0	0	0	0	0	0	0	0
10	Stenhousemuir	0	0	0	0	0	0	0	0

I knew there must be a reason!

Chapter 4

1st. Quarter (The New Season)

It's here! It's another week and another start to a new season. Another dreaded drama, and another obstacle to progress. Another awkward conflict, a wrestling match with ridiculous rules and another reason to feel everything is against you. Don't we just love it! Or is it another chance to show us all just what you are made of and to thrive despite the adversity you face. It's another opportunity to shrug off disappointments and a chance to focus on positive developments. It could apply to us all, in all walks of life, a new challenge, a new season, an opportunity. Let's not throw it away!

A step closer to a brighter future, hopes are high and this could be the season! Let's just get the first game out of the way-why had Montrose drawn Ross County?

Its like a crescendo, it brings to memory the John Foggerty hit, 'Centerfield' , which refers unfortunately to the game of American Football. Don't you just love them-the Americans- they call it football and distort the shape of the ball! Lyric lines from the song of 'The sun came out today', 'we are born again' and 'there's new grass on the field' give the feeling of the start of the new season. The song with its ever increasing hand clap of a football chant, builds into a crescendo of 'Centerfield' – yes, it's time for kick-off!

First game up, a first round Bell's Cup tie to last year's runners-up Ross County, a First Division side. Montrose are away from home at Victoria Park in Dingwall.

Ross County have had a good pre-season, beating Wick, Blackpool and Inverness but falling foul of Third Division East Fife, being defeated two-one at New Bayview. County's manager John Robertson blamed inconsistency and missed chances for the defeat. One bit of news is that Robertson has been taking an interest in former NAC Breda and Guinea International striker Antoine Conde as he seeks to add to the County squad. I see this game as being a test, an opportunity for Montrose at a difficult venue. If things are kept tight, something the defence is still working on, we might just be in with a chance to shock Robertson's troops. I am keeping positive as it is the best thing at the beginning of the season, when we have hopes and dreams.

Ross will have two experienced ex-Dundee United youngsters, striker David Winters and midfielder Rankin, in their team selection. Montrose have selection problems, Stephen is injured and his retiral last week from the Buckie game obviously was not precautionary after all. Both Stephen and McLean will not play. Doyle and Dodds have returned to training and may secure a start. Ross County was Dodds' previous club before he was loaned out to Montrose and subsequently released. The last minute on-loan signing of a central defender has transpired just in time to blood him today. The player, Jamie McKenzie is a Scottish Youth Internationalist who plys his trade with Hibernian and is used to playing in front of Andy Reid. The addition of a defender to the squad is welcome and now gives adequate cover for the future. McKenzie has signed on a six month loan deal that will end in January. This is another good signing as he will have the luxury of full-time training during the week with his club. Hall, who only has one striker available-Watson-will have to decide who to promote to the front line from midfield. Somehow I think it will be Henner!

It's a long journey to Dingwall, travel is an eight hour round trip but my son is there. I am up in Rotterdam for the day at a South American, Caribbean Carnival and the largest in Europe. As usual with these things it is very busy and the wait is long but worthwhile. After standing over three hours the procession finally arrived with some weary souls as they had already walked for the same amount of time. The lively colourful procession took another two and a half hours to pass and stretched for five kilometres. Your mind wanders to other things, Dingwall and is he there yet? I hope he left in time, its holiday period and the caravan season. When I called on Friday I asked, "Do you know where you are going and do you have a route?"' "Yes" was the dry reply. That doesn't mean you don't get lost, I know that by now with my travels here in the Netherlands. Concentration at the procession is limited as I wonder what the team is and let the mind wander yet again!

No text message with the score and no call that is until Dutch time at ten. I ask about the journey, "Don't you want to know what the score was?" "Montrose played Ross County off the park but we got beaten 2-1."' Martin had scored first before County equalised on half-time and in the second-half they were awarded a soft penalty. Euan Hall equalised but the referee chopped the goal off as Henner got a touch and was offside. A good game and a good showing against a First Division outfit away from home with a small band of supporters, approximately six.

July 30th – ROSS COUNTY report and teams – Bell's Cup 1st.Round
Montrose had a starting eleven 4-4-2 formation with Reid in goal being defended by a back-four of Donnachie, Doyle, new lad McKenzie and Elliot

Smith on the left. Midfield strength came from Webster, Henslee, Fotheringham and Kerrigan. So who was upfront in the striking roles? Lo and behold it is Watson and 'Willie Martin', but it was reported by the press that he is suspend for two games. It transpires that the suspensions apply to the league and not to this cup game. So Willie will not play at Elgin, his former club, and the home Albion Rovers game. Calum Watson is also out of the Elgin game due to a pending one match ban which has been carried over from last year's Reserve League.

The bench consists of Butter, Fraser, Cargill, Hall and ex-County player Dodds. The inclusion of Jim Butter could see the departure or release of young Michael Hankinson.

The game started with a good sized crowd of just over twelve hundred, but with only the six dedicated followers from Montrose. It makes you wonder about those supporters who shout abuse at young Euan Hall. If they were supporters then they would have been at Victoria Park. Their absence was not missed by those in attendance. I remember manager John Holt's promotion winning side and him saying, "The team is winning, just what do they want?" His body language said it all as he would turn in the dugout and look to a section of the crowd. A manager has more to do on a Saturday than be distracted by this element from the balcony of the 'Muppet Show', especially when Henry has pupil Barry Donnachie to keep in check!

In an excellent first period Montrose took the game to the Ross County half by continually pushing them back and putting their goal under pressure. After several attempts, Montrose took a well deserved lead in thirty three minutes. Watson broke down the left riding a couple of challenges before squaring the ball to Willie Martin. Martin's strength and low drive sent the ball past McCaldon in the County goal and into the corner of the net. It looked like Montrose would go in at the interval a goal to the good but it wasn't to be. McKenzie was judged to have fouled a County forward to which referee Frickleton gave a free-kick at the edge of the box. Rankin took the kick, the defence ignoring Reid's plea for four in the wall as the ball curled into the top corner of the net. It was a hard lesson that the defence had learned, as a fourth member in the wall would have prevented the goal. Heads down, the players walked off for half-time and no doubt a few word from manager Hall.

The second period saw County more in the game and it was in the fifty-ninth minute that they were awarded a soft penalty. A routine challenge in the box by Elliot Smith saw McGarry take a convincing dive, enough for Frickleton to make the award and to book Smith. Winters took the spot kick, despatching the ball past an unlucky Reid. During the course of play in the second half, Doyle was withdrawn and young Stephen Fraser partnered McKenzie in central defence. Things were also changed upfront. Henslee joined Martin in attack with Hall moving into the midfield after he had replaced a very tired Watson whose accelerated pace had much troubled County's defenders. Well done Calum! Recent signing Cargill also freshened up the midfield with Fotheringham making way.

Just after the re-organisation, Hall broke down the right sending in a deceptive cross with goalkeeper McCaldon mesmerised. The ball ended up in the net taking a slight touch off Henslee who was deemed to be offside. Celebrations were short lived as the referee handed the ball to goalkeeper McCaldon and chalked off the goal. Ross County were off the hook, there would be no extra time or penalty shoot-out. However there was time for Hall to send in yet another good ball across goal from the right but there were no takers. The final whistle from the referee confirmed defeat in a game in which Montrose had competed well.

Highlights- We are out of the Bells Cup and we can now concentrate on the League. A positive statement, you just need to look at Albion Rovers early days last season. Rovers were firing on all cylinders and on the up by beating higher League clubs in cup competitions before finally running out of steam with games against Premier League teams taking toll. From then on it was a downward slide in their League campaign. The downside for Montrose being eliminated in the first round of the competition is financial; there will be no bonus games or third round bonanzas when the '*Big Guns*' join the draw.

Jamie McKenzie impressed at the heart of the defence. Mentions go to Andy Reid in goal who had another excellent match and the tireless running of strikers Watson and Martin does not go un-noticed.

Montrose have dropped their interest in signing trialist Craig Smart, maybe Henry thinks that there is adequate midfield cover and with pending suspensions his priority is another striker, but negotiations would need to be finalised this week. No names spring to mind for this position but it would have to be a Premier or Division One club fringe player on loan. This coming week could be interesting!

Today, Sunday, it is raining heavily in Breda and it's the aftermath of the yesterday's game. I go out to try to find a British newspaper. I try at the rail station and I am pleasantly surprised and also horrified at the prices€ 3 - 80 cents for a Sunday Mail, without the additional features of supplements, TV guide and promotional CD. What a bargain-I put it back on the stand and settle for a cheap Sunday Mirror which at least had the scores from yesterday's game plus as an added bonus a full report on Celtic's 4-4 draw at Motherwell, featuring a picture of Gordon Strachan with head in hands. The back-page had been held for Manchester United's proposed signing bid of striker Michael Owen. Does manager Hall know that striker Alan Smith may now be available on loan with this impending signing of Owen? Newspaper talk!

From the broad sheets there were no major surprises in the Challenge Cup but there were a few interesting results that could gauge things to come and could be another measure of what we will be up against this season. Stenhousemuir recorded a 4-0 victory away to East Fife which confirms my initial thoughts in tipping them to win the league. It is a long way to go and we will know in nine months time. The other result which caught the eye was Berwick's extra time win at Peterhead who were promoted last term from our division and Berwick were subsequently demoted to join the Montrose fixture list. Ex Montrose players Wood and Sharp who made their debuts for Peterhead, were substituted midway through the second half. Craig Smart now with East Fife only made the substitute's bench, coming on in sixty minutes to be sent off twenty two minutes later. A repeat performance of last season against Stenhousemuir. I wonder if they will regret moving on! A good start is imperative as Montrose must execute this league with professionalism and expertise.

In Breda work is hotting up, final funding approval for the project, more travel and trips, and the execution phase is imminent. It's the part that matters, it's the part that everyone sees and it's not done behind closed doors.

Blood pressure rises once again this Monday morning. I have access to the internet and I settle down to read the reports from various sites on the weekend game. Disappointment, disappointment, disappointment, you would not believe it! The *D.C.Thomson* site, printers of the '*Courier*', greets me with the message,' failure of server *Apache Bridge*' and there's more – 'no backend server available for connection, timed out after ten seconds', it is unreal. I move to the *P&J Sport* and find that Saturday was the last update. Obviously they don't work Sundays. The Club site should have a report on the game, but alas the site has not been updated, the writer is still walking back from Dingwall. I think, where next? Ah, the BBC site, only to find a narrative of nine lines and eighty-eight words, obviously written by two fat ladies. Gable-end Graffiti is my next port of call – why didn't I go there first! There are four pages and pictures, I'm impressed. I just wonder how I am going to survive the month of August as it is a month of travel for me.

My travel takes me to Rotterdam, Amsterdam, Brussels, Zurich, New York, Los Angeles and down the Mexican coast. Some places I will have to visit a few times. I am also home for a few days and will take in the Arbroath derby match at Links Park. Trains and boats and planes, travel adaptors, the joys of travel and the frustrations of not knowing the score. I see the problems mounting already, hotels without internet connections, no dial-ups. I am flying to Zurich, and as I watch others in the airport lounge I realise that some are lucky enough to have wireless connections-all right if you can get a signal and alright if you have an access charge card. On the flight, 'Business Class' resembles the Montrose support at Victoria Park, three to be precise. It reminds me of East Stirling attendances and the times we would count the crowd, which reflected the lack of interest on the park. So today, a change of culture and another change of language from voetbal to 'fussball' and next week will be another change.

First impressions of Switzerland are positive, the train meanders to my lakeside destination. Chalets pepper the hillsides-it sounds nice but when you are going from meeting to meeting you don't see much except airports and the inside of hotel rooms with forty-eight channels of un-interpretable television viewing.

As usual meetings over-run, late arrivals mean there is only time to eat and sleep, no time to connect to broadband and no update in the Montrose FC world. Hotel charges would likely be exorbitant in any case for the use of the 'net.

Holidays beckon, they can't come quickly enough, but with it comes more travel and more communication issues. I will be travelling to America, my mobile is dual band and it will not work in the U.S.A. Communication is further compounded as I am cruising from L.A. down the coast into Mexico, and even if I did have a tri-band phone, there would be no signal at sea. The ship's phone requires a booking slot, which is practically impossible, as it is only available at specific times. I've read signs in the past *'Home is just a phone call away'* but now begin to wonder. At least there is the ship's newspaper, an extract from CNN and the BBC World Service. Typically it caters to the Americans, so it's baseball and football of the oval type. My only hope is that there will be an 'Internet Café' on board. Failing that it could be 'MAY DAY – WHAT'S THE MONTROSE SCORE!'

Today, August 3rd, and with scarcely a kick of the ball, we have the first managerial casualty. Cowdenbeath have parted company with manager Dave Baikie who is facing a jail sentence. Baikie has pleaded guilty to assault. It is regrettable that Baikie who was an excellent manager has put the club in a difficult position leaving the Blue Brazil no option but to terminate his contract. Baikie had success with junior club Tayport and Arbroath before becoming manager of Cowdenbeath. Graeme Irons, Baikie's assistant will meantime take the reins.

I read on the BBC web site Gretna manager Rowan Alexander's Division Three season's preview. He states in his preview that he predicts a close contest with teams taking points from one another. Rowan forecasts Arbroath and Stenhousemuir to lead the pack as early favourites but also says there could be a few surprises. Let's hope that one surprise is Montrose FC. In the review, Montrose are predicted mid table and he feels that they lack that bit extra. After reading this forecast I would consider '*Mystic Meg*' for a crystal football reading as she would be more accurate in her predictions.

Quarter One - League campaign

Aug 6th	Elgin	Away
Aug 13th.	Albion Rovers	Home
Aug 20th.	East Fife	Away
Aug 27th.	Arbroath	Home
Sept 10th.	East Stirling	Away
Sept 17th.	Cowdenbeath	Away
Sept 24th.	Stenhousemuir	Home
Oct 1st.	Berwick	Away
Oct 15th.	Queen's Park	Home

Elgin, first up in the league campaign and another trip north, an away result would be tremendous but Montrose have struggled at Borough Briggs before and if pre-season is anything to go by Elgin have also tightened up their defence. Elgin also put together a creditable display against Raith Rovers taking the game into extra time. Goals may be hard to come by today.

Elgin manger David Robertson had made a few signings through the summer, six in total. Ex Peterhead striker Martin Johnston, signed from Cove Rangers, will be the main threat to the Montrose goal. Meantime Hall is quoted as saying 'The boys are keen to get going now and are well prepared. They have put in some hard graft in recent weeks and fitness levels are good. We want to get off to a positive start'. Don't we all! The Montrose dilemma will be who to play up front, who from midfield will be sharp enough to fill the strike roles. A pairing of Kerrigan and Henslee would be my choice and that would leave a midfield of Hall, Fotheringham, Cargill or Dodds and Webster. Neil Stephen is fit to play again. Doyle is struggling from injury and may be kept for the midweek Challenge Cup tie against his former club Clyde. I would see Reid in goal and a defensive shield of Donnachie, McKenzie, Stephen and Smith. It would be interesting to see how the pairing of McKenzie and Stephen will work or will Stephen Fraser assume the role of sweeper. The bench this week may be filled with cardboard cut-outs or the walking wounded, not a good situation. On the other hand Henry could spring yet another surprise, just like last week in signing McKenzie on loan and have signed a striker!

Last night I watched 'Still Game' and the episode 'Dial-a-Bus'. There is a 'Happy Bus' going to Elgin (obviously a three seater!), it was one of the few games I saw last season. It was a good day out and Montrose eventually won by three goals to one after substitute Graeme Sharp turned the game. A repeat score would do, especially when we have a make-shift team in the offering. Gareth who is making the trip will fill me in.

First league match of this term and first time at the Internet Café which is named '*Surf and Talk*' and situated next to the café '*FLY-N-HY*' I just hope that it's not '*Purple Rain*' come 5.45 Dutch time. It's an experience, sitting for more than an hour behind the screen flicking back and forwards, site to site game to game but as usual there are problems. The *Courier* web site is my first port of call but I shouldn't have even bothered as there is no report. Only clubs which have a higher League status are mentioned. I am quiet sure that in the paper edition that there would be a paragraph.' Henslee backs Hall of fame' is the headline denoted by the *P&J*. Henner is reputed to have said "I am extremely confident about the League campaign and I will consider our season to have been a failure if we have not won promotion to the Second Division."

I look up the Montrose message board and find a cheeky post from an Elgin fan. He asks if we are going to bring more than three to Borough Briggs. The reply that he receives is classic although he may not understand – 'There are two car loads and a tandem leaving the Mo and Hamish (a local worthy) is hitch-hiking'!

The game has started in Elgin meanwhile in Breda I try Sky Sports and click the link to live scores. There is a box that appears on the screen, it states, 'Software for flash player required.' (I didn't know that Montrose had any flash players.) I check the install software box as it is a free download and start to download. The temperature bar starts to rise, but suddenly stops and a security box flashes up stating that I do not have access to load software on the '*Surf and Talk*' computer. Foiled yet again! So I can't see the scores as they come in live, but just maybe if I click on results there will be a live link score. Yes there it is, the fixtures for today.Oh, I see Forfar are one up against Gretna. I go into the game direct, and the first page gives the score again along with scorers. Wait a minute, it says that it is 2-1 Gretna. I flick back-no definitely 1-0 Forfar. So back again I look at the teams and the referee and it is now 3-1 Gretna! You see my problem, I decide to click the Montrose link to see what the team selection is and what referee is in charge, or better still who we have been saddled with today. No matter how many times I click nothing happens. I try other teams in the Division; the East Fife-Berwick match and teams appear but that is the only one. It's another case of poor relations. What can I try next- will I go into 'Ask Jeeves'? Then I remember BBC.co.uk has a vide-printer and the page refreshes every two minutes. I log in, Queen's Park have equalised, Berwick go three up and Young scores for Albion Rovers against Arbroath. Phew, that was hard work. I flick back to the match scores for all divisions and just when I do I see that there is life at Elgin. I can hear Henry Hall from the Borough Brigg's dug-out, it's that plaintive cry of "Barry, Barry, Barry!" Yes it's that Barry Donnachie moment, first league game, twenty-three minutes on the clock and Barry's name goes into the referee's black book and he is shown the yellow card. I doubt if 'William Hill' would give odds on this stonewall certainty. Half-time rolls in, no score, I sit for a while, the computer has gone to sleep and just then as my thoughts drift to what am I doing here, it flashes up that Garry Wood of Queen of the South has been sent-off in 53 minutes. By this time I am irritated by the time delay, it may be updated every two minutes but the details are not what had happened in the last two minutes, if you know what I mean. I decide to retire and head for home to catch 'Final Score' on BBC, I remember thinking as I left the café, things could be worse, it could be raining and it was!

Aug 6th ELGIN CITY, Away - report and teams
The 'Happy Bus' is back from Elgin, I ask the usual questions and I get the reply of 'It was dire'. There is a new offside rule, where a player who moves towards the ball is deemed offside as he is seen as interfering with play. I don't understand it and by the sounds of Gareth neither does the referee. It was also a day of too many bad performances compared to last Saturdays blinding performance. I don't think I have seen Barry Donnachie play badly but he seemingly did today. My son thinks that Henry's 4-4-2 formation is suspect-it doesn't work- and that they need to adopt a 4-5-1 system hitting on the break. I don't know, I wasn't there, but I wish I was to see for myself. Rome wasn't built in a day but we do need another striker.

It was a no score draw, a point in the bag or is it two points dropped? Team changes from last week were always going to be as Martin and Watson would not be available and Doyle was nursing an injury. Henry had no surprise signing up his sleeve either this week. Montrose started the match with Reid in goal followed by Donnachie, the return of Stephen, partnering loan signing McKenzie in central defence and Smith on the left side. Fotheringham and Kerrigan operated in midfield with Webster and 'Evan' Hall (as the Elgin announcer so kindly referred) on the respective flanks. Henslee assumed the striking role, partnering Calum Watson! It is the same Calum Watson who is reported to be suspended. It transpires that the club have appealed to the SFA concerning the suspension as it was acquired during a reserve match and as there is no reserve team, it is found to be a bit unfair. The bench sported Jim Butter, Fraser and Dodds. Paul Doyle and a ninety-nine percent fit McLean filled the last two spots beside the management team.

In wet conditions, Montrose took the field of play and threatened the Elgin goal in the first five minutes. Fotheringham broke down the left chipping a ball through to Watson who flicked on to Henslee. However, keeper Renton collected the ball from Henslee's outstretched leg. A few minutes later Fotheringham sent a free-kick across the face of goal, but the strikers did not react. After that, chances were few and far between with Montrose having taken their foot off the pedal. Elgin came more into the match and started to create chances, as Reid made a fine save in turning away a Johnston effort. A full-stretch save from Reid also denied Elgin the opener. Montrose struggled to take command of the game, a few flashes from Euan Hall, Watson and a goal-line clearance from a Webster shot with the Elgin keeper beaten, was all that transpired before the half-time whistle blew. Manager Hall would have a few words for his troops as he was obviously not enamoured with the way things had gone in the first half.

The second-half commenced and it seemed that the half-time talk had done the trick as Montrose had their best spell of the game. It was Fotheringham who from midfield beat three defenders with a jinking run before bearing down on goal with only Renton to beat from six yards. The simple task of sliding the ball home seemed easy but Fotheringham's weak shot was in Renton's midriff. Another chance to be on the score sheet lost, it was going to be one of those frustrating days. Elgin, on the other hand, hit on the counter attack and before long besieged the Montrose goal with set pieces and a series of corners. Reid defended his goal like a scene from a 'Custer's last stand' episode as the defence looked on and on one occasion only the woodwork denied Johnston of Elgin a goal.

Substitution changes were made, Duncan McLean replaced a jaded Watson, and Hall was swapped for Dodds on the right of midfield. This seemed to be the injection of life that Montrose needed as the game started to pick up pace. There was now a sense of urgency in play with some crunching tackles but it was all too late as the chances that fell were not converted into goals. Elgin's defender, Dickson was booked before Montrose made the final substitution which saw Doyle come on for Webster and it was Doyle who almost won the game for Montrose, when after a good run he scaifed his shot as he was goal bound. The final minutes saw McLean come close as Renton saved from a tight angle. Relief greeted the 'Happy Bus' as the whistle sounded for full-time.

Today's Referee, Hornby, is new, but one to note. Plumpish, and has difficulty in keeping up with play. Who would be a referee, you are loved or hated by both sets of supporters in a no win situation. On this occasion I am assured that Barry Donnachie's tackle was a 'cleanish' challenge and was most surprisingly booked. Referee Hornby flashed the yellow card in his direction. Donnachie, as he walked away asked the referee if he knew his name. "No, but I got your number" was the reply. What a legend!

Highlights- not many- Andy Reid kept a clean-sheet and Montrose in the game with a series of notable saves. His handling of the ball was competent and mention should go to him for his tremendous double stop midway through the second half. Young McKenzie put in a good shift and substitute Kerr Dodds provided a bit of grit and determination in his twenty minute role and must be in contention for a start in the Cup match on Tuesday. Entertainment value in the first half goes to Elliot Smith for his ongoing comical battle with the inept track-side linesman, who obviously is a contender for 'Spec-savers' offer of two pairs for the price of one.

This game has confirmed Montrose's need for more striking options and that this should now be a priority. Chances were created, but there were no takers and the will to win was just not there today. Emerging from the light of a cold shower, the players have to treat this game as a wake-up call for games to come and be more competitive as there are better sides than Elgin in this League.

On the striking front, I see that Gretna have signed James Grady from Dundee United, yet another striker to their ranks. Surely they must have someone to spare or share another loan signing; perhaps it would be worth a call. Failing that, what about our friends at St. Johnstone or our new best-friends Hibs. It is a problem with a small squad but we need to dig deep for someone and soon!

From Saturday's games Stenhousemuir, Cowdenbeath and Berwick all secure three away points. Berwick put a creditable four goals past East Fife, manager-less Cowdenbeath notched a 1-0 win at East Stirling and '*Mowgli*' (Paul McGrillen) came off the bench to give Stenny a 2-1 win at Hampden. Albion Rovers and Arbroath shared the spoils at Cliftonhill with the game ending 2-2. So on the first Saturday night the table reads Berwick, Cowdenbeath and Stenhousemuir with East Fife holding the bottom spot but there are another thirty-five games to go.

I am making a fleeting visit home on Thursday flying into Aberdeen from Amsterdam and leave again early Saturday morning from Edinburgh to New York. My planning ability is suspect and I <u>am</u> a planner. Why can't I plan things a bit better as I miss the Clyde game by two days and leave prior to kick-off for the Albion Rovers match, I have nae luck!

Clyde are at Links Park on Tuesday in the Challenge Cup. Montrose have home advantage and stand a good chance of a surprise result. The '*Bully Wee*' under a new management team of Graham Roberts and his assistant Joe Miller signed eleven players in an amazing twenty-four hours. Signings include goalkeeper Paul Jarvie, released from Dundee United, former Morton striker Alex Williams and for some reason Gordon Parks of the '*Daily Record*'. Parks warmed the bench for wooden-spoon holders East Stirling last season but the club did receive substantial media coverage for the privilege. It is a young Clyde squad with ex Old Firm pairing, of Celtic reserve Arbuckle and his Rangers counterpart Tom Brighton. Days earlier Clyde lost three goals to Ross County, who Montrose matched in a previous week. This tie has extra time written all over it. At least the strike force of Willie Martin and Watson will be free to play as Martin's suspension does not affect cup games. Just maybe, Henry will be able to play the team of his choice with a settled defence and strike force. Let's hope so.

I was disappointed when I looked for the Elgin match reports on the internet, a few lines on BBC, not a 'dickie' from the '*Courier*' site and likewise from the '*P&J*' although they had posted extensive coverage of the Highland League weekend games. Prior to tonight's game, the review of the Montrose game was attached as a foot-note to a Forfar article and even then they can't get it right as 'Paul Boyle' may also feature in the side. The other piece of news is Andy Reid is suffering from a knee strain from Saturday and a decision will be taken prior to kick-off on whether he will play. The article then goes on to say that Willie Martin comes back after completing his suspension. I thought it was two games he was suspended for? Don't tell me, as I begin to wonder how accurate the article really is! In linking into the '*P&J*', I soon found that their reporting had a bit of substance as they referred to Martin being available for tonight's game before serving the second and final match suspension this coming weekend.

Just how long does it take to get home and call! No word, is that good news or bad. The game on the other hand could be in extra-time. What do I assume, I need to go to Rotterdam tomorrow, do I go to bed or do I wait? If I had teletext, I could see the score and I could see if there was extra-time, but the Dutch only have a limited service, only enough to see the TV guide. I will just have to wait!

They say patience is a virtue," Has it paid-off?" I ask. "What was the score?" but I could tell by the lilt in his voice that a victory had escaped Montrose and that a next round tie would not be. The game was different from Saturday and there was no cohesion in their play. No turnaround in fortune and no scalp claimed from tonight's game and a 1-0 defeat.

Aug 9th. CLYDE, Home - report and teams – Challenge Cup 1st.Round
A drab game in dreich conditions, an early sign that winter is approaching fast. In heavy conditions Montrose made heavy weather in a game that they created little chances. Four changes to Saturday's team were made. Reid didn't make it in goal but was on the bench as back-up to Jim Butter. In a re-arranged defensive line-up, Dodds started in place of Barry Donnachie who was demoted to the bench for his weekend display. Doyle and Stephen partnered each other in central defence and Smith resumed his role at left-back. The midfield was along the usual lines of Webster, Fotheringham, Kerrigan and Henslee with Watson and Martin taking the front striking places. As well as Reid and Donnachie on the bench, the remaining substitution places were taken by McKenzie, McLean and Hall.

Montrose struggled to adapt quickly to the conditions as passes went astray, as the ball stuck and slithered around the field of play. It was no surprise when Clyde took the lead in eleven minutes. The visitors played a ball in from the right after some swift play, Clyde striker Tom Brighton rose to head home despite the efforts of attendance from Butter and full-back Dodds. One down and the heads also slumped in that direction as Montrose from then on scarcely troubled the Clyde defence. After Watson had been fouled Fotheringham took a free-kick, which he sent past the post. In 28 minutes Montrose lost the services of Watson who sustained a calf injury to be replaced by Duncan McLean. At the other end, the Montrose defended with goal-line clearances as Butter was beaten once again to the ball by Brighton.

The interval resumption saw a marked improvement in team play by Montrose as Clyde some what lost their way. Webster and Fotheringham were the architects in creating chances but once again there were no takers. The best chance fell to McLean, who from a Henslee flick, swung wildly at the ball only helping the Clyde defence to clear their lines. After that Kerrigan headed wide from a corner and there was not much else to report. Henry Hall introduced McKenzie for Doyle and Donnachie for a struggling Willie Martin who seemed to have picked up a knock. The game from then on fizzled out as Clyde regained control. Tonight we were even beaten on the bookings front with Clyde receiving three and Smith of Montrose getting his second of the season and over-taking Barry Donnachie in these stakes. It is evident that the players are taking longer to adjust but we need a settled team and a line-up that trips off the tongues of the supporters. That is how leagues are won.

Highlights – Paul Doyle had the much rated Alex Williams in his pocket and gave no change. Kerrigan was back to his hard tackling, ball winning self in midfield, which was good to see. On the down side once again chances that were created were not taken and a striker is even more of a priority as McLean may be the only striker available for the match with Albion Rovers. A settled side is required and a change of formation may or may not help. Tonight Webster was lost for long periods of the game, often swapping flanks. Dodds is better in central midfield and gives a bit of graft, grit and a myriad of hairstyles, Henslee didn't look comfortable in his role and may be better pushed forward. You see many teams playing a diamond formation which releases three on the break. This would mean a further shuffle of personnel with the dropping of Webster in favour of a more central minded midfielder. I don't know, Henry is the tactician, but one thing is for certain, Montrose must get into a winning way and three points on Saturday is a must.

While travelling to work this morning, I listened to ''*Talk Sport*'' on the car radio, and lo and behold the CIS Challenge Cup got a mention. Very unusual but it was only to take the 'mick' out of Scottish football and especially the lower league sides. One or two scores were mentioned but the main target was the crowds at the games as one presenter asked "Do you have their names and addresses?" The Crowd at Links Park last night was 400, with approximately 50 brave souls making the trek from Glasgow. It is a sad state of affairs when you considered that Cup-ties in the past were special and pulled a larger than normal crowd.

On the web front it is the same old story, the MFC site contains the same old news and the Montrose game does not even make the '*Courier*' postings. The '*P&J*' site hasn't broken from its slumbers yet as yesterday's news is the most current offering.

There are no surprises in the Cup, except that Stenhousemuir lost at home to Peterhead, who hadn't won a game. Cowdenbeath put up a notable display against St Johnstone impressing their new manager Mixu Paatelainen who was in the stand. Cowden finally lost out 3-2. Thirty-eight year old Paatelainen has a few goals left in him yet and will be seen as a major threat in this division. Paatelainen, a Finnish international has had a career that has seen service with Finnish side FC Haka, Dundee United, Aberdeen and Strasbourg before returning to the UK to continue his playing career. A firm favourite at most clubs, Mixu, once fit, will be a great signing for Cowdenbeath as he starts his managerial career.

Saturday's fixtures sees East Fife visiting Arbroath, a home tie for Berwick to collect another three points against East Stirling and a dogged affair at Central Park as Cowdenbeath take on Queen's Park. Elgin City make their way to the Warriors of Stenhousemuir, a game sure to see a few bookings and possibly the first dismissal of the season. Links Park is the setting of Montrose's first home league fixture against Albion Rovers who are an unknown quantity having just signed almost a full team. A bit like previous visitors Clyde I suppose, but I hope we can reverse the result in our favour as the side needs a win, if only as a confidence booster.

The *Algemeen Dagblad* newspaper gives today a review of the Dutch League clubs and how their preparations have gone in pre-season. I can't believe some of the scores and just who were they playing. They list the top five scoring games like a league table. RKC sit in prime spot having recorded a 24-0 result against Cluzona away from home. Second to fifth read as 21, 17, 16 and 15 -0 with FC Groningen scoring thirty-three of the goals. You wonder what good these games must serve. They even list the top scorers for pre-season. Pierre van Hooijdonk of NAC Breda leads the field with fifteen to his tally. There is even a photograph of Pierre sandwiched between two players as he goes for goal. The caption reads 'Met 15 goals mag NAC'er Pierre van Hooijdonk (midden) zich topscorer van de oefencampagne noemen.' We always knew that Pierre was a midden at Celtic and I am just surprised they had to print it or is it Dutch for middle? The Dutch League has eighteen teams with each team playing each other home and away. There are times that I think that Scottish Football should revert to two bigger leagues as it would give some of the smaller sides a bit more revenue. As usual, greed prevails and it is the Old Firm of Celtic and Rangers who call the shots in this competitive game.

One game that I didn't realise was played was a NAC home friendly against Spanish side Celta de Vigo, as I would have attended. I find advertising of matches in the Netherlands very strange. There are no posters in the shops or posts in the local free papers, you really need internet access. The games could be on a Friday evening, Saturday afternoon or evening or a Sunday at lunchtime, afternoon or evening. There is no regimented 3 pm deadlines, as kick-offs are also at weird times and vary from match to match. In the way we would say 7.30 meaning half past seven the Dutch would interpret this as thirty minutes before seven. It's all very confusing and I find myself feeling very stupid as I arrive an hour late to functions.

I am on holiday, a ten day break, but also the longest ten days of limited access as I am all at sea. I wake up on Sunday morning wondering, what was the Montrose score!

Having booked into a Los Angeles hotel, the next morning I tripped over a bound package outside the room door which resembled the death of several trees. It's a dilemma, $1.50 or 38cents. Always read the small print as the paper is delivered to you whether you want it or not, but it will cost you thirty-eight cents if you don't want it. The Los Angeles Times, supplements ranging alphabetically from A to M plus a barrage of typical American advertising offers. At least the sports supplement had the English Premiership and Scottish Premier results but they were incomplete with games missing. It was a final edition of the paper and if you consider the eight hour time difference you would think that they could give a complete report of classified results. I remember the newspaper sellers who would come around at half-time to the games, the stop press listing the scores and scorers. Before the end of the game you would hear the cry of 'Full Time Results' and 'Final Score' with the ink still wet.

Having spent the morning scoreless, I took a yellow cab to Long Beach which was a short ten minute journey. Sitting in the rear, I took in the scenery through the side windows of the cab as the dividing viewing panel was obscured with a series of awareness notices for the passenger. I thought, you don't tell a Scotsman to 'belt-up', another read that the first 32 seconds will be charged at $2. It is hardly time to sit down. Large letters also signified not to ask for change as the driver only dealt in $5 bills. But the icing on the cake was the post stating that there would be an additional 50cent charge during the 'gas crisis'. My heart bleeds, £1. 50 pence a gallon. Oh what a shame, poor Uncle Sam, then I realise that it is me who is getting ripped-off.

Within minutes of stepping out of the taxi, the memories of working in Boston returned immediately along with the American endearment. "You guys all set?"', "My name is Tracey, I'm your server" and the ultimate "'Ya'll have a nice day now, ya hear?". 'It's an understatement' my sub-conscience uttered. One thing for certain is that 'I can hear you' and remember thinking 'Were they that loud?" What the heck, another couple of hours and I will be off to Mexico.

For all that 9-11 brought, security at Newark airport had been very sloppy as I found out. Once you are in the US, it can be just as difficult to get back out again, as I was taken to the side because my passport had not been stamped twice and there was also the question of the stamp containing the wrong date of entry. Why does this always happen to me? After some discussion I was allowed to proceed on my journey once finger prints and mug-shot had been completed. The only thing missing was a conviction number and a state penitentiary shirt. As I walked away I heard the stuck record of 'Have a nice day, sir'. Don't you just love them!

8-15 am and still scoreless. It's Monday and another day another dollar. I contemplate my day's options over breakfast. There is no ship's newspaper, the internet, which only Andrew Carnegie could afford, is down, as the signal has been lost. Just when all hope is gone, you find that prayers are answered. "Sir, can I get you a fruit juice?" It was the voice of a young Macedonian waiter. He asks if we are from England, and shares that his girlfriend is from Newcastle. "No" I replied," I am from Montrose in Scotland". Without taking a breath he started to recite all of the teams in the Scottish Third Division, including 'El-gin City'. What a tonic!

He had been educated at a private school overseas and his tutor was a Scottish school-mistress from Cromarty. "Speak to you tomorrow" he said, as I explained that I did not know how Montrose had fared at the weekend. With unlimited access to the internet I pinned my hopes on this crew member. Till tomorrow!

Reading material on this short trip consisted of Saturday's newspapers and a book called 'Pointless' which I had found on the bargain basement bookshelf even though it had just been published. The book 'Pointless' covers a season of Britain's worst football team, namely East Stirling. As I have said before, my previous life was East Stirling. Memories flashed back as I read through the pages, Board names, special games, the 2-2 draw with Hibs in the Cup, John Donnachie's goals and a sell-out crowd of eleven thousand, five-hundred. Changed days, I can even remember the greats of Chelsea gracing Firs Park, but that didn't get a mention. Deja-vu crept into one chapter; the game last season's match against Stenhousemuir, when a father complete with pushchair and eighteen month old son were part of the attendance. It reminded me of Gareth's first game, it was November '83 and a Scottish first round tie at Firs Park against Stenhousemuir. Sitting in the comfort of a Silver Cross pram dressed like the *Michelin Man'* eight-month old Gareth watched his first match. He has since graduated to writing articles this season for the Montrose programme. Start them young!

Another day goes by, I had thought on Saturday about phoning but by the time I reached LA it was nine at night, five a.m. UK time and I don't think Gareth would have appreciated a call and once he was wide awake, we were sleeping. It's difficult.

I think about my new made Macedonian friend, a contractor like myself but seven and a half months on the ship and six weeks home. We think that we are hard done by with four and four or six and two, even twelve and two is a luxury compared to his contract. Sometimes you don't get a choice, I could see the symptoms of missing his family, girlfriend,and the only thing keeping him going was his six weeks leave on the ships horizon. We 'contractors', we've all been there, it's like an illness or a disease in many ways, it's routine and through time we end up as creatures of habit. When you are working, you think of going home. When you are home you think of going back to your small extended family who nurse each other till it's time to go home again!

No score at breakfast from my Macedonian friend, but we are anchored off-shore at Cabo San Lucas and the chance of an internet café. On walking into Cabo, signs were plentiful in this picturesque but scorched town. *'El Squid-Roe'*, not the most appetising of names for a restaurant, is advertising its food. One night-club features, *'Dance till you Sweat'* – charming- but that was not what I was looking for.

I've found it! It's only taken four days and you know what they say 'no news is good news'. Four PC's situated in a convenience store charging 10 peso's for fifteen minutes, about a dollar, that will do me! Enough time to form an opinion and a report. No dialect was required, all was done by sign language, a wave of the hand to sit down and an outstretched palm for their dollar. It couldn't be easier as I uttered *'gracias'* as a way of thanks. For Saturday's results I just looked up the BBC web site and scrolled down taking note as I went. Arbroath 1 – East Fife 0, Berwick 3 - East Stirling 2, Cowdenbeath 0 – Queen's Park 2, then disaster struck, Montrose 0 – Albion Rovers 2, am I seeing things. First reaction-I've just spent a dollar, why did I bother? But that's not the spirit, remember, through thick and thin, good and bad, you support the team.

As I move around the other sites and message boards, I soon realise that the knives are out already. I can't believe this, two games into the season and posts read, Hall and Gilzean must go, from the 'shaky nail', to the signing of wrong players. There is also an attack on the Board- sorry- they have given the required support to the management. Knee-jerk reactions from Montrose supporters, the same supporters who complimented Henry and the Board in financing the player signings back in June. Short memories or possible amnesia has struck Links Park. As *'Steeplejack'* tries to quell the unrest on the message boards, he also reports on the mass exodus after the second goal. What message does that give to players? Certainly not one of support. So we were beaten at home, one point gained from six and a goal difference of minus two doesn't mean it is the end of promotion. I know, however, that Henry Hall had stressed the importance of a good start. At this point last season we didn't even have a point and Brechin also had an atrocious start to Division Two, yet lifted the championship flag. Eighty points is still the target, it can be done.

Aug 13th. ALBION ROVERS, Home - report and teams
A report, days late, old news but it did start back on Saturday the 13th at Edinburgh Airport whist waiting for a delayed flight to Newark. On finding a seat in the departures lounge, I had to clear away the previous occupier's debris from the seat. There is nothing like a second hand newspaper, pages torn and mis-filed but this was the *Airdrie and Coatbridge Advertiser'* a paper similar in content to the *Montrose Review* and is *'The Voice of Monklands'*. The new Albion Rovers' manager is looking forward to today's match but is still raging that his side did not give fans an opening day win over title favourites Arbroath. Chapman, in one breath hailed the battling qualities of his young side but fumed over the two goals that were conceded to Arbroath. The Rovers' boss feels that the visit to Links Park is another big test for his side but a more realistic one than Wednesday's Cup game against Gretna.

Meanwhile Henry Hall has a selection headache according to today's papers. Striker Willie Martin is out, which we knew, as he is suspended. McLean and Watson are both carrying injuries and are very doubtful. Henry states that it is unfortunate that they are out at the same time but someone is going to have to fill the gap. He concedes that we need another striker and that it will be addressed in the coming weeks. Speaking about Rovers' young enthusiastic side, he quotes, "It will be a difficult one and that it is really down to the players as to how the game goes". The *P&J* lead with 'The Goal is clear for Gable Endies' with Henry stating that he is encouraged by the two narrow defeats to First Division opposition. He also issues a warning to his players not to underestimate the Lanarkshire men, as there are no easy games in this League.

Henry Hall changed the team line up from Tuesday's Cup-tie against Clyde with Martin, Dodds, Doyle and Mclean dropping out. Reid also returned in goal replacing Jim Butter. Henslee assumed the role of lone striker supported by Fotheringham in the void between a midfield of Webster, Fraser, Kerrigan and young Euan Hall playing down the left side. A bench of substitutes containing Butter, Doyle, Dodds, Cargill and Watson filled the dug-out to capacity.

In a disjointed first half Montrose played as if they had Dutch clogs for boots with passes going astray and general poor ball control. The conditions contributed to this lack of control as Links Park had become the target of a rainstorm just before kick-off. This first half display lacked commitment as moves continually broke down. Communication on the field of play was non-existent and by all accounts players were uncomfortable, both with the conditions and roles, which they were not accustomed to playing. Chances in the first period were few and far between, with Rovers making the early play creating a few chances, before Andy Reid had to look lively when Rovers' number seven broke through the defence only to lose control. At the other end, Webster directed a header at Ewings in the Rovers' goal and Hall from a Henslee knock-down, ballooned a ball over the cross-bar. Albion Rovers won a series of corners which were cleared, but in different circumstance some of these opportunities could have been converted into goals by a stronger side. Most of the play now seemed to be down the right side of the park. Barry Donnachie and Webster linked well but the end product dwindled into oblivion. From a Reid kick-out, Henslee drove a ball high over the bar as the ball would not fall kindly for him.

The second period of time started with Montrose still searching for that vital goal with most chance falling to Henslee. When Montrose did score in sixty-nine minutes, it was from a Henslee header from a free-kick. This goal was disallowed for some unknown reason, possibly pushing, and this signified that this was not going to be Montrose's day. Changes to play were made immediately; Hall and Fraser were replaced by Watson and Cargill. The team formation reverted to a 4-4-2 system with Watson and Fotheringham leading the attack and Henslee was positioned on the left side of midfield with Cargill. With 72 minutes gone Albion Rovers took the lead as Montrose tried to settle into their new formation. A through ball found Chisholm who had the simple task of rounding Reid before netting. Montrose retaliated with a Cargill drive which went wide of the goal. A minute later things got worse for Montrose when Rovers penetrated the defence yet again to score number two. With 78 minutes on the clock McKenzie failed to cut out a routine low cross from Lennox which was glanced in for the striker's second goal of the match. This goal seemed to spur Montrose on but it was not going to be their day and Fotheringham missed from six-yards and Kerrigan headed over. Resultant shots from Elliot Smith, Henslee and Cargill were tipped over by keeper Ewings or were wide of the target. Frantic goalmouth scrambles ensued as time counted down for the referee to blow his final whistle in concluding the game.

Highlights – Only Greg Henslee and Barry Donnachie came out of this match with any credibility in a lacklustre performance. The front line was changed and changed again to conjure up some magic pairing formula with Kerrigan and Watson being Henry's final attempt. Today we carried no threat to goal, with the killer touch just not there.

Henry reflects, "It's the same as last year and I warned them about it. We missed chances and should have hit the target and if you don't score you will suffer." When asked if an out and out striker would have made a difference, Hall replied that Henslee had scored goals with Arbroath and that he is getting chances, he just has to take them. I also think that with there being no reserve league, there is no opportunity to help players increase their fitness levels. I also feel sorry for goalkeeper Hankinson who is relegated to third choice with virtually no chance of a game. It would be better for the club to farm him out to the Junior League where his reactions in goal would at least be tested. The club have amateur Marc Connelly spending time at Dundee North End this season and similarly winger James Russell and Robert Smith who are playing with junior side East Craigie. These lads in previous seasons would have got a run in the reserves mid-week.

NAC Breda kick-off their League season, it's a Sunday match against the might of Feyenoord and it's away from home. In their first home game they welcome neighbours Willem II from nearby Tilburg. I plan to take in a few games whilst I am here but on seeing the fixture list the better home games are not until the turn of the year. NAC lose their first game twee – nil (2-0) to a strong Feyenoord side.

Elgin City are in the news, and it's good and bad publicity. Assistant manager Kenny Black has launched a takeover bid for the club to which the Board has recommended approval. If his bid is successful the Black's have plans which will see the creation of a soccer academy with accommodation, sports bar, restaurant and indoor training facilities. His aim is to take the club to a First Division status with the club being the centre-piece of the Morayshire community. Black would also retain the services of current manager David (ex Montrose) Robertson. Robertson on the other hand has given the media a field day having just left his childhood sweetheart for the tea lady. El - gin someone!

Heavy successive defeats at home for East Fife has seen the Bayview faithful discontented with manager Jim Moffat. Losing four goals in consecutive weeks to Stenhousemuir in the cup and Berwick along with another defeat at Arbroath last Saturday puts pressure on both manager and players to break their duck in the points market. Montrose, on the other hand travel to New Bayview under no illusions as they play a side that was considered their bogey team last term. Three points for them too is a must from this fixture.

The ships internet system is still down, no e-mail to replace the writing of post cards. Weather hot, food good and having a great time – PS what was the Montrose score!

Puerto Vallarta is below the Tropic of Cancer, you can see the climate change, a humid heat and green landscape to match. A taxi ride through the streets takes me to the 'new town', a hovel. I remember thinking what must the old town be like and even seeing 'Woolworths' did not change my opinion of this town. There is no courtesy between drivers, with indicators being a luxury for most and anticipation an even bigger rarity as they plough into the tail lights of the car in front.

The reason for my journey is to send an email for travel home and to make arrangements for the Arbroath match. The internet café is sparse of decoration but much cheaper than the last if that is possible. I work out the Spanish screen commands and proceed to pull up e-mail or rather Outlook Express. Fingers and thumbs I start to manipulate the keyboard typing away with the backspace key groaning from overwork. It's a Spanish keyboard operated by a clumsy Scot who thinks the key operations are the same positions as at home or at least that is what the brain is telling him. It has taken 15 minutes to write a short email and that was only after help from my amigo in the next booth as the thumping and prodding of the keys got louder as the @ sign had failed to show. Fifteen minutes of work, something that can disappear down the Mexican Rio Grande as soon as you click what you hastily interpreted for send, but was in fact recycle. Whoops! Or words to that effect. Take two was executed successfully as the owner decided to change the operating language to English before I demolished his keyboard. I find out later on returning home that my e-mail had been to no avail as it had been detected as SPAM and subsequently deleted. I spend my remaining time catching up on the news at home. Henry expects more from Henslee and Fotheringham but does not mention the addition of another striker to the squad. The tone indicates that the two lads are the whipping boys for Saturday's defeat to Rovers. Gable End Graffiti reviews the coming Saturday's encounter at East Fife, depicting Montrose playing Jim Moffat's 'Bores of the Season', a comment which I hope does not backfire. After all we have to win sometime but so do they! The 'Pie and Bovril' site, aptly named after the fans half-time purvey, questioned in the general chatter message board, whether anyone had read Jeff Connor's book 'Pointless'. I didn't realise it was just on the shelf, as I had received a four pound reduction on the price. There were the usual comments, one punter questioning the £16.99p price tag and its worth. Another points out a £3 reduction at a certain bookshop but the question was 'What did you think of it?'

Having just read the book and taking my background into consideration I probably know more than most and can reflect on the characters and the happenings at Firs Park. My early recollection was of a promoted side, having just won promotion along with St. Johnstone. The first home game in Division One was against a strong Kilmarnock side before going down 2-0. The faces of goalkeeper Ronnie Swan, Ernie Collumbine, who captained the side, and a team peppered with players whose careers took them to Montrose. The Kemp brothers, Jimmy and Roy, inside man Sandeman, left winger Jimmy McIntosh and the ginger locks of the late Jimmy Kilgannon. He would kick his granny!

But the book was about sadder times, bottom of the pile for three seasons running and a pointless existence. A Manchurian who has had the luxury of watching United or City does not know the meaning of 'Die-hard' or the pain that is involved. Just who would play for £10 a week, it's not enough to cover your train fare. The supporters deserved a bigger input into the book, their tales of travel, their frustrations at finding games are off and the demoralising factor of getting beaten week in, week out. All in all, it's good to see someone taking an interest in a smaller club and other fans buying the book. You also get the wise-guys on the site posting 'pointless' and saying 'Are we talking about East Fife here!' It will soon be derby day and this Cowdenbeath supporter just maybe will regret his 'pointless' post. (As it happens East Fife did win 1-0)

It's full-time and time is up at the café, 'Adios Amigo', or a possible good riddance as the café owner thought I was more bother than I was worth. Taking another white knuckle ride back, I passed the 'Golden Arches' of American fine dining (McDonald's). Only then did I remember that I had not looked up this Saturday's fixtures. Oh well, by 8 am Saturday morning they will be results.

"Weh aye man!", its Roska the Macedonian waiter, obviously converted to the Geordie language by his girlfriend. He takes great delight to tell me that England were 'gubbed ' by Denmark and then gives me the bad news which I already knew. Saturday's score, I got it. Montrose 0 – Albion Rovers 2, "Aw rite man", and with that he departed.

A delayed reaction in hearing the scores of the previous week, but that is the reality of being away from home. I remember whilst working in Boston, five hours behind, ten o'clock kick-offs but I would tune into Radio Scotland's live games via the net. It was the days of Ivano Bonnetti at Dundee and his squad of non-nationals, Speroni, Carranza, Nemsabse, Cabberello and Canniggia. The only real MacKay (Dave) was on the bench. Scottish Football, BRILLIANT!

It's six days later and although it is mid-morning here, another six hours and it will be Saturday at New Bayview. Commitment is needed from Montrose for this game, belief and a will to win installed in the players by manager Hall. I've no doubt that goals will come if sleeves are rolled up and a bit of bite is introduced to their play. It's about time we had a settled team as there have been too many positional changes to the side, some of which have been enforced by injury and suspension, but not all. From reports that I have read it seem Montrose lacks formation and that a 4-4-2 system doesn't suit. A change of tactics to 4-5-1 may be the answer but this requires a lot of co-ordination with players knowing exactly what their roles are in supporting one another. It also puts a heavy burden on the lone striker who has the soul-destroying task of chasing every ball that is pushed through. Andy Reid is definitely Henry's first choice for goalkeeper, the defence should pick itself but there seems to be some doubt whether Paul Doyle should play alongside Stephen or in midfield. Neil Stephen does not look comfortable when Doyle is not by his side as they seem to have an intuition when playing together. Injury has also affected Henry securing a regular back four. The usually reliable Donnachie has also had a few unsettling moments but I hope his game returns as he would be my first choice for the number two spot. Elliot Smith is possibly the most consistent performer in the squad and operates well on the left side of defence. Midfield seems to be the crux of Hall's problems having eight possibilities and players of varying styles. Now may be the time to try five in the middle with Fotheringham just in front of two ball winners who would need to be Dodds and Kerrigan. Webster or Watson and Henslee would play right and left of midfield respectively. Support for Martin upfront would break from Fotheringham, Henslee and Watson or Webster but this has to be co-ordinated and could take some time to master. Holding a strong front line should work against the stronger sides of Stenhousemuir and Berwick but again may not work at Berwick's park of Shielfield because of its tight pitch. Tactically, it's Henry's call but the players have to be comfortable as well, organisation is key and a win can change people's views thus delaying the P60's for the management team.

It's 7a.m. Pacific time, but also kick-off at New Bayview. I am up and the sun is heading for eighty-six degrees, weather conditions at Methil certainly won't reach that. I wonder if Gareth has made the game, he certainly knows where it is as he has been to the ground before. Once a ship building area and now an unemployment black-spot, Methil has never been a happy hunting ground for any Montrose side and on this occasion both managers know that they must win to preserve their positions.

We are at sea today and half-time signals breakfast, at least food takes your mind off things momentarily, but as soon as the final whistle blows I head to the ships internet which is now back up and running, food of another kind, a balanced diet of football and football. Access is expensive as there is a $4 charge to log-on and 75 cents per minute there after. Why did I bother, the results were there for all to see. Things come in three's, three league games, three games without a win and we are on the receiving end of three goals, two of which were scored in the remaining minutes of the game in a 3-2 defeat. Even the Shire won and are no longer 'pointless'. The only thing that saves Montrose from the bottom league spot is goal difference, at least in my dream we were eighth!

Was it worth it? No. Connections were slow, it was just seven minutes and it was robbery on both accounts, two late goals by East Fife and a bill for $9.20.

Aug 20th. EAST FIFE, Away - report and teams
Late summer sunshine made the conditions for fans and players alike first class. With a surprisingly good following from Montrose fans, the team showed a few changes from the previous week. Willie Martin returned to the fold and Doyle took a place in the midfield. Reid was in goal, the defence repeated itself from the Rovers match and starting midfield places were found for Webster, Fotheringham, Kerrigan and Doyle. Martin and Henslee assumed roles in the front line. There was no place on the bench for Calum Watson as Hall, Cargill, Dodds, Fraser and Butter were the Montrose substitutes.

In an open first half both teams failed to make the grade. East Fife's long ball ploy cancelled out any chance of football at ground level. The referee further compounded frustrations on the field by being whistle happy as he awarded free-kick after free-kick. There was no rhythm in this staccato game which was again delayed by the referee's insistence that throw-ins and free-kicks be taken exactly at the point of award.

Early first half chances fell to both teams, long balls from East Fife saw their forwards compete one to one with Andy Reid and at the other end a couple of Fotheringham free-kicks caused considerable anguish for the Fife support. Henslee also headed over from 8 yards from another free-kick. The game bounced from end to end, ex- Montrose player Craig Smart coming close and Paul Doyle landing a shot on top of John Dodds net with the keeper stranded. Andy Reid then pulled off a good save again from Smart. After this Montrose somewhat lost the plot for the remainder of the first half by conceding needless fouls on their own doorstep. The half ended with a Montrose attack, Willie Martin taking the final shot after good link play from Webster and Fotheringham. Unfortunately for Martin his low angled drive was just out of reach of the on-rushing Henslee. Not quiet a repeat of last week's first half, but at times it came close.

The second half started as the first had ended with a midfield battle but it was not long before Montrose regained the territory with the game finally coming to life in sixty-four minutes. A thirty yard free-kick awarded on the edge of the East Fife box was curled by Fotheringham around the wall and past the helpless John Dodds. 1-0 Montrose, but this was short lived as in 69 minutes the equaliser for East Fife was scored by Craig Smart. At this stage many supporters would feel things were over, but this was soon lifted when Fotheringham again restored the Montrose lead. Willie Martin chased down a long pass holding off the East Fife challenge to the bye-line where he played a short pass to Fotheringham who made no mistake as he buried his shot past Dodds and into the net for his second goal. It was all Montrose at this point, some good running from Willie Martin could have sealed victory, Kerr Dodds was in a better scoring position and despite screaming for the ball, and Martin elected to shoot for goal himself from an incredible angle. Dodds who had replaced Webster would most certainly have scored to put the game out of reach of the Fifers. Henslee headed wide a Donnachie free-kick, a Fotheringham corner was held by keeper Dodds and it really looked as if three points were heading to Links Park.

Then disaster struck! A long kick-out from Dodds saw full-back Donnachie tussling with his opposing number for a ball which rolled out of play. The referee deemed to favour East Fife in this tussle by awarding a free-kick. Donnachie for his part was booked but only after verbally abusing the decision making man. With three minutes remaining, lighting struck not only once but twice. A repeat of last week, a routine ball fired low across goal saw McKenzie kicking fresh air and McDonald bundled the ball past a startled

Andy Reid in goal. With injury time being played out, Donnachie's simmering feud came to the boil when hesitation in clearing the ball saw the East Fife forward rob him of the ball. The forward played a shot across goal to John Martin who calmly stroked the ball home. A largely undeserved win for East Fife and a carbon copy of last year's steal at the death, another game from which Montrose should have taken something. Heads bowed the players left the field as supporters vented their anger toward the dugout. It was reminiscent of scenes which have not been seen since the days of ex-manager John Sheran who finally resigned.

❖ – <u>No Trust</u> – ❖

The game at East Fife it caused Henry strife
As we suffered a three – two defeat
Two goals at the end says we cannot defend
As supporters took to their feet
Poor Henry was slammed and even harangued
As the team left the field heads down
Supporters it's said left Henry for dead
Requesting a new manager be found

Highlights – Plaudits go to Martyn Fotheringham for his all round contribution and two goals, which he took with precise execution. Kerrigan also is worth a mention for regaining supremacy in midfield. In defeat we must be humble, no matter how un-merited this win for East Fife may have been. The score cannot be changed so there is no point in dwelling, but the manager has to ask himself why the players lost control of a match that was won. Or is it a case of, we just beat ourselves, thinking that it was won. In the end two individual errors cost Montrose the match.

A target of eighteen points from the first quarter is still possible, but it also means that every game must now be won and the chances of that seem remote. Can we put together a run of six games?

Los Angeles, 'City of Hope', a couple of days here and then back home, where ever home is in this nomadic life. One thing, communication here will be easier as I purchase a thirty minute international calling card only to find that to the UK I have a call time of fourteen minutes. I call home but speak for only a few minutes, no time for a father and son talk but enough time to realise that things were not good at Links Park." It was dreadful today, you have no idea and you should see the damming reports on the web sites and message boards". I had forgotten that this was the first time that I had been in contact with Gareth, no report on the Albion Rovers match and just a few minutes today on yesterday's debacle. The tone in his voice tells me that it is serious, three strikes and you are out! I am a bit shocked as I for one like Henry Hall as a manager. He has given the team stability and tries to play a passing game, but what now! The Board have a dilemma, do they weather the storm, which I think they should do, and give Henry time to turn things around, possibly incurring the wrath of the fans and losing out on play-off places or do they call time, depending on the result of Saturday's important derby clash?

Just what is wrong I do not know. It's hard to tell at a distance, but there is some sorting out required in the home dressing room. A few closed door matches may be all that is required to settle the side. Back in July, Henry Hall and Ian Gilzean had on paper the safest jobs in the division, lack of success changes everything in a very short time and puts more pressure than normal not only on the manager but also the Board. There is no one standing in the wings to take over, so let's hope for a victory against Arbroath as it will restore the faith of this cynical support and give Henry some time get a settled side together. At times we expect too much, so heads up lads!

I thought a few days holiday would do me good, this is not a nightmare, this is real and that about sums up our season so far and our three games to date, but don't panic!

The local derby is a few days away, and Saturday's fixture has caused controversy in the past. The safety of players became a risk, ex- Montrose goalkeeper Dave Larter will remember having been in the firing line of the Arbroath support. Larter, having played for Arbroath couldn't possibly now play for the enemy. Two of Henry's recent signings Andy Cargill and young Greg Henslee fit the same bill, Duncan McLean also comes into this category. Surely, in this day and age of civility, fans should not need to be segregated from each other at this level of football. It's good to see Arbroath back at Links Park. In a preview to the eagerly awaited match, manager Hall emphasis the importance of the game. Hoping that lessons have been learned he states that his players are too attack minded and that we have to be focused more defensively. Added to this he quotes "We have imperfections at either end that we have to work on." The manager knows that a lot is riding on this tie as D-day approaches in more ways than one. Aptly the '*P&J*' headlines 'Hall feels the draught of Gable Endies back door'.

The day has arrived; no waiting for a phone call at five o'clock or a text message and no sitting in an internet café following the score and scorers. Today I can attend and see things for myself and draw my own opinions, without depending on someone giving me a match report second hand. It's a completely different feeling from other Saturdays of sitting in the wings, today I can be centre stage, well behind the goal!

You may find this report is tinged with a helping of Montrose bias as it is a welcome return of the derby matches with our neighbours Arbroath. As you enter the town, travel safely, 'Here's the Basin, there's Montrose, shut your een and haud your nose'.

Aug 27th. ARBROATH, Home - report and teams
Deflated, yes a bit, BUT WE WON! A schoolboy performance, over celebrated by the fans, players and management, but it is three welcome points.

Expecting a larger than normal crowd I entered the park at two-forty. As I walked down Wellington Street, my eye caught sight of the notices posted to warn opposing supporters that segregation was in place. On filing through the turnstile I picked up a match day programme before making my way to the terrace behind the goal. The ground at that time was fairly empty with the Arbroath fans having received the freedom of Links Park definitely outnumbering the few Montrose fans that were in place. We are all creatures of habit; we sit in the same seats, we stand at the same parts of the ground. When segregation is in force some parts of the ground are no longer accessible. The 'Knoll' had been given to the away support, a stand point for many Montrose supporters including a contingent of die-hard old stagers. When I looked across, there they stood, slightly down from their normal position, undeterred at what was going on around them. I thought old habits die hard and Willie even had his bike with him!

A few young lads, stood close to the barriers exchanging verbal niceties with the opposing support. 'We've got soap, youse havnae, we've got soap, youse havnae' or a chorus of 'You only sing when you're fishing'. It was good to hear later on the songs of the 'Links Park Dynamo' and 'I was born under a Gable End', this time songs of support for the team.

The crowd grew to a staggering 888, I had expected more but it also included five Rangers fans in their late twenties sporting their favoured team shirts. Why were they not at Ibrox where Rangers were playing Hibs? It soon became obvious that they were only there for one reason as they made a beeline for the barriers, and that was to cause trouble. As with the young lads, no one had seen these characters at Links Park before. After twenty minutes of the game 'Plod' complete with CCTV footage took steps to eject two of them along with a third a few minutes later. The blue of Rangers could easily be mistaken for the Montrose colours if it hadn't been for the crest on the shirt and at a distance this may not be seen. This is only one reason for the need for segregation today as Arbroath brought the tally of ejected fans to seven.

The Montrose side lined up with a change to formation with Henry favouring a 4-5-1 counter-attacking system. Reid retained his place in goal. Donnachie was axed after last week's vendetta and held a place in the stand (one less booking for him). The defence for the accused read Dodds, Doyle, Stephen and Smith. The five in the middle were made up of Webster, Fotheringham, Fraser, Kerrigan and Henslee. Virus sufferer, Willie Martin passed himself fit to play upfront. McKenzie, Hall, Cargill, Watson and goalkeeper Butter made the bench.

The teams emerge from the tunnel and I hear myself say "You guy's all set?" for a derby game which is the first of four this season. Let battle commence!

The game started at pace with Arbroath being the more active side stringing a number of fast exchange passing movements but never troubling the defence. It was obvious from the first minute that the defence were under instruction to clear the lines as they booted and scaifed away anything resembling a football. Kerr Dodds sharp tackling also intimated that he is after the right back spot, as he fought hard for every ball. Montrose's first attack on the Arbroath goal came some 13 minutes into the game.
 Ex-club servant Roddy Black held Willie Martin and from the resultant free-kick, Fotheringham came close, shooting just over goalkeeper Cairns' bar. In nineteen minutes Montrose took the lead, just when Arbroath were looking the better team. A short passing one-two between Fotheringham and Webster saw Webster break free to sprint down the right, leaving the Arbroath defence in his wake, to feed a ball across goal for it to come off Willie Martin's shin, trundling into the empty net. There was silence, but then again there was jubilation but only after the initial relief.

The remainder of the first half ground down to a midfield battle. Too many times when the ball did break to Martin he had no support. I would have thought that Webster and Henslee would break forward and support to the middle would be given from Dodds and Smith moving up. Elliot Smith had played well in keeping any traffic from the left at bay, breaking up play on more than one occasion. However on one occasion he lost out, but Reid pulled off a point-blank save to save the day. The resultant corner was bulleted over the bar after Reid had palmed the initial ball away.

The game restarted for the second half much as it had ended with some scrappy play in midfield. Arbroath were the hungrier for the game and soon made a few chances only for the final pass to go astray. In 59 minutes the burley ex Arbroath player Andy Cargill, serenaded by his faithful with 'You're no stranger to a pie', replaced a tiring Fraser who is still lacking match fitness, in midfield. At this stage the game once again sprang into life when Henslee headed in, after some Montrose pressure, only for the assistant referee to disallow the goal for some infringement that was not apparent. A clumsy challenge at the edge of the box on Henslee saw Webster curl a ball against the bar. The resultant rammy in the box saw Fotheringham repeat the feat as it then cannoned onto the post. Arbroath were clearly shaken as the match started to boil over. The referee had already booked McMullen and Reilly of Arbroath but the flash-point really developed when Kerrigan and Jackson scrapped furiously for a ball in front of the dug-outs as it went out of play. Kerrigan was fouled and clutching his face with one hand he sent Jackson crashing to the ground. Both players were booked, a stricter referee may have red carded both players for their actions. Even at this stage of activity when Montrose were giving a lot of effort some supporters were continually heard haranguing Hall with shouts of 'Get it sorted!!'. Some will moan all of the time.

As the game dwindled to an end Arbroath increased the pressure on the Montrose goal. A series of three corners had Andy Reid punching away and a Bishop header came off the post as Arbroath fought for an equaliser. Almost on time Arbroath had goalkeeper Cairns booked for unsporting behaviour as he booted the ball out of the park when it was a Montrose corner. From the corner which was taken short Montrose lost the ball and lost advantage. This was a complete waste of an attacking chance on goal. The final minute saw Fotheringham enter the referee's book. When the whistle did sound (by the way, no one left early this week) there were scenes of jubilation all round but I did think some players did go over the top considering they were posted missing during parts of the game.

Highlights – Steve Kerrigan's efforts in midfield today were tremendous as he fought to win every ball in the middle of the park. His timely tackles to break up play and his heading ability in the air made him, for me, man of the match. Andy Reid also gets a mention. It is also the first time that I have seen Reid play, and I thought the goalkeeper showed his ability when dealing with crosses, sometimes clutching and at other times knowing when to punch clear. He also seems relaxed when receiving pass-backs from the defence as he gives the ball a good solid boot back up the park. Full backs Dodds and

Smith stuck to their tasks well, as they shadowed their opponents throughout the game with Kerr Dodds making some no nonsense crucial tackles. This is the type of aggression that is required in midfield as he is a ball winner and would give much needed support to Kerrigan in this department. Maybe Henry will move Dodds forward once Barry Donnachie has completed his one hundred lines of 'I must stay clear of vendettas.'

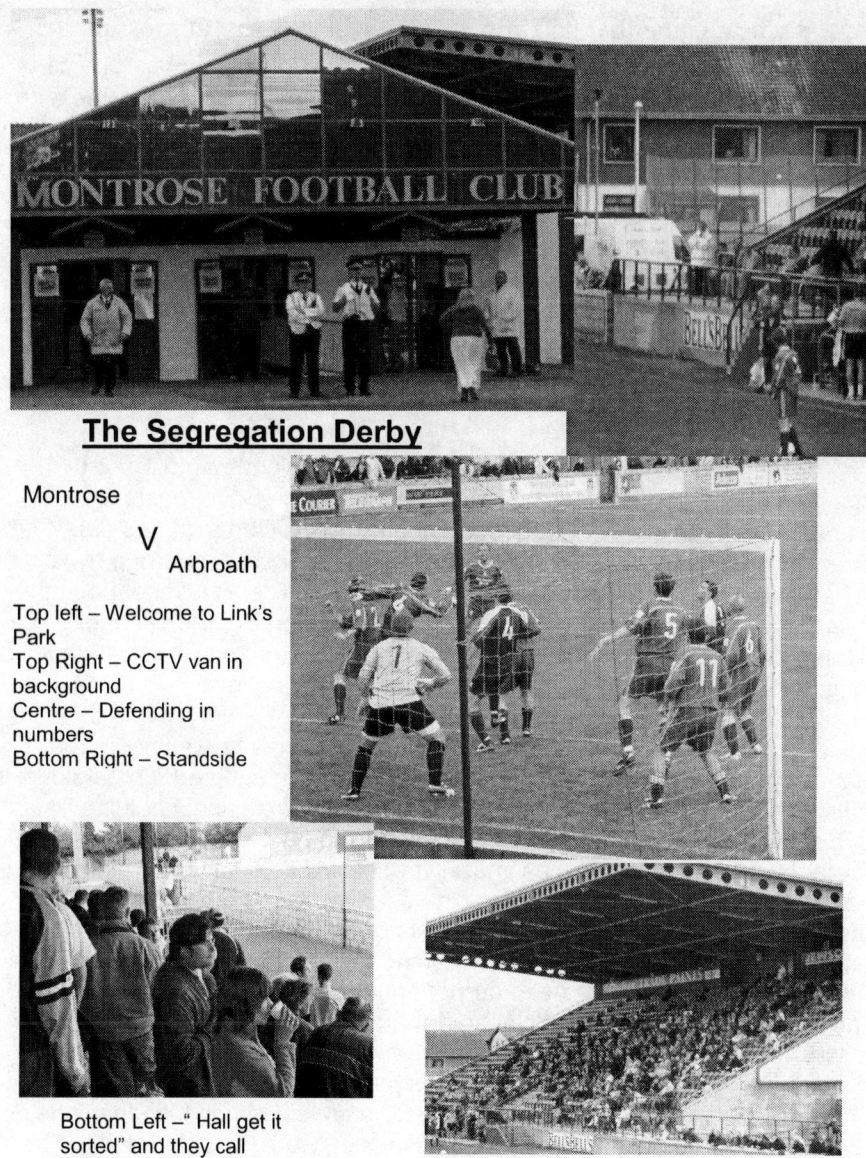

The Segregation Derby

Montrose

V

Arbroath

Top left – Welcome to Link's Park
Top Right – CCTV van in background
Centre – Defending in numbers
Bottom Right – Standside

Bottom Left –" Hall get it sorted" and they call themselves supporters

It was good to hear plenty of singing at the game, and a bigger turn-out than usual. Although the actual match was not a classic, at least it was a game that had atmosphere which is lost at most home games. Winning has helped but there is still a lot of work to be done as fitness and sharpness still at this stage needs to be honed to bring the team up to the level of other outfits. There is a free Saturday this coming week and this should be used to sort things out on the playing side. A closed door match should be arranged where Henry can roar and shout, and even stop play when he wants so that players are aware of their roles in supporting others when the breaks are on. Hall should be given credit for playing a 4-5-1 formation today as it was the right choice for a game in which Montrose had to battle hard to achieve the result that they did. Hall said later that Montrose had defended well and that the players had worked for each other. He also agreed that Arbroath did have more of the ball but rubbed salt into the wound by adding "We got the goal."

The derby weekend saw East Fife take first blood with a 1-0 win against visitors Cowdenbeath. Stenhousemuir hit the Shire for six and Queen's Park ran out 3-1 winners to Albion Rovers. Derby games are normally against your near neighbours with whom there is a strong rivalry. What do Berwick and Elgin City have in common? They could not be further apart, one located South and the other in the far North. This scenario happened to Montrose last season when they were paired with Gretna. It's a long trek on a New Year's Day. Berwick won the encounter 3-1.

The Review reports that Neil Stephen suffered a broken nose from Saturdays match and on top of that Duncan McLean suffered a breakdown in training which revealed after an x-ray that he had sustained a hairline fracture of his tibia. It seems he has been carrying this injury since the friendly with Forfar back in mid-July. It is estimated that he will be out for six weeks and if Henry wants to sign a striker before the deadline then he has six hours till midnight. Meanwhile it never rains, but it pours, Barry Donnachie will also be unavailable till the end of September as he gets married this weekend. All of this brings home the need for not only another striker to bolster the front line but an additional outfield player. Although the transfer window will be closed there is also the option that the manager can still sign unattached players and he also has two 'wild card' signing opportunities at his disposal. One web site hints a whisper of a move for a left-sided unattached midfield player which would possibly mean that Henslee would be promoted to the strike force. One thing for certain, we need to add to the squad before the game with East Stirling.

Thursday was not only a work day but a team building day. We are a small team and can only just muster eleven, no room for substitutes in this small squad. It was a morning of team pictures and winding each other up as we were going paint-balling to shoot the hell out of each other. On travelling to Zeist, I was pleasantly surprised at the event complex to find that it was KNVB Dutch International Soccer Academy. The massive grounds boast training pitches, running racks, swimming pools, tennis courts, indoor training facilities and accommodation of hotels, dormitories and restaurants. The facility is used to coach youngsters from an early age, to rehabilitate players who have suffered serious injury and also by the Dutch League and International sides. Bruised and battered from the paint-balling, we ate in the Jan Nieskeen restaurant, a fitting tribute to a great international player. It was an enjoyable day, but it also made you realise just how well the Dutch are set up to coach and develop the youth of Holland into football greats. The SFA coaching facility at Largs is not a patch on this. Scotland really needs to improve its standard of amenities in order to move forward in sport.

A Saturday without a game – what will we do? Scotland play Italy at Hampden Park but there is little chance of seeing that. Holland will also be playing in the World Cup Qualifiers. It will be Northern Ireland and not the Republic that will take pride of place in O'Meara's, the Irish bar, as the Republic does not play France until Wednesday. So its support Northern Ireland or watch the Dutch qualifier game against Armenia. When we were young we would listen to coverage on the radio or get up to all sorts of tricks. This discussion took place with some work acquaintances, all were from different countries and cultures, but just the usual things that young lads got up to at that time. One colleague looked embarrassed and he said quietly,"' I remember one thing we did. We collected dog dirt in paper bags, we would place them on a neighbour's doorstep and we would set fire to them and ring the doorbell. The neighbour would come to the door, see the fire and immediately extinguish it with his feet." Safer to watch the Dutch game!

I've changed my mind - setting fire to paper bags is more exciting, as the Dutch game transpired to be one of the most boring games imaginable. Where are the matches!

I mentioned last Saturday about match fitness and the need to sharpen up. Henry Hall has taken that on board as a friendly match has been arranged for Tuesday (6th September) with Peterhead visitors to Links Park. It also means the return of summer departures Wood and Sharp and previous defectors, Michie and Gibson. It is now the right time for players to take a sharp look at themselves, giving the manager the commitment and attitude required. The manager has put his faith in them by making the signing and it is now their turn to reciprocate. The game should be a good work-out for all but let's hope that there are no injuries to add to Henry's woes as he prepares for Saturday's East Stirling match.

Sept 6th. Peterhead (friendly)

Montrose lost narrowly by two goals to one at Links Park against Peterhead in an arranged bounce game. Manager Henry Hall saw fit to play the bench warmers, and blooded farmed-out signings James Russell, a winger, and full-back Robert Smith. Even young Hankinson got a run in goal during the second half. Henry also fielded a trialist on the left side of midfield, Graham Fyfe, who had previously had a trial in the pre-season friendly against Deveronvale.

With 5 minutes on the clock, Calum Watson opened the scoring at his second attempt. In a flowing passing move involving Elliot Smith to trialist Fyfe to winger Russell who then squared for Watson to score. In a sluggish first half, Peterhead, who had more of the possession, equalised in thirty-five minutes when manager Iain Stewart struck home during a stramash in the box after Butter had parried a Sharp drive. Honours even at half-time and more changes as the second half began with Henry giving everyone a run out to make up for the blank Saturday. Peterhead's winner came from the penalty spot with Michie netting after Sharp had been pulled down by Elliot Smith.

In a game of multiple substitutions, young Russell with his running and taking on of players caught the eye and looks a good addition to the club through time. The game provided a good work-out for the players and it would also give the manager a heads up for Saturday's team selection.

Tonight was an enjoyable evening and was an evening of culture, as we sat in the Grote Markt having a pre-match drink. Cokes all round. The group could be mistaken for being the butt of so many jokes as there was a Scotsman, an Englishman and an Irishman all with international priorities and depending on who's telling the joke there is always a fall guy. We were just work colleagues trying to see their teams on the big screen. As we headed for the Irish bar 'O'Meara's', one of us was always going to lose-out and it was me. The Republic who played France dominated the big screen with England having been relegated to a twenty inch TV situated at the far end of the bar. This meant poor old Scotland who played Norway being reduced to score updates. On arriving at O'Meara's it was packed to capacity, there were even people camped-out, sitting on the floor. It did not take long to realize which team they supported, for as soon as the teams took the field they belted-out the French national anthem. As one person said,' I thought this was an Irish Bar!'

The atmosphere in a normally quite bar was tremendous due to the non-drinking French student contingent who flaunted their arrogance by using the owner's facilities. Until now I didn't realize the French were as passionate about their football as their faces reflected every passing move, distorting this way and that. "Alay, Alay," they shout passionately, along with a very English "you only sing when you're winning!". The second half brought the only goal of the match as Henry curled a shot past the outstretched Given. Celebrations took over from them, hugs, kisses and another rendition of the national anthem. Meanwhile at the other end of the bar stood a solitary figure, our work colleague from that mega city of Doncaster as he watched the demise of England losing to Northern Ireland. At full-time he filtered past saying "I need to go home, Sven has to go, they've got to sack him, I need to go home" and he left!

As we headed back to the square for post mortems and coffee the Dutch were also celebrating having beaten Andora but my thoughts were with Scotland and their 2-1 win in Norway, a Kenny Miller brace taking the points. A good win considering the times we endured under Bertie Voghts, I bet the fans are still *'reeling'* yet!

It's back to league business as Montrose look forward to Saturday's away clash with East Stirling who are on a high. Fortunes for the Falkirk club seem to be changing, a win against Arbroath, victory on Tuesday night in front of a sell-out crowd against Premier League club neighbours Falkirk in the Stirlingshire Cup and the book 'Pointless' which seems to have become very popular. Taking this into consideration and the fact that Montrose had not been getting results, this tie has the potential of disaster, so it is important that Montrose score first and as early on as possible.

The Shire's main strike threat will come from man of many clubs Ally Graham and Ian Diack who has been scoring well in games so far. For Montrose, no signings have transpired even though there is acknowledgement from the manager that he needs another striker. Graham Fyfe a left midfielder who played as a trialist against Peterhead seems to be interesting Dundee manager Alan Kernaghan and has been invited to the First Division club for trials, indicating that Montrose have lost out on his services. On the plus side, Watson scored in Tuesday's friendly and may return to support Willie Martin upfront as Montrose may revert to a   4-4-2 system at Firs Park. But things are far worse than it seems, Neil Stephen has undergone an operation on his nose and is out of today's game, McLean and Ferguson are long term walking wounded and it also transpires that Webster has a groin injury. Add to this the unavailability of Donnachie and the three goalkeeper scenario you will find that we have serious problems in fielding a team and furnishing the bench with five substitutes. I think that Henry realised on Tuesday that he would have five out and would have to call up farmed-out signings Russell and Robert Smith from East Craigie in order to fill the bench for today's game.

This morning I shop in s-Hertogenbosch and add two pennants from ADO Den Haag and FC Groningen to the Dutch collection. In returning mid afternoon I walk to town to look up some home related information I require that is on the internet. It's a baking hot day, the temperature is twenty-nine degrees and the last thing that was on my mind was looking at financial information. Suddenly there is a text message as the sound of frog's croaking reverberates from my phone. I think what a sad person I am as a normal call would play La Bamba! The message was from Gareth, it was short and sweet, '0-0, pretty even, not good to watch', what more can you say? After sifting through the information I needed the matches were in the last fifteen minutes and it was still 0-0, the only highlights that showed on the Sky timeline site were two bookings, one a piece with Willie Martin receiving his for unsporting behaviour. The team lines read, Reid in goal, Dodds, Doyle, McKenzie and Elliot Smith. Henry fielded a midfield consisting of Hall, Fotheringham, Kerrigan, Cargill and Henslee, with Martin leading the lone charge on goal. So I presume we are on a 4-5-1 and the bench has Russell, Robert Smith, Fraser, Watson and Butter in place. Watson has since replaced Cargill in sixty five minutes as Henry pushes to win this game.

Joy in 82 minutes as Henslee scores, the screens are changed, just eight minutes to hold out, surely we can do it. I don't know what it is, when you are down on your luck, you are down. Just like Bayview, we have a goal in the last minute of the match as East Stirling equalise through Dymock. Talk about being deflated, I cut the connection at the internet cafe and I go. It is not long till I am croaking again, the message '1-1, lost goal final minute, we missed penalty, Henslee scored, should have scored more.' I stop off at the Hotel Ham to reply to his message but just can't understand today's results and Montrose's missed penalty. East Stirling had beaten Arbroath and Stenhousemuir thumped the Shire 6-1 and today Arbroath recorded a 1-0 win against Stenny. It just shows that in this league, teams are much on a level par and there is not much between them. Just as I start to go over the penalty miss and what it would have meant in points, Hotel Ham provided some respite as I watched the ingenious waitress clean the outside table-tops with a window squeegee, and a pizza delivery guy whizzing across the precinct on a moped doing a wheelie. Someone's pizza is certainly going to be lop-sided tonight! It's time to go home. No more post-mortems till I speak to Gareth.

Sept 10th. East Stirling, Away – report

Another 'Happy Bus' travels to Firs Park and another draw is the outcome. The mood on the bus was despondent to say the least but this time there were no scenes of New Bayview calling for the manager's resignation.

The *Courier* reported, 'Montrose threw away a fistful of chances', Henry said "We are really disappointed with the end result" and "It should have been a win for us." Earlier in the match Henslee missed from close range, Fotheringham sent in a curling ball which rebounded of the inside post and Euan Hall missed a sitter. It about summed up the afternoon, Kerrigan squandered two chances from slick passing movements and Willie Martin missed a penalty with keeper Jackson making the save after Cargill had been up-ended by Mackay. The rebound fell for Fotheringham who failed to score.

The first half saw both teams competing well and at pace. It was pretty even by all accounts. The Firs Park turf was re-laid during the summer and Montrose easily produced their best football display to date. Hall, Cargill, Dodds and Fotheringham all linked well in neat passing moves. It was the delivery of the final ball into the box that either went astray or drifted out of play which put paid to creating even more chances. Time and again, Montrose attacking moves were started by Kerr Dodds, who had urgency in his play and strode forward on many occasions, as Montrose sought the first goal. Shire came close before half-time, Diack the culprit heading over with Reid having been beaten to the ball.

The second period of time saw Montrose take control, firmly entrenched in the East Stirling half. There was a hunger in their play, but scoring was not on the agenda. A missed penalty that was not on Sky Sports, but it was clearly yet again not to be. Even when Henslee scored, doom and gloom set in a minute from time. There is not a lot you can say, Henslee picked up a booking five minutes from time and a stunned silence greeted the final whistle as the crowd headed home (all 195 of them, the lowest of the season).

Highlights – Kerr Dodds today was a winner in 50-50 tackles and committed in attack. Fotheringham and Kerrigan stuck to their roles in midfield reading the game well and controlling the area. Henry stated that a number of regulars were missing but the side didn't look the worse for that. It was a good performance but Montrose lacked that cutting edge. Calum Watson caused problems for the Shire defence when he replaced Cargill but we sadly need a striker who can take advantage of the chances and opportunities which are created.

There was a poor team called the Shire
With performances totally dire
Montrose could not score and the game was a bore
Who thinks Henry Hall should retire?

Not a lot is going well for Montrose at present, once again the message boards are looking for a new manager, some have taken to poetry, while others are quelling the posts and putting out the fire. I personally don't see the point of changing the manager as things will eventually come good in the end. Chances are being created and one of these days -----! Remember the Forfar Cup game? Everything is going to happen at one time and some team in the not too distant future will receive a hammering!

Ever the optimist, there are four games left until the first quarter of the season is over. That's twelve points, plus the five we already have and a possible seventeen points. Two games at home and two away brings the first quarter to a close. We can dream or we can do it!

Berwick head the league after five games having recorded a 1-0 away win at Cowdenbeath. Spoils were shared at Borough Briggs after Elgin surrendered a two goal lead to Queen's Park and East Fife had a good win against Albion Rovers scoring four goals with their long ball tactics. Stenhousemuir dropped two points at Arbroath after leaving it late with McGrillen equalising in 89 minutes from the penalty spot to counter Arbroath's opener. Montrose, are sitting in seventh position in the league with five points, that's one point a game!

The Graham Fyfe saga goes on! Fyfe appeared as a trialist last Saturday as Dundee played Airdrie at Dens Park. Substituted at the half-time break, the former Celtic midfielder has failed to secure a contract with Dundee and is again a free agent. Whether Henry Hall will pursue Fyfe for a third time is yet to be seen.

The merry-go-round at Elgin City is still also ongoing but the wait is almost over as the Board and shareholders come to a decision. Elgin are without a win and believe that the take-over bid by the Black's has affected the players both on and off the field. An early evening meeting is arranged for tomorrow night at Borough Briggs when a final decision could be taken. Whatever the outcome from the meeting, Elgin supporters will be looking for a home win, as they entertain Albion Rovers on Saturday.

This Saturday is the Qualifying Cup quarter-finals, for the North and South Leagues with the eight victors taking their place in the first round proper. It makes you realise that the draw will soon be taking place. In previous years in the early rounds Montrose have been drawn away, so just for once it would be good to receive a home tie. The first round is not due to be played until November 19th with the draw taking place mid-October-some time till we know our fate. We look forward in anticipation, as the draw can be a money-spinner, especially in the later stages once the elite from the Premier League join the minnows.

Montrose prepare to play Cowdenbeath at Central Park and in the past these games have been very tight. It is not a favourite venue for Gareth, as going there twice last season he witnessed two equally bad matches ending scoreless. One match was straight from that memorable win in the Cup at Station Park, Forfar. Central Park is a ground that lacks atmosphere as the small playing surface is surrounded by a stock car racing track with fans standing some distance from the pitch. The stand on my last visit did not keep-out the elements and the general facilities were much in need of maintenance. I just get this feeling that Gareth will decline to go on Saturday, so it will be a phone call or a text message as I will be in Rotterdam for a different type of ball-game.

Cowdenbeath, under new management since Baikie's resignation, have had a sluggish start under Mixu Paatelainen. Losing both home games under his charge he will be looking for a win against Montrose. Meanwhile the P&J lead with the headline 'Time for Gable Endies Push, Says Manager'. Henry remains confident that his team can be pushing the teams at the top despite a poor start. The walking wounded are listed yet again, Webster is fit but Barry Donnachie is still unavailable. Andy Cargill who showed up well against the Shire faces a late fitness test on a hamstring injury.

Sitting in brilliant sunshine in Rotterdam, just finishing a meal with family and my mobile sounds. It's a text, but it's one of these texts that you have been dreading all day. You know what you want it to say but realistically you know what it will say. I wasn't quick enough to react as I was paying the bill at the time, but there it is – you have a message! The message was short and to the point, '2-0 Cowden, we were clueless', end of message. No sign-off, not even 'G', or his alias Fred –What's going on?

The reason for my trip to Rotterdam was to see the XXXVI World Cup Baseball Final which was being held at Familiestadion Neptunus, not far from the Mosque and Rotterdam Spartak's ground. I was expecting a Cuba-Netherlands final and a good atmosphere as the semis were played the night before. So I was a bit surprised when we arrived. It was South Korea who were the opponents of Cuba. You would think that the USA would be strong candidates for a final place but it was a lesser side that had been sent to compete in the World Cup as the baseball season is in full flow competing for the 'World Series'. Wait a minute, how can you have a 'World Series' when it is only American home based teams that take part? Another thing that has been screwed up! The Cubans have won this tournament twenty-four times since 1938 and out of thirty-five occasions that the tournament has taken place. Tonight there only looked one winner. As always with these games the American hype takes over, even in the Netherlands. Between innings in this glorified game of professional rounders the music reflected the mood of the game. 'What's going on' boomed out from the speaker system.' Hey, hey, hey, I say hey, what's going on?' A reflection of today at Central Park, but something that I will not know until reading reports on Monday. I wonder what excuses will be given, will the hatchets be out, and maybe it's me 'optimistic Tam', who has been wrong, thinking things will come good for Henry, may be it *is* time to go. Monday will tell it as it is.

> There was a post on the web
> The kind you usually dread
> It calls to resign, but all in good time
> As Henry hangs on by a thread

A quick phone call to Gareth tells me that one web site had published its match report earlier than normal. It did not dwell much on the game, but it did give reasons why time for Henry was up. Time for a change bullet pointed fitness, out of date training methods and no youth policy, a situation that needs rectified after the Central Park fiasco. If it continues Montrose will be the laughing stock of the league. You might ask what happened, but by all accounts we could not fill the substitutes bench or maybe I should say we did but with two goalkeepers, one of whom was stripped for out-field. We have spoken about this before and reflected that the team could not support three keepers and that if one was released then funds would be available for another out-field player. The small squad is coming home to roost. Last week Henry was able to call on Russell and Smith who are farmed out for the season. This week Russell's club, East Craigie were unable to release the player, but at least we got Robert Smith, failing that it would have been really embarrassing having to list Ian Gilzean as a twelfth man. Glitches like this need to be addressed before they happen. I know we have five or so injuries and so should the manager, he must plan ahead to fill the gaps. It's not often that I would say that it's worse than I thought but after hearing this it brings it home that time is clearly up and that it is time for a new face. The writer of the web report states that Henry Hall is a decent man and that he is sad in writing his article. He positively points out that Henry can be astute and that he was responsible for turning around the side of 2003/4 after John Sheran's departure.

There are younger managers in the field today with new coaching methods and tactical awareness. The players need lifted and that will only come from someone who has new ideas. Eddie Wolecki, an ex-player and current manager of junior side Lochee United is a name that keeps coming up. Lochee, which has sports psychologists and dieticians, do well in the Junior Super League. Wolecki led them to the Scottish Junior Cup Final in 2004. I personally would look for a player-manager, a striker, an ex-senior who is looking to management, someone who is good for a few goals and years yet. The decision is now up to the Board. If the decision is left too late, then for any new manager coming in, the play-offs could be out of reach and promotion for another season out the question.

The league is starting to take some shape now and a gap is forming at the top. Berwick are on eighteen points, Stenhousemuir sixteen, Queen's Park ten, with Cowdenbeath and East Fife sharing nine points. Montrose, still on five points, *are* still within reach of Cowdenbeath and East Fife. Results at the weekend saw Berwick, record a 3-0 win at home against Arbroath and second placed Stenhousemuir taking three points from East Fife in a 2-1 win. Elgin battled out a 2-2 draw with Albion Rovers and Queen's Park defeated East Stirling 3-0.

Sept 17th. COWDENBEATH, Away - report and teams

Gales and rain, not the best of weather conditions for playing football or for supporters at Central Park today. Montrose made one change with Andy Cargill failing a fitness check before the game. Henry stuck with a 4-5-1 formation of Reid in goal, covered by Dodds, Doyle, McKenzie and Elliott Smith. Hall, Fotheringham, Kerrigan, Webster and Henslee were the midfield fit-out and once again Willie Martin continued out front.

In the first half Montrose played into the wind with the Blue Brazil taking the advantage. It was an attacking first half performance from them as Montrose defended to keep their goal intact. Andy Reid once again showed his skills with a tip-over save early on from a dipping shot. His acrobatics were called upon again and again as he pulled off save after save with Montrose showing little reply. When chances did come, goalkeeper Hay saved from Kerrigan with Fotheringham sending the rebound wide of goal. Martin and Henslee also had opportunities but failed to even draw a save from Hay. The first period ended in stalemate, but Montrose could now look forward to the wind at their backs.

Henry's half-time team talk did not cut any mustard, as there was no improvement on the first half performance. 'Clueless' possibly summed it up as Henry persisted with a 4-5-1 system instead of reducing the midfield to four and pushing a player forward to support Martin, especially when we had wind advantage. When the break-through did come it was Cowdenbeath who were on the score sheet. In 53 minutes the defence failed to deal with a ball from the left and after several attempts to clear in the six-yard box, McCallum drove home. Four minutes later Cowden made it two when Graham Guy dispatched a free-kick from the corner edge of the box after Fotheringham had fouled. The final 15 minutes saw some attempt to salvage a point from this encounter with Montrose winning a series of corners but did not hit the target. In front of a poor crowd, Kerrigan, Dodds and Fotheringham collected bookings for today's exploits.

Highlights – Only Andy Reid showed commitment with a string of fine saves. Today was a lack-lustre performance, which was reflected in the players' body language. There was no passion in the Montrose play and it is sad to say but there was no direction from the dugout. Heads must be raised and attitudes changed in the dressing room. Obviously the players are uncomfortable with present tactics and Henry should revert to 4-4-2. I hope next Saturday, if Henry is still in place, that the supporters give him a chance and that they do not inflict their attention directly to the dugout from kick-off.

It's Monday, and there is nothing on the *Courier* web site, not even a report. There was no mention of the match or any other Third Division side; in fact Brechin didn't even get a mention. Was this because Dundee United won on Saturday, as most articles were directed towards them? As expected the message board was full of statements, 'We are definitely going backwards', 'He has lost the dressing room' and 'We are a disgrace'. Things even go back to losing three strikers and only bringing in one replacement. No matter what is said the fact is that Henry is still manager. One 'Mori Pole' post has heard on the grapevine that the Board will have a chat with Henry this week. It's all doom and gloom - according to one fan, Saturday's home task when we play Stenhousemuir is already lost, but we will see.

Funding is all about moving forward, today we received full funding for our project. As one colleague said it is all downhill from now on! It is a major milestone in the execution procedure, a step that was taken by the Montrose Board earlier. To authorise this kind of money you have to demonstrate a confidence that will meet expectations and the end target. It will only be downhill if we let it as now is the time to manage and take decisions. Some decisions that we make are neither right nor wrong, as they only turn out wrong if we let them, by not making them work. It is worse not to take the decision and face the real challenge that awaits. In a business where timescales matter, it is a team game, where if one fails we all fail. Tomorrow I hope we can cut ground.

The Elgin takeover saga goes on for another two weeks as their team captain states that he will leave if the Black's offer is rejected. Their manager David Robertson has also indicated that he may leave the club. The longer negotiations are protracted the more the playing side on the field is going to be affected. Elgin's Board really need to decide quickly for the future of the club and its support.

Stenhousemuir are visitors this Saturday, the good news is that striker Colin Cramb is suspended and will miss the match. Manager Des McKeown, fresh from a SFA fine for bringing the game into disrepute, still has the best strike options available to him even with Cramb suspended, pair any two from Carroll, McGrillen, Savage and Mercer. This week is a tough test as I reckon Stenhousemuir are better equipped than Berwick who have yet to lose a match. In goalkeeper Willie McCulloch they have the safest pair of hands in the League and if there was a weak spot it could be in defence. Messrs, Denham and Renwick were signed in the summer to plug last season's gaps. Although both are very experienced professionals, they may lack pace, which may allow Montrose an in-road to goal.

From what I can gather in this week's *'Review'* , Henry is most disappointed with the teams showing at Central Park. He goes on to say that he had brought in good players but the team is not showing the quality displayed last season and as a team are not blending yet. Positively, Henry focuses on the next two games against the league's pacesetters. He displays the right attitude by saying, "It might just be the challenge we need to get our season started". There is little doubt in his mind that the team's performance requires to step-up a level as he states "We have to roll our sleeves up and start converting the chances we are creating. The team has been doing a lot of work on finishing at training this week." Stenny beware!

This game could be a make or break situation for Henry, hopefully he will change things around and revert to 4-4-2 if we are to take anything from this match. Barry Donnachie is available and should be able to fill Hankinson's place on the bench or in fact play. Hopefully the Doyle / Stephen partnership can return to the ranks and Dodds can be pushed forward into midfield to give Kerrigan a hand. I would play a midfield formation of Dodds, Fotheringham, Kerrigan and Cargill. Up front a starting pairing of Watson and Henslee is worth a try with Martin relegated to the bench. A drastic change is what is required and it could be the saving of Henry Hall. Saturday's vidi-printer result will be interesting.

Saturday is here again, and that means weekend chores. People say, "You are here or you are there". They have this image of sunshine and adventure, nice surroundings and that everything is hunky-dory. Well, you still have to do your washing. On some occasions I have a washing machine other times it's a laundrette and the risk of your washing coming back misshapen, shrunk and not all there. Sometimes there are a few additional items added just to make up the quota, would you wear someone else's jocks! It's no joke. In Kazakhstan, your washing was bagged by the maid and done in the basement of the multi storey apartment. A three day turn-around service could stretch to six days ending in an identification parade. There were also times that the good stuff went missing. I did not mind as they were poor people-some only had one set of clothes. It makes you appreciate what we have. In the Netherlands I have a washing machine, but there is a catch, the power doesn't come on till 9 pm at night through the week.

So Saturday it is. I think I will try and find a game to take in today. When I was in Athlone, not the Mecca of Ireland, they did show Scottish League games from time to time. It's that old Celtic connection. I remember venturing one Saturday around the hub, well I walked down the main street to see if any of the local hostelries were advertising a game. There was only one-no names no pack drill - Aberdeen were playing Celtic, but there was a reluctance to venture in as this was the self same pub that a few weeks earlier displayed the poster featuring Celtic versus the Hun's. By the sound of the shouts from inside, the match had already started, what will I do, go in or go home. It's a toss up. Deep breaths, courage brother, courage, I opened the door, suddenly I could hear the Tremeloes sing 'Silence is Golden' except there isn't a juke box. Heads are turned and eyes are on me, a sea of green and white hoop's and a stranger in their midst. I sat in the corner by myself before being flanked by a family of green and white clad late-comers. Thankfully no smoking laws in Ireland dictate smoke free premises and fortunately for me at half-time, it gave this non-smoker an excuse to depart, never to return. 'How do I get into these situations?' I ask myself. You would think I would be wise enough, big enough, old and ugly enough to have learned by now.

Today, I decide to walk to the railway station to buy a ticket for going home next week. My walk takes me down and along the inner ring road. Time to think. Two more games after today's match and the first quarter of the league season will be gone.

Heading back into town I pass *'Purple Rain'* circles of smoke drift from the cannabis café portraying a nil-nil draw. 'What's going on' booms out, a reminder for a second consecutive Saturday, but I remain positive as we could get a draw!

I pass the statue in the park of a child pulling away from its father. There is no clue to its body language, the child could be saying 'I want to go to Links Park' or the father could be telling the child, 'You're going to Links Park'. It passed time, as I made my way to *'Surf and Talk'* with my arrival coinciding with kick-off. As I searched the sites, only the *P&J* had a preview of the match and Henry Hall's thoughts. "We need to start scoring and convert the chances that we make." It was a re-run of the manager's Montrose Review comments. Willie Martin is doubtful for today after picking up a pelvic injury from the Cowdenbeath match. As expected Stephen, Donnachie and Webster return to the squad. There is a late fitness test for Dodds who is suffering from a thigh injury.

Stenny's assistant manager makes a good point in saying that only the champions go up automatically as the promoted side this season with the introduction of the play-offs. Smith states that they have to keep things going and be that top team. Mercer scores for Stenhousemuir in 6 minutes, good start! I leave *'Surf and Talk'* at half-time heading for home and just hoping that things will have been turned around by the time I reach home and the vidi-printer of 'Final Score'. How wrong can you be, as McGrillen, 85 minutes flashes up, making it three goals with no reply. It's 5-45pm and *'Purple Rain'* descends!

'Don't worry about the world coming to an end today. It's already tomorrow in Australia.' (CharlesSchult)

Sept 24th. STENHOUSEMUIR, Home - report and teams
The team sheet resembles a 4-5-1formation with no change in tactics which was a bit disappointing. Both Dodds and Martin took to the field, Neil Stephen returned but to partner McKenzie in central defence. Webster was on from the start assisting Kerrigan, Hall, Henslee and Fotheringham in midfield. There was no repeat of last week's bench as Watson, Fraser, Doyle

and Donnachie took their seats along with goalkeeper Butter. The play-offs are running away from us. According to 'Mori-Pole' (I never doubted him) the Board have concerns and did have a word with Henry in mid-week. After today's result, time is only a game or two away.

Notable away wins this week for Berwick, Elgin and Cowdenbeath. Berwick's 2-0 win at Coatbridge ensures they keep top spot. Elgin recorded their first win of the season at the Shire by the same margin. Arbroath went down 3-0 to Cowdenbeath and were also reduced to ten men for all of the second-half. An own-goal was enough for East Fife to take the points from Queen's Park.

NAC Breda v AZ Alkmaar (Sunday 25th Sept.)

It is a sell-out crowd. I didn't know this at the time, you never do when you decide to go to a match on spec. The weather was fine, last of the summer sunshine as fans arrived in their droves, most wearing the yellow and black of NAC Breda. I made my way to the information centre only to find that no tickets were available for today's match. A disappointment, but I should have known better as AZ lead the top of the Dutch league. TV vans, radio stations and reporters line the stadium yard slab. Stretch-limos arrive, businessmen alight but this is a game for all except me. Young fans proudly wear the team colours, families arrive on their bicycles (what else), maw, paw and wean's. The atmosphere builds up, as do queues at the turnstiles as entry is delayed by body searches. The police are in attendance, loitering at each corner of the ground, kitted out for when trouble flares, shin pads and padding to thighs in place and CS gas under their belts, a deterrent for any fan. Vendors litter the extremities of the stadium, selling NAC merchandise, food and a trial of FIFA 06, a football computer game. No programme sellers in sight, boxes of the A6 size edition are left on the corners of the stadium for supporters to help themselves -nice touch. It's almost kick-of, queues increase at the turnstiles, one more wouldn't make any difference as I think back to the days of 'Lift me over Mister!'. "Pierre, Pierre" fills the air prior to the start of the match as the fans chant for their hero, van Hooijdonk. The bike park is full as fans start to park their cycles on the outer fence and the whistle sounds thus starting the match. Ooh's and aah's, whistles and jeers, sound throughout as fans show appreciation for their team's effort.

Right – Fans
wear their
colours

L/Above – Go by limo
Left – Take your girl
Far Left – Search me

**NAC
v AZ**

Above – Locked-out
Left – Sell-out Crowd

Ten minutes gone and so am I, as I take the road home with Pierre van Hooijdonk's name still echoing in the background. I didn't see any of this today, highlights on Dutch TV will be my only hope and a chance to find out the final score.

Before I can watch the highlights I receive a call from home, 'Breda won 2-1 today' - thanks Gareth. 'How was yesterday's match?' Silence ensued before he uttered, 'Harry Cairney resigned as Arbroath manager after yesterday's match and Forfar also lost their manager who resigned for business reasons.' Sad to say, Montrose were no better yesterday, tactics resembled 4-4-1-1 or was it 4-5-1 and someone had stepped out of line? In the second period a 4-4-2 prevailed. Montrose has scored just one goal in the month of September, that statistic reflects the need not only for changes in tactics but the need for a striker, which had been spoken about, but has not yet transpired. The players are obviously not happy with play and this seemingly was demonstrated by Webster at his withdrawal from the field of play when substituted. I wish I had a magic wand, it's not something that you can kiss and make better, as we just have to ride the storm for the time being. Some fans were vocal, calling for Martin Allan and Colin Maver to replace Henry, but this is not the answer as we have had ex-players before in John Sheran and David Larter. The Board must now decide just how long an extension of time they can withstand before gate attendances dwindle and finances are seriously affected. Today I witnessed a sell-out crowd at Breda, the attendance at yesterdays match with Stenhousemuir was three hundred and one, and gates in previous weeks at Firs and Central Park were also low as people will only support a winning team.

The newspapers concentrate on Harry Cairney's resignation with names of replacements submitted by the journalists. Paul Smith, John McCormack and former club captain John McGlashan lead the field and are expected to apply for the vacant position of Arbroath manager. Another paper leads with 'It's all change in the Angus Clubs hot seats' quoting 'Montrose are struggling in the bottom half of the table after a dismal start and sections of the home support were calling for the manager to be sacked during Saturday's match'. But it is how Montrose played that is of interest to me. Finally more information from Saturday's Match is available.

This week good conditions prevailed at Links Park for the visit of Stenhousemuir. Two changes from last week's team sheet with Doyle and Fraser dropping to the bench, with Webster and Stephen filling the vacant slots.

The game started scrappily with passes going astray and being over hit. Henslee combined with Hall but the move frittered out. Fotheringham threaded a pass through to Henslee who chipped the advancing McCulloch in the Stenhousemuir goal only to see the ball sail over the bar. The Warriors took the lead in six minutes. McGrillen sent in a cross from the left which was headed down by Mercer and past Andy Reid.

Poor refereeing decisions led to numerous free-kicks as Stenhousemuir penetrated the Montrose ranks at will. Reid saved the day punching clear crosses targeted for Mercer as the defence struggled to cope with the aerial threat. It was one-way traffic which could not be stemmed. Half-time and manager Hall along with the players made their way down the tunnel to the sound of 'boo's' from the stand. Disgruntled supporters, but over the break the manager could salvage something from the game as we are only one goal down.

Starting the second period, Montrose still sat deep in their half, allowing the Warriors to move forward in numbers unchallenged. McGrillen won a free-kick at the edge of the box but the resulting kick was cleared. Meantime, Willie Martin clashed with his opposite number in front of the dug-out, both players were booked and Hall subsequently replaced Martin for his own good with Watson taking over as the lone striker. Two minutes later Montrose were dealt a further blow when the referee awarded a penalty for a tackle on McGrillen in the box. McGrillen dusted himself down and sent Reid the wrong way to score in sixty minutes. The game was now over, but Montrose did have a chance to claw their way back when a Henslee header rebounded off the inside of the post. Atrocious luck has pursued the youngster, hopefully this will change.

The rest you know, Doyle replaced Stephen, an angry Webster made way for the introduction of Fraser, and McGrillen scored his second on the eighty-five minute mark after a stray Doyle pass.

Highlights – A poor showing, lying too deep and no tempo to the play. As one critic said,' The tempo was flatter than a Dutch meadow.' The players can do better, I know they can, but they are not motivated for some reason. Only Kerrigan, Euan Hall and Martyn Fotheringham deserve a mention from the match. Andy Reid for the first time this season was not on top of his game but still came to the rescue on several occasions. Montrose, sit in eighth spot with only East Stirling providing the buffer from bottom place. That could change next Saturday as Albion Rovers are the visitors to Firs Park. What looked like a good season at the start has turned into a nightmare for all concerned. A change of luck is needed fast!

Bad decisions and poor defending take the rap for Saturday's performance in '*The Courier*'. The manager is quoted as saying, "We were still in the game at 1- 0, but the second goal was a killer and the third was disaster". He also states that Willie Martin was only 75% fit, so it begs the question as to why he was playing when Calum Watson was on the bench as a replacement. Henry closes by saying that it was a better all round performance than last week but admits that there is a lot of work to be done. He asks for all concerned to keep positive, as he can't bring anyone else in at the moment, so basically it is down to the players and that they have to blend.

Attention is diverted from the manager as supporters turn their focus and wrath on the Board. The message boards were full of comments with the first post appearing an hour after Saturday's final whistle. There is nothing like being direct, as the post said – 'The message to the Board is simple, act now or go! I condemn this attitude as the Board have been supportive and have kept the club going in difficult times. This situation is no different, as we just have to bear with them. The Board realise the position, they would not call a Board meeting for Monday night if they were happy with the way things are going. One fan pleads with the Board that they should be able to see that there was no organisation on the park and a lack of respect for the manager. He also focuses on Saturday's crowd and the fact that he could spend a 'tenner' in better ways. This is something that you certainly don't want to hear. A supporter quite rightly asks, ' What has gone wrong, why has Henry lost the respect of the players? What has led to this, as I can't understand why things have deteriorated so quickly into the season?' The poster is quick to say that he is sick and tired of the roundabout of hiring and firing managers and the persistent lack of success at the club. We all have expectations, we all have dreams and we are never happy, but when did Montrose last have a manager poached by another club?

What is it they say, "no news is good news"? Well there 'ain't no news' from last night's Board meeting. Chairman John Paton is on holiday and it looks likely that a decision will not take place until his return. It gives the manager a glimmer of hope in facing undefeated Berwick at Shielfield or is it just delaying the inevitable.

Today was tinged with sadness as I read that the Club's Honorary President, Willie Johnston had passed away. Everyone at Montrose Football Club is saddened by his death. Willie's contribution to the club spanned over many years. He first became a member of the supporters club prior to the war, helping to raise funds. In resurrecting the club post war, he was elected chairman in 1946, holding this office for thirty years. His chairmanship also extended to the Forfarshire Football Association and he was also a member of the Scottish Football Association.

As a mark of respect the club intend to hold a minutes silence prior to the next home game with Queen's Park. It is a fitting tribute to a real gentleman who has done so much for Montrose Football Club.

Montrose make the trip to League leaders Berwick this week and for Berwick fans it will be a game of revenge, a grudge match. Some seasons ago Berwick were drawn against Montrose in the Scottish Cup. It was in the early rounds of the Cup and the match was at Links Park. Berwick who had the ball at the time had a player injured and played the ball out for a Montrose throw in, so that the physio could attend to their man. On resumption the throw-in was passed to Kevin Webster who duly thumped the ball over Berwick's stranded keeper, who was waiting for the ball, back in this day of sportsmanship. The goal stood even after protests and a tunnel ruck. Ever since, Berwick fans have never forgiven Montrose for this act, but memories are short as I remember a young Shire full back (McCluskey) being immediately hassled in similar circumstances when he was forced to hit a rasper of a pass back from the Berwick half, to Willie Duff in the Shire goal. Duff only dived after the ball was in the net as he was caught out on a wet day returning from behind the goal having given his 'bunnet' to a young supporter who was standing in the rain. It was funny at the time but likewise it put Berwick one up.

Berwick are going strong having amassed twenty-one points from the seven games that they have played. It is an impressive start to the season, but it remains to be seen if it can be sustained as complacency will set in. In past years, the leaders at the end of the first quarter seem to fall away and by the time April comes around they are out of contention for the promotion spots. This season could be a bit different due to the play-off positions that are up for grabs, giving another bite at the cherry.

Berwick boast an experienced strike force of Gareth Hutchison and Ian Little. Haynes is another player who has been on the score sheet. Some summer signings have seen Chris McGroarty sign up along with ex- Morton goalkeeper Coyle. Manager John Coughlin has built up a side which earned him the Manager of the month trophy for his efforts and results.

According to the Manager, Montrose are still struggling with injuries. Willie Martin will not feature but could make up the bench; Calum Watson looks to take Martin's place in the front line of one, if we stick with 4-5-1. Neil

Stephen should be fit to play and could partner either Doyle or McKenzie. Henry is also demanding more from the players and is calling for Kevin Webster to exploit the open space of Shielfield.

Berwick are sitting pretty, it's time for a fall and their minds will be on next weeks encounter with Stenhousemuir at Ochilview. The message boards are full of predictions of three and four nil. The Berwick support are cocky and I can't see many fans travelling down from Montrose to take the match in. So as luck may have it this could just be the game that Montrose will win. When the chips are down something turns up. Let's hope so as anyone who travels that distance deserves a bit of enjoyment and a score that will reflect a good day out.

Arbroath have appointed ex Montrose player John McGlashan as manager. The former Arbroath player who went to the Junior ranks at the end of last season takes over from Harry Cairney who resigned. November 5th will be an interesting match when Montrose travel to Gayfield for the next derby game.

Run time errors and opportunities to de-bug- what more can one ask for. It's part of the scenario that the club is currently going through. Hopefully a fix can be made shortly. It's just a pity that the *P&J* web site did not work as it should today for the same reason, but it is now rectified and there is no news of the pending situation ------

But the next day 'I won't be next, says defiant Hall' headlines the *P&J*. An angry Henry Hall states that it is business as usual. After changes to the Arbroath and Forfar managerial hot seats, Henry is adamant that he will not be next to collect his P60. Speculation after last week's defeat to Stenhousemuir and Monday's Board meeting, has added fuel to the fire but is seemingly nonsense as the Board meet regularly every fortnight.

The manager turns his focus to today's match stating that injury has led to a poor start to the season and that the injury situation is no better for today's game. The walking wounded are listed, Martin, Cargill, Ferguson and McLean - but we will soldier on! Henry also mentions a free agent, a player that he is running the rule over who is looking to come into Scottish football. I hope he is a striker!

Well you won't believe it but the *P&J* web site is down again! Today I am met with the greeting of 'We're very sorry but we are currently experiencing technical difficulties. Our technical team is working on solving the problems as quickly as possible, but please accept our apologies for any inconvenience we are causing you in the meantime.' When I read this I look at the wording, technical difficulties means we don't know what is wrong and the plural, problems means there is likely to be more than one. The use of the word quickly usually reflects that it could be sometime and it was, but I accept their apology.

After reading four match reports I find that there is no consistency in the reporting, was it Little or Haynes that scored for Berwick and was it Ian Little or Kevin Little? Between that and Coyles getting mixed with Doyles it is all a bit confusing unless your name is Kevin which was used countless times. It's quite obvious nobody can be bothered to check the accuracy at this level of football and that reports are generated to fill a space. This should be worth two pages!

Oct 1st. BERWICK, Away - report and teams

Berwick's one hundred percent record has gone and they can consider themselves fortunate that they did not lose all three points. Montrose lined up in a 4-4-2 formation, a change to recent weeks. Reid took his place in goal and was shielded by Dodds, McKenzie, Stephen and Elliot Smith who returned to Shielfield for the first time since being freed by Berwick. The midfield positions were taken by Webster, Fotheringham, Kerrigan and Hall. This week I am pleased to say we played with two strikers. Calum Watson convinced Henry Hall of his fitness in training and partnered Greg Henslee upfront. As 'Steeplejack' said in his report, 'What a game to miss', I was home but had too much to do, I did get as far as Edinburgh but only as far as IKEA and by the sounds of it I also missed Montrose's best performance of the season so far.

Berwick dictated play in the first half but Montrose showed up well, especially full-backs Dodds, and Smith who seemed to have something to prove to his former employers. Andy Reid denied Berwick chances to open the scoring. Reid saved from both Little and Haynes before Haynes crashed a shot off the bar. Although both teams went in at the interval goal-less they still had produced scoring chances in an even matched game.

Both teams came out for the second period fired up. Montrose started well with Berwick goalkeeper Coyle pulling off an unbelievable save from a Kerrigan header. Andy Reid once again kept his goal intact by pulling off a superb save from a Kevin McLeish penalty which was given by the referee in unconvincing circumstances as Dodds was not booked for his misdemeanour. Berwick however took the lead in 54 minutes from the resultant corner, with Ian Little heading home.

Montrose held their heads high and for the last half hour took complete control of the game. Kevin Webster was instrumental in this turn-around. As expected, Kevin had suffered the taunts of the Berwick support but proved to be a thorn in their side as he silenced the support with an equaliser in 65 minutes. Webster had picked up a pass from Dodds, and swivelled to drive low past keeper Coyle for the Montrose equaliser. Berwick lost all composure from this point and Montrose were deprived of victory as keeper Coyle pulled off saves from Kerrigan and Henslee. Henslee had further chances to open his October scoring account but it wasn't to be, as he missed all three. In 80 minutes Doyle replaced a tired Watson who had showed up well in leading the line. Donnachie, Fraser, Martin and Butter remained unused on the bench.

Before a reasonable attendance of four hundred and sixty-five, referee Boyle allowed play to flow, booking goalkeeper Reid from Montrose, and Shields and Haynes from Berwick. We will give him the benefit of the doubt for his penalty award as there was no way possible that Dodds deliberately handled the ball. Maybe that is why he did not produce a yellow card. In a passionate and committed display Montrose deserved more from this game and it gives hope for the future and also an extension of time for Henry.

Highlights - This certainly was a different Montrose team today which on this performance quiet easily could be in Berwick's shoes. The emphasis should be on the word team as everyone played a part. Special mention should go to Kevin Webster who suffered a torrent of abuse from the Berwick support but he did not let this affect his game and scored the equaliser. Andy Reid confidently pulled off quality saves when it mattered, Dodds and Smith stuck to their tasks in keeping Berwick's wing play at bay. Kerrigan once again won every ball in the middle of the park and was well supported by a much improved Euan Hall. Upfront Henner thrived in his new found freedom and was unlucky not to be on the score sheet. By all accounts Montrose looked good and surely better times lie ahead. Looking at the message boards some who were at the match commended the players for their performance but as usual some are still critical.

'Dynamo Rumble' referred to the manager's 'Courier' preview of today's match as drivel and is highly critical of the Board for not taking action. He also thinks the season is over, but it may only just have begun. There is support for Henry Hall among the support who are rational in their thoughts. 'Mr.Bluenose' (I thought he was a Rangers supporter but then again the Mo play in blue) states in his reply 'So we sack HH and the Board, then what?' As he quiet rightly points out – you just can't sack everyone!

I'm confused, is 'Dynamo Rumble' really 'Mori-Pole' or is he 'Ferryden Mo'? One poster says 'All we ever hear on this message board are demands for sackings - of both the manager and the board, yet very little by way of a constructive and a realistic alternative. When you've worked out what that alternative is, one day maybe people might start taking you seriously'. I don't know if he has been using multiple logons, but it seems that he has been sussed by some and it is time for him to play a different record. This could apply to a few of us!

Has the result at Berwick been a turning point? Let's hope so. We now really need to put this poor start and all the ill feeling that it has aroused behind us and get behind the team. Saturday was a definite improvement and the manager is trying to improve the squad, but we may have to wait to see what Henry brings in during the January transfer window.

Saturday's results – An Ian Diack brace sees East Stirling take the points from Albion Rovers in a 3-1 home win. The Shire now move to sixth place in the table, swapping places with Rovers who are now bottom markers. The surprise result of the day (for Stenny fans at least) was at Central Park where Cowdenbeath run out 4-1 winners with the Stenhousemuir defence having an uncharacteristically bad day. East Fife took the points at Borough Briggs in a 2-0 win and Queen's Park and Arbroath shared the points in a 2-2 draw at Hampden.

I just don't believe it! Today I thought I would have a look at the *Montrose Review* web site to see what Henry was saying about Saturday's match at Shielfield. What do I get – You are not authorized to view this page! It goes on to state that 'The Web server you are attempting to reach has a list of IP addresses that are not allowed to access the Web site, and the IP address of your browsing computer is on the list'. So I am a marked man-for what? I am no terrorist or computer hacker, I don't use multiple logons and just because I am in the Netherlands, does it mean I am under suspicion? After all who in the Netherlands would want to look at the '*Montrose Review*' web site- only an ex-pat!

I thought that Henner's signing for the club was all done and dusted but it seems not. The SFA have set a date of today October 6th for a tribunal to be held to decide a transfer fee as both clubs failed to reach an agreement. The tribunal is to be held at Hampden in Glasgow and both clubs will be represented. I don't know what Arbroath are asking but Montrose should ask for a bit of a rebate due to the fact that he has only been on the score sheet the once.

It is strange how things transpire as I later read the headline 'Rivals reach Henslee compromise'. Arbroath officials had approached Montrose Directors prior to the tribunal to agree a fee to which both parties were in agreement. The fee will remain undisclosed, which suggests to me that Montrose got the better deal.

So it *is* true, as the message boards reveal that Henry's mystery 'free agent' is in fact an Australian and better still he is a striker. Some fans have 'no trust' as author 'Ticketyboo' does not live up to his name when he asks 'So where is this new striker?' It is as if he does not believe that the manager is trying his best. Henry's hands are tied until the January transfer window to bring in any new signings but free agents are different, especially someone coming in from abroad as they can sign and play straight away. I think this is tremendous fore-sight by the manager who has obviously been working hard behind the scenes to acquire a striker. He is on trial and no decision has been made as yet, but it does give hope.

Friday night and East Fife play Arbroath as this Saturday was supposed to be a free due to the internationals. As one newspaper said 'There are usually plenty of things to do in Fife on a Friday night, but seeing a Third Division football match isn't normally one of them'. The match has been brought forward from the bank of midweek fixtures destined to be played on Tuesday 18th of October. Berwick and Elgin have also arranged to play their New Year fixture on Saturday.

I wonder if Friday night football will ever take off. It is not everybody who can make a Saturday due to work commitments and family as 'she that must be obeyed' insists that you go shopping.

When working in Ireland I was amazed at some of the attendances at matches as the quality of football was no better in some instances to public park kick-a-rounds. I think that the locals supported all sport well and some of this was down to the church, as many ran football, soccer and hurling league teams. In the Netherlands, the weekend fixtures are distributed from Friday through to Sunday evening and kick-offs are scheduled at various times. This works in a small country as the logistics of attending an away match is easier as journey times for most are only an hour.

Just out of the house and it happens again. Why me! I don't dress in pink trousers, lime coloured or bright orange shirts. I am not Dutch! I don't even look Dutch! It's like being picked on at school, the car stops, the window rolls down and you are met with a blast of Dutch looking for directions. It's a regular occurrence; you can't even work in the garden without people summoning you over, some even come into the garden then look amazed that you are not Dutch. One car stopped in pre-season, supporters of a Belgian side and asked for directions to the NAC Stadium-I could understand that much. I duly sent them to the north of the City only to find out that they were actually playing at Baronie's ground a kilometre along the road. How was I to know? Dutch is a language that is easier to read than to speak as some pronunciations are difficult. Although you master the niceties, stringing together the spiel takes time. The other night I went to move my car as a parking space had become free to move into nearer the house. I was no sooner on the pavement than a car stopped, the occupants looking for directions. Another barrage of Dutch ending with my reply, that I don't speak Dutch and an apology. "You don't speak Dutch?" "No" I replied, "You are not from here?" "No" I replied, "You don't speak Dutch?" "No" I replied for the third time "You are not Dutch?" " No" I replied again, exasperated, and the window promptly was wound up as the car did a u-turn. Ever wish you had done the same!

There was an increased attendance at the nightspot of New Bayview. East Fife's Friday night game drew over seven hundred brave souls to take in the ambience of the Third Division match. At the end of the day Arbroath shared the points in a 1-1 draw with the Fife support claiming it was two points dropped.

For Berwick, their match with Elgin was a re-run of the previous week as they drew 1-1 and dropped a further two points in their run up to Saturday's game with second placed Stenhousemuir. One asks has Berwick's bubble burst?

Tonight sees Montrose Supporter's Club host a meet the manager session and it is a chance for Henry Hall to give his view and to allay the fans concerns. Henry started off by saying that "The future is looking better" but conceded that we have had a problem in scoring goals as well as creating good chances. He states as fitness returns, we can also expect a better team performance and to 'have faith' as things will get better. In answering questions from the floor, the manager was disappointed to lose Graeme Sharp, a player that he would have liked to keep, but stated that you have to live within your means and budget. Sharp's sprint pace is missed upfront and creating the moves that set up scoring chances. The manager also stated that the players are more relaxed playing away from home. I wonder why! Maybe if the support got behind them they would possibly not feel under so much pressure at home and be more composed.

Some good points were made but it all boils down to winning matches, starting with Saturday!

This weekend's fixtures sees the first quarter of scheduled matches come to a close. Saturday's fixture as I have said, matches the league's top two teams with Stenhousemuir having the home advantage against Berwick. A draw would suit most teams. Albion Rovers entertain Cowdenbeath and their Fife counterparts are at home to an improved East Stirling. Elsewhere, John McGlashan has a home managerial debut against Elgin in the match at Gayfield and will be looking for a winning start. Further up the coast Montrose are at home to Queen's Park and a game that they cannot afford to loose (how many times have we said that recently) as they need to start picking up points not only in this match but in the forthcoming ties as they enter the second quarter of fixtures.

The message boards focus on the 'Big One', I think they mean the Stenny-Berwick tie. There is little chance of it being the Montrose match but predictions by most are for a Queen's Park away win and at a canter! Montrose still have a few missing even with the luxury of a free Saturday the treatment table backlog is not cleared. Henry states that focus will be on attack and I would expect a starting line up similar to the side that took the field at Shielfield with one exception. Neil Stephen may not make it with a recurring injury which may sideline him to the bench with Paul Doyle taking his place. Let's get off to a good start to an important few weeks of fixtures. 1-0 would do as long as it is in Montrose's favour.

Queen's Park is a good, well organised side which, under manager Billy Stark, has adopted a 4-3-1-2 system which works well. Everyone knows their role and responsibility which works for them. Part of this well worked organisation goes back to the grass roots and their youth development set-up from which players trundle through the ranks. Some make it, some don't, but the end product of generating a good first team squad is there to see. I think it is something that Montrose needs to look at, as it is the future of the club.

My extended work family are home for the weekend and I am at a loose end and on my lonesome. I had decided that if the weather was good then I would explore the Netherlands further. It's not quite kick-off. My mind wanders back to today's match. Four minutes past four and I wonder if we are on the score sheet. A mobile phone (what else!) disturbs my thoughts as I wonder yet again. Will the trombone playing Queen's supporter be there at Links Park today, if only to drown out the home support and the Hall must go brigade!

Saturday can be boring without football – without being able to support your home team. Sad, yes, but that is part of being drawn away from home.

No phone call from home, is enthusiasm starting to wane, will I be met with the dreaded words of 'I wish I hadn't bothered' or 'Why did I buy a season ticket?' or 'Montrose were beaten today'. On ringing, I am met with the latter! Despondency sets in as I ask Gareth what the score was and how did Montrose play? 'OK- but another game without scoring.' The score a 1-0 win for Queen's. Montrose lacked Queen's Park's organisation in supporting one another and they had more of the play and could have added to their tally. There is a post already on the message board, it doesn't call for Henry to be sacked but takes a different tack stating that he should do the right thing and resign. Nine games and a miserable six points!

Oct 15th. QUEEN'S PARK, Home - report and teams
As was thought, Montrose kept the 4-4-2 formation and Doyle slotted in for the heavily strapped up Neil Stephen who was sitting on the bench. The remainder of the bench consisted of Donnachie, Fraser, Butter and James Russell, who once again made an appearance but was not used. Before the match got underway a minute's silence was held in memory of Honorary Club President, Willie Johnston.

Montrose created the first chance of the match, Dodds on a raid down the right, floating a ball into the Queen's penalty area and Hall sent a shot wide of goal. Reid turned a curling ball over at the other end before Montrose mounted their next attack. Hall won a free kick on the touchline, Fotheringham took the kick and Henslee shot wide. A run by Fotheringham saw his shot smothered by Queen's keeper Crawford. The keeper then saved from Watson and a double from Webster. Montrose kept the pressure up with Kerrigan heading over from a corner and pinned the Spiders back in their own half. On one of the few breaks that Queen's Park did have saw Andy Reid in superb form, pulling off a tremendous save from close range. Going in at halftime, manager Hall could be satisfied by the team's performance and by the sounds of it, the extra work that had been put in at training was showing positive returns as we had created several chances. No score and it was still hopeful at that point, but unlike Jose Mourinho of Chelsea, Henry did not take the chance to change play and push forward to a 3-4-1-2 and play with three strikers. It worked for Chelsea as they slotted 5 past Bolton in the second half. A radical change but sometimes that is what it takes.

There were no changes in the playing personnel as the teams took the pitch to reconvene battle. A first half that Montrose dominated all was about to change in the second period. In the first 10 minutes Montrose pressed the

Queen's defence and created further opportunities to score but that changed in 55 minutes when Euan Hall was robbed of the ball at the dugout side of the touchline. Completely against the run of play a pass found Weatherstone, Queen's number nine, he turned McKenzie, and duly sent a beautiful shot over the advancing Andy Reid. One goal down and the heads went down as Queen's Park then proceeded to close the game down. Confusion between Reid and McKenzie almost added to Queen's tally before Montrose mounted another attack. Hall almost made amends when he rattled the crossbar with a shot from a rebound the Queen's defence managed to clear. Changes were made in 70 minutes when Fraser replaced Watson with Fotheringham being pushed forward to join Henslee in the strike force. Webster and Hall switched touchlines to stage strategy on attack. The changes made no difference, Henslee headed for Crawford to collect. Doyle could not penetrate the Spider's wall and time ran out. Donnachie replace Dodds in eighty-one minutes but by that time it was out of reach as scoring was not on today's agenda. Luck had run out early on, we cannot score and Elliott Smith added to his tally of bookings, overtaking Barry Donnachie in the stakes.

Highlights- Today the team performance did deserve a point for their efforts in an entertaining game. There were signs of a turnaround as the passing movements of last season returned, but you do have to score! We know there are problems in that department, options are limited but it needs to be addressed. Kevin Webster today turned in a good committed performance, Doyle and McKenzie looked solid in defence and Kerrigan yet again put in his usual ball winning shift in midfield. It's three dropped points and the hope of twelve points in the month of October has disappeared. Priority is a striker, but we know that already. Let's hope that the injury list clears in that department.

Today Montrose had the lowest recorded crowd of three hundred and twenty, two bodies less than the Albion Rovers-Cowdenbeath tie but it is a sign of times to come unless we start winning! The game is hardly over and all we hear is, 'Yet again another poor performance', 'Enough is enough and simply not good enough'. One poster puts it down to 'No forwards, no shape and virtually no crowd'. Our friend 'Dynamo Rumble' relives his previous postings and states that we have now reached the point where the Board must act or stand down. What good does this do, as he covers his tracks and identity with a smokescreen, in claiming he is walking back to the Borrowfield area of Montrose? It's like give us a clue on these message boards and a who's who of aliases.

Player of the month, do they deserve it? Well this one does and credit where credit is due to Euan Hall, who would probably have been our best player in September. Well done to Euan as being the manager's son is never easy and this presentation award may just get a few of the support off his back (they can be found behind the goal) as he often takes the rap for his dad. A good choice indeed by Montrose Supporters Club!

The weekend saw Berwick's bubble still intact as they won the battle of the top two at Ochilview and remain undefeated. In a hard fought match it took a 25th minute penalty to separate the two teams giving Berwick the three points. Elsewhere the Kingdom of Fife won both games with Cowdenbeath recording an away victory at Coatbridge, with 3 goals in their favour and East Fife repeating the goal feast in a 3-1 home rout against East Stirling. Our neighbours Arbroath and friend John McGlashan received that managerial boost from a convincing 2-0 home win against Elgin.

It's the end of the first quarter, nine games played and six points attained, but it could have been a lot more. There were games early on that we possibly threw away; the most notable was at Bayview which I see as three points dropped. We did not start well in the first two matches and possibly should have killed off both Elgin and Albion Rovers early in the game instead of being on the receiving end. We had created numerous chances to win these games twice over but failed to convert. All in all we have dropped more points in these games than we have accumulated. It is disappointing to say the least, only achieving a third of the first quarter's point's target. The statistics reflect a league position of ninth (one off the bottom) and that we have been hit badly by injuries, but there is still the underlying effect due to not having depth in the squad to overcome the situation. The added factor of no youth system to call on has not helped, as it does help fill the bench. Too many players have been sitting out and their fitness must be questioned as knocks have been picked up too easily. Goals have not been forth coming, partly due to the formation of 4-5-1, which hasn't worked and the lack of a striker to convert the chances provided. September in particular was a dry month with Henslee the only player to net. Montrose, the only team not to hit double figures with five goals to their credit have only scored once at home giving the fans little to cheer.

On the positive side, it is good to see that we are now starting with an attacking formation as the best form of defence is attack. Spirits seem lifted once again due to the result at Berwick. There are signs of playing as a team and the players now have the chance to rectify things in this coming second quarter of matches. We have good players but they need to find their self-belief again and a bit of organization wouldn't go wrong.

Montrose are now twelve points off fourth place and a play-off spot!

Quarter One

POS		P	W	L	D	F	A	GD	PTS
1	Berwick	10	8	0	2	22	6	+16	26
2	Stenhousemuir	9	6	2	1	20	10	+10	19
3	East Fife	10	6	3	1	16	14	+2	19
4	Cowdenbeath	9	6	3	0	16	5	+11	18
5	Queen's Park	9	4	3	2	15	11	+4	14
6	Arbroath	10	2	4	4	10	16	-6	10
7	Elgin	10	1	5	4	10	18	-8	7
8	East Stirling	9	2	6	1	11	21	-10	7
9	Montrose	9	1	5	3	5	13	-8	6
10	Albion Rovers	9	1	6	2	10	21	-11	5

Looking at our league position, maybe my dream was true after all!

We have had little to celebrate !
Except against ARBROATH !

Chapter 5

2nd. Quarter (Joy to the World)

It is the start of that all important week and a chance to build on the previous week's results by putting a winning run together. Two home games and a midweek trip to Coatbridge could just be the confidence booster that is required. It should also be noted that the next four matches see Montrose play all the bottom-half league teams. If Montrose can attain maximum points from the first four games then it will double their current points tally and hopefully raise their ninth place league status.

After this week fans have only two further home games to look forward to between now and Boxing Day, that's unless we get a home tie in the first round of the Scottish Cup, or consider the short trip to Arbroath at the beginning of November as being home. I think not!

Sixty-six shopping days to Christmas, can you believe that and eighty-seven days till the transfer window opens. Some players had been given six-month contracts during the summer so this is the period to prove themselves if they expect their contract to be renewed. Hopefully by then the likes of defender Stuart Ferguson who has resumed light training will be fit and Duncan McLean will also be up for selection before Henry goes shopping.

With bated breath I await the outcome of this coming week!

Quarter Two - League campaign

Oct 22nd.	Elgin	Home
Oct 25th.	Albion Rovers (mid-week)	Away
Oct 29th.	East Stirling	Home
Nov 5th.	Arbroath	Away
Nov 12th.	Cowdenbeath	Home
Nov 26th.	Stenhousemuir	Away
Dec 3rd.	Queen's Park	Away
Dec 17th.	Berwick	Home
Dec 26th.	Elgin	Away

Monday brings the first round (proper) of the Scottish Cup draw. It sees the North and South League team qualifiers join the big time. The fact that we don't join the big time until the third round doesn't matter as we first have to win the early round games, which is easier said than done. From the Highland League, teams such as Inverurie Loco's and Forres will be difficult to beat. Threave and Spartans from the South qualifiers are always strong as well. A home tie is the wish although many supporters would like a jolly to some seaside resort such as Lossiemouth or Girvan. Some years back Montrose fell foul to a first round exit at the hands of Cove Rangers. It's better the devil you know!

The draw has taken place and Montrose had made it through to the second round on a bye. They were awarded an away match but it is not a simple straight forward tie as Alloa await their first round opponents from the yet to be decided outcome of Selkirk and Girvan. On paper there should be only one winner and that is Alloa but as we know in the past that is the romance of the cup as David takes on Goliath!

Alloa have suffered some heavy defeats lately in losing 6 to Partick, 5 to Morton and 3 at home to Gretna. If it is any consolation, Alloa recorded the narrowest of victories over Arbroath earlier on in the season.

It's a reasonable draw whether it is Alloa, Selkirk or Girvan and I hope that it is Montrose's name that is in the money spinning third round. It may be a selfish thought as I will still be at home when the third round ties are played on January 7th and I would like to see Montrose play in the Cup!

The message boards disclose a week of unrest. Links Park does not seem a happy place at the moment. In message board language, there is a split among posters. On one hand you have the 'Montrose Supporter's Trust' who claim to be the voice of the support and on the other you have the Montrose Supporters Club. It is a political nightmare! The Supporters Club are true to the cause and back the manager Henry Hall and the 'Trust'; well let's just say they want a new manager. They see themselves in a strong position after an injection of money from Gretna's chairman Brooks Mileson and the acquisition of some additional shares which gives them a voice on the Board, but is it a voice that we want to be heard? The post says that if you want to join the 'Trust' then they can be found behind the goal.

The Board, well, they are livid as that undisclosed fee for Henner has been disclosed!

It's not a happy place!

Weekend matches – Arbroath will be hoping to continue their recent form against Albion Rovers in securing three points. East Fife would be happy with a draw at Berwick but I would expect Berwick to take the points to continue their unbeaten run. Stenhousemuir's home tie with Queen's Park looks likely to be a draw and Cowdenbeath should add to their points total when they play East Stirling at home. I can't see positions in the top half of the league changing but there could be a shuffle between the bottom four sides.

This week's opponents, Elgin, are fresh from the Black's anticipated takeover and the pending installation of ex-Ross County manager Alex Smith as Director of Football, but all is not well, as club captain Jamie McKenzie is ready to quit the club if he is not selected to make a start. Elgin have played ten and accumulated seven points, one more than Montrose. It's an opportunity to jump a couple of places in the league which we must take. When you look at the fixture it could be the beginning of one chapter or the end of another, depending on the score.

At Borough Briggs, we should have taken all the points but we didn't and eventually escaped. As someone said," If we can't beat Elgin." Well let me remind them that Elgin also took a point off Berwick at Shielfield recently. It is a game of caution, yes, Montrose must attack, but they must also keep a clean sheet.

On the strike front, I would expect Martin's return and the prospect of him facing his old club for the first time as he missed the Borough Briggs match due to suspension. Whether he will partner Watson or Henslee upfront I don't know but have been thinking that Webster who has pace may be a candidate. It would mean a complete re-shuffle of the 4-4-2 system and like the 4-5-1 it may not work. It would have to be a 4-3-1-2 which would mean Donnachie returning to his berth at full back and Dodds moving into midfield in place of Kerrigan who would move forward to support the front pairing of Martin and Webster. Would it work? Who knows but we might have a better chance of scoring with 'three' up front.

We don't have three! A brief scan of the news web pages tells me we are without three strikers. McLean is a long term injury which we knew, and Willie Martin is still not 100%, but will possibly fill a berth on the bench. Calum Watson is on holiday!

The word 'failure' instantly springs to mind – a word that when typed into 'Google' draws up the web site of 'The White House' and President George Bush. Enough said!

To add to our misery, Neil Stephen is also out and there is no sign of long term injury victim Stuart Ferguson. Cargill however, just might feature at some point from the bench as he returns to fitness. Henry Hall is quoted as saying, "The injury list is not as long as it has been. Things are looking a bit more positive and confidence is still high." He goes on to say, "We have played well this season with the exception of the game against Cowdenbeath. We just haven't scored enough. The opportunities are there and we have been working hard in training. Hopefully, it will come together for us against Elgin."

The *P & J* are more down to earth with the headline, 'Gable Endies ready to recall players farmed out to Junior clubs'.

'Things can only get better', boom's out in mono over the Links Park tannoy system, while in Breda it is the Stones and 'This could be the Last Time' but I don't know! I don't see today's crowd breaking any records and for the few that are in attendance, I hope that they see a home win, if only to boost morale amongst the diehards. It is a game that I would blood James Russell from the Junior ranks and it will be a chance to see just what he can do. It may be the case that he will give the width that is required to penetrate the Elgin defence. He has something to prove in stepping to a higher level, so let him prove it and give him the chance to be a hero for the day. Will farmed out striker Marc Connelly feature? Once again Montrose are under pressure at home, to score not just one goal, but many, to restore the faith of the support. This is what is required to bring them onside but can it be done without strikers?

An invitation to dinner early on Saturday night means no score. I moan when I travel, when mobile phones go off and your ozone space is interrupted by all sorts of conversations that you do not want to hear, so tonight my mobile will be on mute. I receive a text, its four-twenty and it only says, '1- 0 Montrose - Henner '. So we must have scored in 16 or 17 minutes. Texts like that change the rest of your evening as you start to wonder what is happening. However before I reach my dinner date another text is received, '2-0, Keggsy'. There was a sigh of relief, I know the match is not over but two goals is a better cushion, I can now enjoy my evening.

Oct 22nd. ELGIN, Home - report and teams
To start with, who buys newspapers? The public do, to find out information, whether it is front page news or your Saturday sport update. There are times when I would question what is published.

Montrose made some positional changes to last weeks eleven. Lining up for the Gable Endies were Reid in goal supported by a back four of Dodds, McKenzie, Neil Stephen and Elliot Smith. Webster, Fotheringham, Doyle and Hall represented the midfield and Kerrigan who moved forward partnered Henslee as the stand-in strikers. Butter, Donnachie, Cargill, Fraser, and Martin were the substitutes.

Immediately I noticed two things, one is Stephen, who according to one newspaper was definitely out, is playing and secondly there does not appear to be any Juniors in the team or on the bench. So much for the *P & J* headline!

Winter is approaching, and floodlights are required to watch this encounter. After a sticky start with Reid saving from Elgin's Johnston, Montrose finally started to take control of this match. The defence put in a comfortable shift with good running from Dodds and Smith on the flanks. Henslee and Webster linked up well on the right and it wasn't long before their efforts were rewarded with a goal. In thirteen minutes, after some swift passing from Dodds to Kerrigan to Henslee, who found Webster on the right, the winger cut back for Henslee to side-foot home. Sustained pressure from Montrose saw Webster shoot wide from eight yards, Henslee fail to reach a Fotheringham flick-on and Webster fire another shot in, for it to be cleared off the line. Henslee then headed down for Hall to rifle a shot at keeper Renton who held at the second attempt. A good first period which does not reflect the one goal half-time advantage as Montrose should have been further ahead.

No changes for the second half and Montrose continued from where they left off. Hall and Henslee pressurised the Elgin defence with Hall's shot beaten away by Renton. Henslee then hit the side netting followed by Renton blocking a Webster drive. From the resultant corner, an in-swinger from Hall, the Elgin defence were at sixes and sevens allowing Kerrigan to nod home. The 61st minute goal gave Montrose the required cushion and a comfortable 2– 0 lead. Tempers flared after the re-start with Elgin substitute McKenzie (barely on the field) and Henslee going into the referee's book. Scullion of Elgin soon followed for a challenge on Hall and Kerrigan rounded off his striking debut with a yellow card. The last ten minutes saw Kerrigan, Webster and Fraser all coming close before the referee blew for time.

In 70 minutes Fraser had replaced Hall. Donnachie then made an appearance for Doyle and Martin for Kerrigan as manager Hall used substitutions to play for time.

Highlights – Kerrigan today was easily the best player on the field of play and was a constant threat to Elgin. It seems no matter what position Steve is asked to play, he gives more than the one hundred percent required of him. His commitment is a testimony to his captaincy. Jamie McKenzie today also stood-out in defence as he confidently dealt with any Elgin threat. Webster and Henslee created opportunities and were well supported by Euan Hall who was unfortunate not to be on the score sheet.

Supporter comments are more favourable, from 'a decent performance' to 'a convincing win and deserved result, but Elgin were shocking!'

Saturday's results from other games saw East Fife on the receiving end of a three-goal defeat at Berwick. Cowdenbeath however draw ever closer to the leaders as they secure another three points by beating East Stirling comfortably by 5-1 in a match that was over at half-time. Queen's Park received an 89th minute sucker punch yet again at Ochilview with Stenhousemuir's Cramb scoring at the death. Queen's previously lost out to a McGrillen late penalty award at Hampden. I had hoped that our neighbours Arbroath would soften up the opposition for Tuesday night's game at Coatbridge. Albion Rovers, however, record their second win of the season with a 2-1 win. Arbroath remain in sixth position but it is all change between the bottom four. Montrose moved from ninth to seventh, followed by Albion Rovers, Elgin and the Shire regain their familiar spot as bottom markers, but that could change in mid-week.

The Crowd – recorded at 308, I can spot ten on the 'Knoll' without taking my shoes off!

There is a change to routine for some this week as there is a midweek fixture list. East Stirling entertain Berwick at Firs Park and Stehousemuir have a long journey north to play Elgin at Borough Briggs. Queen's Park and Cowdenbeath will battle it out at Hampden. Montrose travel to Coatbridge, and both sides are fresh from much needed confidence boosting wins. Albion are within a point of Montrose so tonight's match has great significance for both teams as they fight for three points. Rovers had sent an advance party to Links Park on Saturday to spy on their opponents. Hopefully they received a good impression and a noted improvement. Manager Henry Hall is quoted as saying that he will have the same squad available, and that he is reluctant to do more than maybe tinker a bit round the edges. "I'll be giving a bit of thought tonight to my final selection," said Hall, "but I don't want to make too many changes after Saturday." I should think not!

So barring injuries in the warm-up, Montrose's line up will be the same as Saturday. The bench could see a change with a doubt over the fitness of Cargill. No speculation of Juniors, no dissenters on the message boards and no pressure playing at home. Let's get a result!

A midweek match and no access to 'Surf and Talk', as it closes at eight. No teletext, the probability of no support at the game with the chance of a text message, what am I going to do? There are times when you find yourself in a little world of your own and the reality of this ex-pat life is far less glamorous than it sounds. Conversation is limited, unless you want to argue with yourself and when someone does speak to you, it's in Dutch and they are usually looking for directions.

I end up thinking of Henry's summer signings, the January transfer window and where we go from here!

Two text messages on Saturday told me that things were going a bit better at Links Park. It is good to see Montrose win and win comfortably, but by the sounds of some reports there is still a long way to go and a clear-out is required in January. Meantime we must build, starting with tonight's match, which is not a foregone conclusion. We face the Shire on Saturday and I think we can record a narrow victory at Gayfield. Winning these games would certainly put us on a better footing come the onslaught of the teams vying for promotion. Whether Henry will be there come January, I don't really know as there have been times that I thought that's it, he's away. Some summer signings have not worked out- do we need three keepers and so many midfielders? I would favour the release of Butter, Cargill (who hasn't really played) and Fraser or Hall to bring in two strikers and possibly a left sided player with pace. In addition to this McLean may also be released in favour of

Russell being called up from the Juniors. If money is available then it may be the case that the Board will give it to a new broom, one with bristles who can regain the respect of the players.

As I hope that the score is positive tonight, I try my radio as a last resort and joy, yes I have a signal. You would not believe it, the signal is Radio Scotland and commentary from tonight's Aberdeen match at Pittodrie. Imagine, Radio Scotland in Breda, it's made my night and it is not long till I hear good news as Henner scores in ten minutes to put Montrose one up. Wallace equalises shortly afterwards for Rovers.

Half-time shocks filter over the air waves, two matches in particular get my attention as East Stirling are one up against Berwick and Elgin are also ahead by the same margin. But as luck would have it, Berwick ran out winners 2-1 and that man McGrillen stole in at the death as he often does for Stehousemuir to win by the same margin. Cowdenbeath had a fine 2-0 win at Hampden. Crowd attendances at last night's matches were alarmingly low. A total of one thousand and forty-three brave souls ventured out to the four matches with only one hundred and eighty one spectators at Cliftonhill. I think that East Fife and Arbroath were wise to play on the Friday night as the attendance rose to 742.

What do you need to do to get a report on last night's match? The local papers had no match reports posted on their web sites and the '*Daily Ranger*' (Record) has more English Premiership team coverage than is normal. They have totally ignored the lower divisions of the Scottish League. It's 'Bang out of Order' which reflects their headline of the day concerning gun crime.

There is nothing on the Club web site or 'MoMoSuperMo' and there is desertion in the ranks at 'GableEndGraffiti' as 'Steeplejack' is away in Estonia receiving a taste of ex-pat life and the frustrations encountered in finding out the Montrose SCORE! Alas, I am subjected to the BBC web page of four sentences and a bit of Glasgow bias to the Lanarkshire team.

Nothing short of a miracle, later in the day from the other side of the Baltic Sea and with the help of technology, 'Steeplejack' was able to post a report.

Oct 25th. ALBION ROVERS (mid-week), Away - report and teams
Henry Hall stuck with the exact same line-up as Saturday, including the bench. Any doubts about Cargill's fitness were unfounded although he wasn't used. It was Montrose who created a first minute chance with Fotheringham blasting over. Stephen then headed into the hands of keeper Ewings from a

corner before Fotheringham hit the side net from a Kerrigan pass. The match swung into action when Henslee struck in ten minutes to score with a good strike of the ball as he steered Kevin Webster's cross under the diving Ewings in the Rover's goal. This goal should have given Montrose confidence but their early lead was short lived as Albion equalised in eighteen minutes. From a Lennox cross, Rovers striker Wallace headed home.

After a rapid start the teams settled down with both defences struggling to cope with conditions, opportunities arose from this but neither side took advantage.

As the BBC reported 'Albion Rovers could only muster a draw despite their domination for long periods'. Our man at the match – well he thought it was a poor game and that the teams cancelled one another out.

Reid was the busier keeper pulling off saves from Bonnar, Lennon and Chisholm to deny Rovers taking the lead.

The match had been played in farcical weather conditions, possibly one of the reasons that goalkeeper Reid was replaced in goal by substitute Jim Butter during the second half of the continuous downpour. This was part of a double substitution with Willie Martin coming on for McKenzie. Hall reshaped the side with Doyle dropping in for McKenzie, Kerrigan withdrawing back from the firing line and Martin slotting in up front. Montrose had a great chance to regain the lead when the ball fell for Henslee after an attempted clearance bounced off a Rovers player. From six yards Henslee shot wide when it seemed easier to score. A final substitution was made in eighty minutes with Fraser replacing Hall in midfield but to no avail as a draw was played out. In the final minute Butter earned credit when he parried a Chaplain shot to ensure a point.

Highlights – A point was taken from the match but Montrose can thank goalkeepers Andy Reid and Jim Butter for that as they turned in five star performances in atrocious conditions. It was later revealed that Reid had been suffering from stomach cramps or was it a Coatbridge pie!

Montrose move from seventh to sixth place in the league and are on the same points as Arbroath but are plus one on goal difference. Henslee's good strike tonight and his goal at the weekend will give a much needed boost to the striker as there had been a number of occasions that you could have thought that his luck had deserted him as it did in the second period tonight. In saying that, Henslee worked tirelessly in attack.

On the bookings front, Elliott Smith picked up another yellow card (fifth), along with Martyn Fotheringham (fourth) who was also booked on Saturday. The thought of suspensions looms. Another card and Barry Donnachie may be back in full flow slotting in on the right with Dodds moving left. A win this weekend would see Montrose on a run and set for the Gayfield encounter.

It is announced that Scotland will meet the United States in a friendly international at Hampden Park on Saturday, November 12th. Montrose are due to play Cowdenbeath at home. The SFA are asking league clubs to play on the Friday night or Sunday to accommodate this friendly match. Cowdenbeath have requested that the match be played on Friday night but Montrose are unable to change dates for hospitality reasons. So the match kicks-off as usual at 3 pm.

The Cowden family are not happy- one poster states that the crowd will be lower but adds that Montrose will add another 200 to fudge the attendance as they normally do. Another, an Arbroath Red Lichtie, chances his luck in saying that Montrose are lucky to get a crowd of 200. Quite sad really considering our league position and a goal difference of one over his side! You can't blame Montrose for not changing as in this case the blame lies firmly with the Scottish League as this international date had been set aside for a meet some time ago. It's a situation that we should not be in, as we shouldn't have to choose between club and country. Yes I would love to see Scotland play but if it's a choice then my colours are firmly pinned to the mast of Montrose. 'Henry's Cat' gets it right when he posts, 'I know where I'll be'!

'Trade Me', is a New Zealand auction site. There are all sorts of things for sale but this one took my eye! It read, 'Time Machine-unfinished project. Started making a machine to facilitate time travel. Unfortunately I don't have the time to complete it.' It goes on, 'Have had mixed results so no guarantees. Would suit - DIY handyman with quantum physics background, or similar interests.' There is also a statement – 'No time wasters please'!

You've got to admit, it could be handy for those long weekends that we enjoy so much. If only we could turn this season back in time!

A third game in eight days for most sides and the Berwick-Cowdenbeath fixture looks to be a strong contest for the teams involved. East Fife, have home advantage at Bayview to Albion Rovers and the return of the 'Black and White' takes place at Hampden as Elgin are the opposition. It is also the battle of the maroons at Ochilview where Stenny take on Arbroath. This match may see the return of John McGlashan from dugout to the field of play as Arbroath have apparently clarified the position concerning their manager's registration. If he doesn't play this week then he will certainly not resist temptation to play against Montrose on derby day.

Two defeats in Fife and no points from Berwick midweek sums up East Stirling's last three games. No points from nine, let's make it none today again and collect another three points to add to the four secured in the past seven days. It is important that Montrose get the required result before going into the Arbroath derby game next Saturday. For the team, today is a confidence booster for next weekend.

If things would only click! Our last encounter ended with Dymock's last kick of the ball equalising in a game that Montrose completely dominated. As well as paying the penalty, Willie Martin also missed one. Like the previous Saturday we must be wary of being hit on the break and again it is important to make that break-through by scoring early on. On a cautionary note, East Stirling have not won at Links Park for five years now. We are due goals today, Fotheringham has not scored since his double at East Fife, Hall has had misfortune in front of goal, and Webster is due a strike. If they are once again partnered up front, either Henslee or Kerrigan could score.

I am looking forward to a dose of Tam Cowan this afternoon on Stuart Cosgrove's programme "Off the Ball", broadcast on Radio Scotland. Thereafter I will listen in, as they troll around the grounds with updates north and south. It was a great find this week, as Radio Scotland must have increased the signal strength as I could only ever receive it on my car radio. I may be desperate but I am not so desperate, that I would sit in my car, engine running, listening to Tam Cowan!

I remember one contract, when a certain person would call his wife on a Saturday and ask her to turn the radio on. The broadcast match would likely be Rangers (surprise, surprise), and his wife stood with the telephone receiver held to the radio. Now that is desperate! The same person flew home to Glasgow to watch a European match involving Rangers. The game was televised and his wife and son could not believe their eyes when they saw a familiar face in the stand on their television screen. After the match he flew directly back to work. All, his wife could say was, "I wondered why you hadn't called to switch on the radio'!

The press reports Montrose as having drawn themselves up the league to a mid table position, but like a game of snakes and ladders a defeat today and we will slither back down. I hope the Shire is not the snake that we slither on.

Manager Hall states on one hand that he might freshen the team up but on the other says that in the past two games he has had a settled side for the first time. At the end of the day, I don't think that it will be far from any recent line-ups. Hall reports that Martin, Kerrigan and McKenzie are all carrying niggling strains but are expected to be available. Andy Cargill is now back in full training and may receive a run later in the match. Duncan McLean has resumed training but is not ready to return to the play. The *P&J* greeting of 'Real Montrose ready, says Hall' headlines their article. Now, is it Real as in Madrid or just plain get real! Either way 'Judge us now is the call' and we are a much stronger side now provided that we stay injury free.

East Stirling will be missing three players, McKay, Walker and Blair. Boss Dennis Newall claims on paper that the Shire have the edge that is required over their opponents to grind out a result.

Dutch radio stations block the Radio Scotland signal. It was fine this morning, then this afternoon, nothing. I've got to say I am disappointed. As the final whistle approached I thought that I would try one more time and Hey Presto or was it Chic Young, the signal was back with brief interruptions from some singer. So I was reduced to BBC sport for the afternoon and a small yellow box in the bottom right hand corner of the screen. Press RED button for live scores and reports-that's ok if you HAVE a red button!

Who needs a red button when you have a dedicated son and staunch Montrose supporter (Gareth). The first text message was in ten minutes followed by two more. They were simple, '1-0 - Henslee, 2-0 - Henner, 3-0 - Henner hat-trick, but it could have been more'. Fotheringham who played up front with Henslee had five good chances, Webster three, but he finished poorly and Hall had two opportunities. Henslee's hat trick at least takes our goal scoring tally into double figures and gives a personal tally of six for the lad as we move onto thirteen points. On the down side Steve Kerrigan was stretchered off minutes before the final whistle after a nasty challenge. It is not known just how bad the injury is but he would be a big miss as he is the ball winner.

Oct 29th. EAST STIRLING, Home - report and teams
Changes, changes, changes! Henry Hall made three notable changes from Cliftonhill. Donnachie wearing the number three shirt played at right back with Dodds moving to the left, Fraser replaced Doyle in the midfield as the holding man and Fotheringham partnered Henslee in the front-line with Kerrigan resuming duties in midfield. Montrose lined up with Reid resuming his place in goal having got over his stomach cramps. Donnachie, McKenzie, Stephen and Dodds formed the defence. Webster and Hall sat on either flank,

Kerrigan along with Stephen Fraser filled the remaining midfield roles, and Fotheringham and Henslee were upfront. Butter and the outfield players of Doyle, Cargill, Martin and Elliot Smith sat on the bench.

Montrose started off well. In 2 minutes Fotheringham found Hall on the left side of the touchline, whose pass inside to Henslee found the striker in space as he curled a shot beyond the reach of keeper Jackson, to see his shot go just over. It did not take long for Montrose to take control of midfield as they out manoeuvred their visitors. There was no surprise when Montrose took the lead in 11 minutes. Webster started off the move on the right, passing inside to Fraser, who threaded a ball wide down the line for Barry Donnachie on the overlap to cut back into the box. Henner placed the ball past Jackson to the left of the goal into the net.

The Shire, who up till then looked an improved side from last term, immediately lost the plot as heads went down. Henslee picked up a loose ball leaving three players in his wake before being shepherded wide of goal. Fotheringham shot over when well placed, then followed this with a free kick that he screwed wide of the upright. It was one-way traffic at this stage with Montrose doing the pressing. A long clearance from Andy Reid down the middle escaped the Shire defence finding Henslee who blasted the ball off keeper Jackson. Jackson was again in action saving a volley from Kerrigan after good work from Euan Hall. The onslaught on East Stirling's goal continued, and in 35 minutes Montrose were rewarded with a second goal. A Dodd's run saw the full-back unleash a superb drive on the turn with the in-form Jackson brilliantly turning over for a corner. Kerrigan showed his skill from the corner when he shielded the ball before turning the Shire defence with a back-heel pass and crossing for Henslee to head home his second goal, with the Shire all at sea. The last attack of the first half fell to Fotheringham, who had a great chance to make it three, but failed to connect a Webster cross. Montrose dominated throughout and deserved their 2-0 lead.

The second period saw a change in tactics by East Stirling as they tried to show their presence, committing several fouls in the process, before Tyrrell was booked for a foul on Hall. Stephen's name then followed the Shire player into the referee's notebook for a similar challenge. Montrose were soon back into harness when a Tyrrell slip allowed Webster to pick-up speed to send in an inch perfect pass to Fotheringham who also slipped at the crucial moment in front of goal. Miss of the season? No that was being saved for the next attack!

A one-two between Henslee and Fotheringham saw Martyn Fotheringham in the six-yard box, directly in front of goal. It seemed a certain goal but he somehow managed to send the ball over the bar from an impossible position. Another miss when it seemed easier to score and the fans behind the goal let him know as they vented their anger yet again! I find it hard that the support can be like this. It does not give the player any confidence and the emphasis seems to have moved from young Euan Hall to Fotheringham to receive the critics' wrath!

Smiles however (if that is possible) were back on the faces of the support a few minutes later. An inter-passing move between Webster and Henslee saw the winger brought down at the edge of the box. From the resultant 67th minute kick, Webster floats a ball across the six-yard box with Henslee chesting the ball across the goal-line as the Shire full-back attempted to clear. With a 3-0 lead Doyle replaced Fraser in the holding role, Martin then came on for Hall and Andy Cargill made an appearance for the last 10 minutes when he replaced Fotheringham.

The match closed with Steve Kerrigan unable to get up from a 50-50 challenge. Clutching his fore-arm the player was stretchered off. At first there were fears that he had broken his arm, an injury that he had received in January of last term. But there is good news, as it seems the injury is not as bad as first thought and that Kerrigan's damage is down to bad bruising.

Tonight the clocks change and with it we hope that our luck now changes too.

Highlights – Henner's hat-trick, his fourth goal against the Shire this season. Greg worked tirelessly throughout the match with some good runs and he also linked up well with Webster and Fotheringham. From today's match one thing is certain, Martyn Fotheringham is not a finisher and it is unfair to put a player of his ability in a position that he is not suited too. Barry Donnachie was back to his best along the 'Knoll', entertainer and master of abuse, and today he was also on his best behaviour, not one booking. All in all, it was a team performance and the team deserves credit for their play.

Let's not get carried away, it was a solid performance against a poor team and we should have killed off the game earlier on, but it also keeps a good run going. The Shire can consider themselves lucky that they escaped in only losing three goals. Next week will be a different story, preparation is key in getting a result and a greater commitment will be required from some of the players and I'll be there!

Yet again, this Monday morning, Montrose are neglected by the local press. What is the point of posting a match preview on Saturday and then not giving a report on Monday? It is a similar situation with the *P&J*, but somehow Arbroath feature on their web site and teams outwith the Grampian Region also take priority.

At the weekend, Berwick brought Cowdenbeath's run to an end with a 1-0 home win. Stenhousemuir demolished Arbroath with a goal in either half. East Fife left it late in pulling level against Albion Rovers to retain a point at home and Queen's Park saw off Elgin in a 3-0 rout at Hampden. It changes nothing, league positions remain the same after Saturday's matches.

Next week sees the return of the derby matches, close encounters between neighbours, a term that is used loosely as there is no love lost. The Angus and Fife derbies lead the charge this Saturday, Stenhousemuir make the short walk to Firs Park and Albion Rovers similarly are at home to Queen's Park. Berwick meantime take a hike, as they are paired with Elgin!

Sense at long last finally prevails as Montrose have confirmed that the kick-off for the Cowdenbeath clash has been brought forward an hour to 2 pm.

There is no Scottish Cup trip to the seaside and that is definite. Borders side Selkirk were outright winners of Saturdays replay tie. Selkirk recorded a 4-1 victory to give them a next round away match at Alloa in two week's time.

The month of October has been a five match month for Montrose. Henry's troops have recorded two wins, two draws and suffered defeat at home to Queen's Park. Eight points from fifteen, seven goals and three given away signifies a much improved month. Room for improvement, yes, are we on schedule, the answer must be no and what is our recovery plan?

Seventeen miles and three points is all that separates Montrose from the smoke shelters of Arbroath but what will separate their support tomorrow? In the past at Gayfield there has been extra policing but no need for segregation, as the fans go through the ritual of changing ends at half time, using a clockwise movement so as not to meet.

For Henslee, it is his first return to the dressing rooms since swapping maroon for blue and he can expect a change in attitude from what was his home support for so long. He may have been a hero for the Smokies in scoring crucial goals but the rattle is now out of the pram on several counts and one is the disclosed / undisclosed fee as the support claim he was worth more. The encouragement Greg experienced in the past will now be venomous, a Judas in their eyes, and if he scores as many do when they return to their old stomping ground, then it will not be forgotten for derby matches to come!

Expect a hostile atmosphere and a match that will be more open than the last encounter as Arbroath's manager, John McGlashan's emphasis is on attacking football. Montrose cannot allow themselves to sit back and lie too deep, as they need to push forward with an element of surprise. McGlashan on the other hand is an ex- Montrose favourite and will be out to prove his managerial skills by putting one over on his old side (he may even lead from the front) but I still think that Henslee will have the last laugh!

A steady stream of cars filtered its way down the coast to Arbroath, a convoy heading for the 'Pleasureland' end of Gayfield Park. Segregation unusually was in force, a CCTV van advertised its wares and the eight hundred and thirty attendees were yet again serenaded with old and new songs. 'Sign On' with words put to the song from the classic musical Carousel ('You'll Never Walk Alone', just in case any Arbroath fans read this), to the taunts of 'Giro's and crime'. As before there is no love lost between either fan base. The Arbroath end is boosted by the attendance of the 'Ayrshire Nuttin Crew' and 'Aberdeen Service Crew'. Casuals on a day out- but why pick this match?

Nov 5th. ARBROATH, Away - report and teams
Today, Montrose are without Steve Kerrigan as it was revealed that he *has* broken a bone in his lower arm. Dodds seems the likely replacement but when the teams are announced, Dodds was named as a substitute along with Cargill, Martin, McLean and Butter. Montrose lined with Reid in goal, a back four of Donnachie, McKenzie, Stephen and Smith. Webster, Fraser, Doyle and Hall filled midfield. Henslee and Fotheringham were again paired up front.

A stunned silence encompassed the Arbroath support in only 4 minutes, as Montrose fans were jubilant. What a brilliant start!

Henslee had been fouled outside the box and Montrose were awarded a direct free-kick by the referee. Fotheringham took the kick curling the ball round the wall beyond the reach of keeper Peat. A few minutes later Henslee had a chance to kill the tie but the ball went wide. Montrose started to lose their way, letting Arbroath come to them. There was no grip on midfield as Montrose backed off into defence which resulted in Stephen or McKenzie having to clear long balls back up the park. Wave after wave, three balls lost to the sea that borders Gayfield and still Montrose stemmed the tide. Arbroath did have the ball in the back of the net only for the linesman to flag offside. It should have been a wake-up call, but once again Montrose hit the snooze button. Glad to be in the lead at half-time, surely the midfield would be changed for the second half, but there were no substitutions and the flow of one-way traffic continued where it had left off. When a substitution was made in 60 minutes, Martin replaced Fraser and Fotheringham returned to midfield.

Montrose were clearly struggling and things exploded when the referee allowed play to continue when McKenzie lay on the ground suffering from a head knock. This and further controversy in 71 minutes threw Montrose into turmoil in a few minutes of madness and the game was lost. With the linesman clearly flagging for off-side the referee chose on this occasion to ignore his decision and allowed play to continue. From the ball that was played in towards goal Dobbin headed home by a neck! Protests were to no avail as the referee had decided but obviously Fotheringham still had a few words to impart and was duly red carded for his wisdom, having previously been booked for a foul immediately after the restart. So now down to ten men we struggled along like a wagon that had lost more than one wheel. It was not until the 81st minute that Dodds was finally introduced for Euan Hall. He was barely on the park when Arbroath scored the clincher for the three points. Montrose failed to clear their line and Clarke volleyed home from twelve yards. It was our time to be silent but we new it was coming as there had not been one attempt on goal during the second half.

In the light of the day manager Hall admitted that we simply didn't play well enough to win but was also critical of referee Colin Brown as he felt his side had been harshly treated.

For Montrose now, Queen's Park and East Fife are the teams to catch but they can only do that by taking points from Stenhousemuir, Berwick and of course Cowdenbeath (our next match) in this league. That is the challenge and must be the Montrose goal in this second quarter of league games. It was a disappointing afternoon.

Highlights – In a below par team performance few can take any credit. Barry Donnachie who captained today's side played with heart, tackled well and was a saviour on many occasions. Hall worked hard, harried and chased, Stephen along with McKenzie put in the effort but ultimately today after the early goal we never looked like winning as we tried to defend a 1-0 lead, falling deeper and deeper into defence. The midfield looked anonymous, and needed the injection of a ball winner. Why was Dodds on the bench? Doyle looked uncomfortable in midfield and plays better in a central defensive position. Second half substitutions seemed strange as the midfield required to be shored-up. The introduction of Dodds and possibly Cargill may have secured our lead but the inevitable happened and when we lost one, another was destined to come. It's a game that is best forgotten, Arbroath fully deserved their win but the test for Montrose will come on Saturday. It is one thing beating East Stirling and Elgin but you have to be able to beat the better sides especially at home as it is the only way to climb the league.

Seven points from the last four games and they are still at it. What I mean is, there is still a section of the support not behind the team or should I say the manager and his son, Euan Hall. I witnessed it at the match again today. The last match I saw was a game that Montrose won and again today the very same people were being abusive. It was the same in pre-season. There is a post on the message board, 'Will the Supporters Trust who slag-off young Hall stop. He wasn't the worst player today; in fact he worked his socks off'. I just have to look at Thursday's '*Montrose Review*' (it's a ritual when I come home, thumbing through back issues) and the picture of Montrose Supporters Trust Committee members receiving a share certificate for one thousand, eight hundred shares from club chairman John Paton to add to the two hundred presently held. The 'Supporters Trust' was set up to give a voice at Board meetings and a way of helping the club. So what has gone wrong?

I can confirm that a letter was written to the Montrose Review some time ago from a concerned supporter but it was never printed due to an increase in dog fouling. This is an extract of the letter –

This letter is an attack on the behaviour of some members of the MST (Montrose Supporters Trust), who are so called supporters. I have been a supporter of Montrose Football Club for a number of years and have the best interests of the club at heart, but cannot bear to see and hear such behaviour from this faction. The Trust Society Board state that they " will continue to make constructive representations on behalf of Montrose supporters, on any issues that are brought to them".

It is particularly hard to believe the criticism of Euan Hall who like it or not puts in a good shift in a Montrose shirt and will likely develop over-time as his confidence and belief is rebuilt. Over the pre-season he has played some good football in a side that is learning about one another, often out of his position, he is a young player much like the rest of the squad and will of course, like others, suffer dips in form, but his confidence is boosted no-end by the society board 'speaking out'! The abuse is unjust and often unwarranted and is on the point of childish, petty playground taunts.

Why can't you be supportive? Why can't you give all the players, staff and the board a chance? Why do you constantly relive the past, be it success or failure and why do you use this as an excuse for your behaviour?

Everybody can hear you and everybody can see you doing it, you're a disgrace in thinking you have a right to portray yourselves as the voice of the supporters. Think before you speak, support before criticising, you would do so if you actually truly cared about the club.

So please stand-up and remind me, what is the role of the MST? Give the club the backing that it deserves starting with an apology to Euan Hall!

Bearing in mind that this was written back in pre-season, after today's match, it's about time something was said. After all the 'Trust' were all smiles up until the 71st minute. After Arbroath scored, they then proceeded to take their retribution out on Euan Hall, then Gilzean and Henry!

I only wish the letter, which I saw as being a shot across the bows had made its way to the press. Don't get me wrong, a supporter's trust is a great benefit to a club as it can generate much needed revenue and it can also give a voice to the supporters on the Board. We all have a genuine interest in the Club and only want the best, but that can take time-after all Rome was not built in a day. For instance I think that the club has lost a bit of its structure by having no youth policy and that will return in time. I personally would like to see the Trust doing well (2,000 shares is a step in the right direction), but barracking players and team managers is not the way forward and certainly does not constitute representation of the support. If the 'Trust' want their membership to increase, they have to market not only the concept but themselves. Sometimes frustration does takeover, the letter that I quote was possibly written out of frustration, but we have all got to change and seek a clean sheet. I wish them well as one day they might just have enough shares to run the Club. The concept is good, it can be done!

Saturday's derby scores – A couple of strange results as it took Berwick 95 minutes to equalise for a 2-2 draw. Ten man Shire held Stenhousemuir to a 0-0 draw with the Warriors missing a penalty in the process. Cowdenbeath turned a one goal deficit around at half-time, by scoring three in the second period. Albion Rovers also snatched a draw from Queen's Park by scoring a late equaliser. The league positions have not changed, but will we be able to say that after Saturday!

Joy to the world, I am really speechless as this morning I read a post on the message board and can't believe what is written. The post reads-' It's not the Trust who get on Euan Hall's back, it is individuals who do the slagging. Just because you are a Trust member, or indeed a Supporter's Club member, there is no need to toe the party line; you are entitled to your opinion – whether or not that opinion is held by the organisation that you are part of.' He or she (it's hard to tell) ends the post with – 'Now that I have that off my fairly ample chest, I do agree with the rest of your post.' If that is not guilt, what is and why drag in the Supporters Club?

So why is the Trust not doing anything to rid this mind-set element? As to who would want to join an organisation which is clearly not in charge of its membership is beyond me. There has got to be some code of conduct, after all it does reflect badly on those holding prominent positions on the Trust Board. If you agree with this post then take a leaf out of David Blunkett's book who resigned under similar circumstances for having a foot in both camps after breaking the ministerial code. You are either with the 'Trust' and give support to the Club including Board, manager and players or be man enough to resign instead of hiding behind aliases.

It's a moral dilemma -

MORAL QUESTION

This test only has one question, but it's a very important one. By giving an honest answer, you will discover where you stand morally. The test features an unlikely, completely fictional situation in which you will have to make a decision. Remember that your answer needs to be honest, yet spontaneous. Please give due consideration to each line.

THE SITUATION

You are in Florida, Miami to be specific. There is chaos all around you caused by a hurricane with severe flooding.
This is a flood of biblical proportions.
You are a photo-journalist working for a major newspaper, and you're caught in the middle of this epic disaster.
The situation is nearly hopeless.
You're trying to shoot career-making photos.
There are houses and people swirling around you, some disappearing under the water.
Nature is unleashing all of its destructive fury.

THE TEST

Suddenly you see a man in the water.
 He is fighting for his life, trying not to be taken down with the debris.
You move closer.
Somehow the man looks familiar.
You suddenly realise who it is.
It's George W. Bush!
At the same time you notice that the raging waters are about to take him under forever.
You have two options--you can save the life of George W. Bush, or you can shoot a dramatic Pulitzer Prize-winning photo, documenting the death of one of the world's most powerful politicians.

THE QUESTION

Here's the question, and please give an honest answer:
Would you select high contrast colour film, or would you go with the classic simplicity of black and white?

There was another post stating that the Club Board now read the message board. It's about time. They may even recognise who's writing what as it doesn't take a genius!

As 'Remembrance Day' approaches-a holiday in many countries- and a day to remember lives lost in the war years, there is still a deep resentment here in the Netherlands at the treatment of Jews. Many years have passed by but wounds are fresh. I have visited Ann Frank's house in Amsterdam and left with a chill that reminded me of the 'Holocaust' memorial in Boston and a feeling that I had never encountered before.

In Dutch football, Ajax Amsterdam 'ultras' have taken to supporting the Israeli illegal occupation of Arab lands and show their support by waving or hanging Israeli flags at games. This in turn has led the corresponding Feyenoord fans to show support to the Palestinian cause by flying flags and singing anti-Semetic songs. This has added further fuel to the fire of an already overheated derby match, often ignored by the hardcore fans who favour songs and chants which ultimately ends in a 'Battle Royal' at the end of the game between both sets of supporters and the police also like to be included.

I was speaking to one of our design consultants, who told me that for a company to be 'chartered' which allows them to put the word 'Royal' in front of their name they need to meet a certain criteria before being considered. Firstly they have to have been in business for more than a hundred years. Secondly they have to be seen not to have collaborated with the Germans during the war. The cut is deep, there are people who speak Dutch but hide the fact that they are German. It is a side of the culture that an outsider may not see, the healing process has started but the history is still there and will always be remembered by the population.

Another round of fixtures this weekend but they are disjointed, with some playing Friday and others keeping to the routine Saturday kick-of, but not at the usual scheduled time. All this reorganisation just to appease Scotland fans and a friendly match with the USA.

East Stirling and Queen's Park have opted for a Friday evening start. East Fife who play Stenhousemuir, have gone for a lunchtime kick-off of 1 pm. Albion Rovers and Montrose kick-off their home games at 2 pm. Which leaves our neighbours, Arbroath entertaining Berwick down the road, keeping the statutory three o'clock time. Obviously satellite technology hasn't reach Arbroath yet!

I am dreading kick-off, I am back in Breda and after Saturday's disappointment I hope that the team selection for today's match is right. Henry Hall seems under pressure to win yet again as a defeat could cost him the manager's job. Some sites go through the A to Z of who is available; others give a run down of the managerial career pattern.

Many have said that we need a settled team but too many injuries had seen to that and now Fotheringham is suspended. Cowdenbeath have been free scoring and Montrose will need to be on their guard. If it was me, which it is not, I would play 3-5-2 with McKenzie, Doyle and Stephen in front of Reid and five in the midfield. Wing-backs, Donnachie and Smith running the flanks with Hall, Dodds, and Cargill filling the middle slots. Upfront, McLean should be given the first half along with Henslee.

Cowdenbeath are always a well organised side and matches with Montrose are never high scoring, keeping it tight is Henry's only option. Cowdenbeath are the in-form league side at present, and as with the last match, we will be lucky to be able to fill the bench. Could another call for Hankinson to appear as an outfield player be on the cards? It's looking bleak, but sometimes these circumstances can be the coupon buster, but on this occasion I don't think so, as even a point seems out of reach.

Today's papers reported Dodds and Butter as slight doubts with calf strains. Henry Hall states that he will have to rethink midfield and that Cargill may step in. Duncan McLean will be on the subs bench in order that he is brought back from injury gradually.

In one paper, Hall states that Cowdenbeath are the best team that Montrose have played in the league, yet in another he states that Montrose's worst performance of the season was at Central Park. No matter what, a result against Cowdenbeath is the best way to put the Arbroath defeat behind them.

3 minutes gone, there is a text message and Montrose are one down. Like last week, what a start and it's a gift!

I suppose it was quite apt really as Breda celebrated the start of Christmas with their Sinter Klass festival as Sint Nic rode through the streets on his white horse. You should have seen the kid's faces. It's all about believing!

Nov 12th. COWDENBEATH, Home - report and teams
Cowdenbeath manager Mixu Paatelainen is fresh from celebrating his manager of the month award and it only takes 3 minutes for him to celebrate his brother Markus' goal.

Montrose started of with a 4-4-2 system with Reid in goal, a back-four of Donnachie, McKenzie, Stephen and Smith. Dodds and Cargill took midfield spots with Webster and Hall on the flanks. Martin and Henslee partner each other up front. Watson reappears on the bench along with McLean, Fraser, Doyle and Butter.

Montrose were caught cold, a quickly taken corner found Paatelainen who was able walk through the defence unchallenged to volley home. One down through lack of concentration and from then on Cowdenbeath dominated the first half. More chances fell to the Fife side when Ward headed over and Paatelainen headed wide. It was hard to believe that the score remained 1-0 at the interval as Cowdenbeath were faster, stronger and more committed.

No changes at the interval and another let-off straight from the re-start with Cowden's Guy heading against the woodwork. Montrose did not look like scoring and it took until the 51st minute for them to win their first corner of the match. An Elliott Smith long range drive, which was pushed over by goalkeeper Hay, was their only real shot at the visitor's goal.

Henry Hall freshened things up by introducing McLean for Martin up front. Doyle then replaced Jamie McKenzie who was suffering from a heavy cold and had been a doubtful starter. The final substitution saw Fraser take over from Cargill in midfield but as the final whistle blew the changes that had been made were to no avail. A 1-0 defeat and a reported crowd of 305, with some 125 in hiding as the attendance was considerably lower. To further compound things, Neil Stephen was red carded for a second bookable offence, Elliot Smith picked up another yellow and must be up for suspension after collecting a sixth card. Euan Hall also picked up a booking for his trouble.

We are going nowhere! There is no determination, no structure in our play and a distinct lack of effort. It's only a matter of time before the Board see the light and seek a replacement manager. It's a cost that Montrose can ill afford but sadly have to consider.

Our next match is against Stenhousemuir at Ochilview. Team selection will most certainly be a problem. Fotheringham is still suspended, Stephen will be out after today's red card and Smith could also be on a charge.

Will Kerrigan be back from injury? I doubt it, which means the bench may be scant and on top of that we need to sort out our problems in attack. Anybody coming in will have a job on their hands and it will take someone of strong character to sort it out. No game this coming Saturday lets the dust settle once again and allows the message boards to cool!

The other game of the day, Scotland's friendly with the USA ends in a 1-1 draw, preparation for the USA for the World Cup finals taking place in Germany in June 2006. A creditable result for a Scotland team placed 63rd in the FIFA world rankings. The USA on the other hand currently lies in 7th place and could swallow the nation of Scotland ten fold where population is concerned. For Scotland signs are good as Walter Smith has rejuvenated the side, but after today's display by the United States I'm even more convinced, there is no way they put men on the moon!

There was one other match, a friendly between rivals Argentina and England. We are seven months away from the World Cup, the draw destined for December has not yet taken place for the finals and on one friendly result we are subjected to a barrage of headlines. It is truly unbelievable – 'Best friendly ever played', 'A dress rehearsal for the World Cup Final' and 'Historic

145

day in English Football'. Radio shows are no better – are you now convinced that England can go on and win the World Cup, Sven is the right manager and who's the biggest threat to England? One rag even had a picture of Sven holding the World Cup trophy. Will we have to endure this for the foreseeable future? The answer is yes, well at least until the end of June.

On this day as Christmas approaches it reminds you of the part football played on a day of cease-fire during the First World War. It was played in no-mans land, a kick about, friends for a day before returning to their trenches and the hostilities of war.

So much for playing on a Friday night! East Stirling's match with Queen's Park was postponed due to high winds. In the other matches East Fife surrendered a two goal home lead to be beaten by Stenhousemuir with an 89th minute winner (no it wasn't a penalty!). Elgin recorded a rare 2-0 away win at Coatbridge and Berwick's unbeaten record has gone. Arbroath did it in style putting 4 past the Border's outfit which means Arbroath climbing above Montrose in the league and their turn to gloat!

It's been a quite week, message boards are quiet and it seems that nobody now cares any longer, as someone says that the season for Montrose is now over. The towel from the support has been thrown into the ring, the fight has gone and with it any belief that was there. I now think I know why young kids want an old firm football strip for Christmas. Some kids asked one of their youth coaches, who is wearing a Montrose top, "But who do you really support - Rangers or Celtic." The coach bravely replies "Montrose" and explains to the young ears that they should support their local team, but as they walk away one youngster questions why you would support Montrose when you can support Rangers or Celtic. Why indeed? It's a question at this precise time that I could not answer but maybe the answer was in last week's match programme, as there was an article concerning youth structure and the polices that some clubs have developed over several years. Youth involvement from an early age, giving awareness that there is a team in the town and that they can take part. I remember Ross Jack running an early touches coaching week in pre-season. It was well attended, and by the end of the week the Rangers and Celtic shirts had diminished as kids changed their allegiance to the blue of Montrose. Change is required, better interface with the community and schools. The players also have to play their part and spend time promoting the club and giving encouragement by putting something back in. The gain would be long term, it has worked for Cowdenbeath with the introduction of a youth system, and they have benefited financially as young players have moved on for a transfer fee. It would take work but the effort I am sure would be worthwhile for club and community.

A free weekend next week and some respite from the League and also a free Saturday as Montrose have a bye in the first round of the Scottish Cup. Montrose will play the winners of the Alloa - Selkirk tie. We have been drawn against both sides before but it was some time ago. Montrose have met Alloa on three occasions, two were first round ties and in the first instance we were on the end of an 8-3 defeat in 1948-49. In the second, season 1963/64, we managed a replay after holding Alloa to a 1-1 draw at home. The replay at Alloa saw the home side run out as 3-2 winners. In the 1966-67 Cup preliminary rounds Alloa were 2-1 winners at Recreation Park. Our fortunes have not been good in Cup competitions where Alloa are concerned.

We have only played Selkirk once, in 1974/75, again a first round match, and this time we were victorious, recording a 5-1 win at home. It looks to be a trek to Alloa if the form book is right!

Car trouble, it's always difficult when you are away from home and something happens to your car. In this instance someone had a greater need for my blind-side wing mirror than I did. It wasn't until I returned to the car park where I had left my car that I saw that it was gone. The individual had taken great care to remove the mirrored glass and disconnecting the electrics for which I should be grateful. There has been a problem not only in the Netherlands but other countries too where Eastern Europeans not only steal cars to order but also parts. It's incredible!

In this game you can have all the continental cover of the AA that you like, but for small things like a mirror it is worthless as you have to sort it out yourself and that can be a task on its own. A mirror on a right-hand drive car is something that you cannot do without in a left-hand drive country as it is difficult enough to drive with both mirrors. After a few phone calls I was asked to take the car to the dealership, it was a simple enough job, there was no need to leave the car and there was no need for a courtesy car, which was just as well. You see the courtesy cars, complete with sponsorship, that were on offer only had two wheels, you've guess it, the good old Dutch form of transport. You want a courtesy car, get on yer bike!

Nov 19th. Alloa v Selkirk
Match postponed – only two matches in the Scottish Cup first round survived the cold overnight hard frost. Firhill is lucky enough to have under soil heating which allowed the Partick Thistle game to go ahead with Albion Rovers. Rovers managed a creditable draw and a replay at Coatbridge. In the

other match Gretna recorded a 6-2 win at Edinburgh where non-leaguers Preston Athletic play.

What does this all mean for Montrose? We can't book the bus for our day out to Alloa or Selkirk and it looks like our match against Stenhousemuir could be cancelled if Stenny re-arranges their cup-tie with East Stirling for Saturday week. It would mean another blank Saturday to practice our skills, healing time for Steve Kerrigan and prolongation for the management team.

The bias is so unbelievable! BBC half-time scores squeezed into a slot during the interval break in the Ireland - Australia rugby match. They go through the English half-times including the Conference league and low and behold the voice says that's all we have time for as we return to the rugby at Lansdowne Road. Don't they know that it is Scottish Cup Day! It is different when it is the FA Cup, as it is given pride of place. We all pay the same licence fee and once again we are short changed. I have been sitting here for an hour for just a glimpse of the scores and didn't even get that.

Humbug! The doorbell rings the letter box is rattled, someone is impatient, someone else disgruntled with the days events. I rise from my seat as there is no ignoring it and prepare myself for a barrage of Dutch and a hasty interpretation before retreating indoors. On opening the door I find a brightly coloured chap, black face, dressed in period costume. He utters a few words in Dutch, takes my hand and placed some ginger nuts into my palm before shaking his can for money. Halloween is past, he ain't a guyser but is Sinter Klasses helper, 'Black Piet' as he is known. Obviously, the racial discrimination act has not reached the Netherlands! The Dutch myth is that Piet carries the bags for Sint Nic and if you are not good then you will be put in Piets bag and return with Piet to Spain as he sails away. There is history somewhere there as the Netherlands was once ruled by the Spanish. Speechless I parted with my cash and returned indoors.

It has not been a good day, car trouble, the BBC score service, Sint Piet and O'Meara's did not have the Celtic-Rangers match televised. Imagine an Irish Bar without the required satellite link! As I had walked through the Grote Markt, I watched kids send their balloons high up into the sky, with a wish for Christmas attached. We all have wishes, aspirations and hopes. Let's hope that it is a Merry Christmas for Montrose Football Club whatever happens!

Tuesday evening, November 22nd and a Forfarshire Cup first round match against Brechin takes place at Links Park. I suppose that it is a welcome game especially when there has been another vacant Saturday.

Neighbours Brechin, a first division side, have also had their troubles this season with injuries and have struggled to make any impact after being promoted last term. It gives Henry Hall a chance to play Saturday's team selection and a chance to see if it works. Lose on Saturday and it could be the last chance saloon as fourth place would now seem out of reach!

Yes! Saturday's match with Stenhousemuir could be on as they play East Stirling tonight in the re-arranged cup tie. The match just has to survive another heavy morning frost and referee's inspection. Alloa are also down to play Selkirk tonight. Two matches and they both have an outcome for Montrose.

Nov. 22nd. Brechin, Home – Forfarshire Cup 1st. Round
Match postponed, but it was a late cancellation as the game was called off at 18.40hrs. just fifty minutes before kick-off. After a heavy morning frost the referee's inspection deemed that the goal-mouths were unplayable. There is no date yet for the rescheduled match.

It wasn't the only match to fall foul of the weather, as the two relevant cup-ties at Alloa and Stenhousemuir also bit the dust for a second time. These games however have been rescheduled to take place on Monday now, so Saturday looks to be still on at Ochilview if it thaws out, contrary to the Montrose web site, which has the game being played at Stair Park, home of Stranraer. However for this weekend there is a severe weather warning of heavy snow falls and the match may be postponed. Another free weekend looms!

NAC play FC Groningen tonight and it's the televised Friday night match. I was looking forward to watching Erik Neveland, a player with FC Groningen who I admire, but heavy snow and thunder and lightning has put paid to that, as the match is postponed late in the afternoon. It's starting to be a habit and if the weatherman's prediction of a truly brutal winter is correct, then a backlog of fixtures will ensue, affecting most teams come March, when they have to play two games a week in heavy conditions.

The' Montrose Review' gives a hint of the team lines for the Stenhousemuir match. There is no mention that it is off and I suppose Stenny are in the same boat as Montrose having not played the previous Saturday.

Montrose have Fotheringham and Stephen suspended, Martin has flu-type symptoms and will also not play. Fraser looks set to return as Fotheringham's replacement, Doyle will partner McKenzie in defence for Stephen and it looks like Duncan McLean could be on from the start. McLean has been injured since pre-season and has yet to play a full match, let's hope he gets his chance to prove his fitness before the January transfer window.

Stenhousemuir still occupy second place and will be difficult opponents with home advantage. Mid-fielder McBride destroyed Montrose at Links Park with a first half exhibition of how football should be played. In that match striker Colin Cramb was unavailable and he will be a further threat to the Montrose defence along with 'penalty king'- Paul McGrillen. Signs are not good, we really are up against it, our only hope is postponement but that just delays the evil day!

What a find this Saturday! Whilst browsing through some shops today I found an old wooden football rattle. I hadn't seen one since my childhood and couldn't resist having a shot. As you can imagine the noise did attract attention. The shop owner approached exchanging the niceties of 'mid-dag' and enquired if I knew what it was for. Pleased with myself, I said yes we used them to support our football team. He on the other hand said" No "He informed me that that in the sixties they were used in the Netherlands by the bin men for householders to bring out their rubbish. Highly embarrassed at getting it wrong, I bought it. A Christmas present for my wife but somehow I don't think that it will be appreciated as she takes the bin out on refuse day!

I only got the usual BBC treatment during the half time break at Murrayfield where Scotland are playing the All Blacks. As soon as the English Conference results were shown it was straight to press the red button. Once again for a second week my red button was pressed as I was furious at the treatment and complete disregard for Scottish results by the BBC, all for the sake of another few seconds before returning to Murrayfield. If they had even considered not telling people about the red button it would have been enough time to complete the Scottish matches being played!

I am still not enlightened as to whether the game is on or not and what matches are off in Scotland. Did we survive the referee's inspection? Unfortunately we did!

Having gone to Brabant Noord for dinner I had reconciled myself to finding out, one way or another, on Sunday depending on an English tabloid. Resigned to that fact my mobile rang and it was Gareth.
"Did you see the score?" So the match was on! "Yes" he replied "but did you see the score?"
His eagerness to tell me built up my hopes, had we pulled it out of the bag as I replied "Tell me then."
"Arbroath beat the Shire 7-2"

"Yes but what about Montrose?"
"It was 6-2." I should have known better as I asked the stupid question "Who for?"

Nov 26th. STENHOUSEMUIR, Away - report and teams
Embarrassingly hit for six, a reported crowd of three hundred and twelve says that few travelled down to make the match. One down in 9 minutes, we did draw back level before going in at half-time 3-1 down. Once again 9 minutes after the restart Stenhousemuir added to their total before Montrose pulled another goal back. A further two goals in the last eight minutes rubbed salt into an ever deepening wound to a humiliating defeat. Losing six is bad enough, but neighbours Arbroath scoring seven shows what a management change can do to lift a team. Have the Board left it too late to call time?

The team lined up along the lines I had thought. Reid was in goal, with a defence of Donnachie, McKenzie, Doyle and Elliot Smith. Webster, Dodds, Fraser and Hall camped out in midfield. Henslee's partner for the day was Duncan McLean who has returned to full fitness and hopefully a consistent spell in the team. The bench - there lies a story! Kerrigan made a return to the bench and later played for 15 minutes coming on for Hall. Butter, Watson, Russell and the cardboard cut-out figure of Andy Cargill who did not turn up completed the bench line up.

The Warriors set the pace in early exchanges but Montrose were equal in play until a McBride trundler eluded Andy Reid into the bottom corner of the net. Switching play down either wing Montrose fought back and in 16 minutes levelled the match. In a well worked goal, Webster delivered an inch perfect cross for Henslee to head home past goalkeeper McCulloch. Stenhousemuir regain the lead in 23 minutes; after a series of corners Sinclair finally picked his spot in heading home. Cramb then put the Warriors two ahead lobbing the keeper as the defence backed off. Losing two soft goals saw heads drop and discipline diminish. The front two of Henslee and McLean tried to create opportunities but to no avail. The half-time whistle was a welcome sound for the few individuals who had made the journey to the central belt as at this stage the game was already lost.

After the restart Stenhousemuir proceeded to take command where they had left off, winning corner after corner. Montrose were on the back foot and after clearing one corner, full back McAlpine struck a twenty-five yard drive sweetly into the bottom corner of the net. Undeterred by this, Montrose rallied once again, Fraser had a shot pushed over by McCulloch then McLean sent the keeper scrambling before being substituted by Watson. A long hopeful ball into the Warriors box in seventy–five minutes saw the goalkeeper spill the take and Webster was on hand to follow-up and net. Shortly afterwards James Russell replaced Webster. Stenhousemuir finished the game with two goals from sixteen year-old Templeton, who had come off the bench, toe-poking home both efforts from six-yards to complete the scoring.

Highlights – Fraser and Henslee worked hard, Donnachie and Webster never gave up and earned pass marks for their performance. Henry Hall made no excuses in his '*Courier*' comments, in which he gave full credit to Stenhousemuir for taking their goals. He goes on to state that it was a bad day for the back-four and the goalkeeper, failing to recognise that it was also a bad day for the support and the few die-hards who attended. Henry concludes by saying that we never really attacked at all and that it was a poor game but that we did look better going forward. I can't work these comments out but we do agree on one thing and that is you should never lose six goals!

Message boards are a- wash with posts, 'Pie and Bovril'- just what you need on a cold day- has the thread of 'Sack Hall' running with some thirty odd contributors. The Montrose Supporters Trust urge fans to come to their annual general meeting this Friday. The run up to the previous manager, John Sheran's resignation is re-lived and some supporters call for the Board to go public in supporting the manager. Oh to turn the clock back to the successful period of the seventies! For the first time in football history Montrose have something else in common with the mighty Glasgow Rangers. Not only do both clubs play in blue but neither side has won in the month of November and both managers are under scrutiny by the fans.

In the weekend's matches, it is the Scottish Cup that produces the shock of the day. Non-league Spartans knock out high flying Berwick with a single goal win. Spartans now play Lossiemouth in round two and Berwick's travelling support can now cancel their trip to the seaside! It's another lesson learned as most of the Berwick posts when the cup was first drawn had the 'Who will we meet in the third round?' bias as if the ties were a foregone conclusion.

A Brazil and Clark hat-trick for Arbroath sees the Smokies bring their points tally to within a couple of points off fourth place in the league. Queen's Park leap-frog East Fife to take fourth place with a 2-0 win at Hampden.

Nov 28th. Alloa v Selkirk
Finally the postponed Scottish Cup tie is played and Selkirk suffer a 9-0 defeat at the hands of Alloa. It is a bit better than season 1984-85 when

Stirling Albion took twenty goals off Selkirk in the same competition. So that's it then, Alloa here we come!

Posts are still appearing on the message boards but they are tempered and rational to a point. A think before you write attitude has taken over and some good points are brought out. This post in particular made me think – 'Don't know if there is a board meeting tonight, but even if they do decide its time for a new manager, it is only the start. They also need to rebuild relationships with the businesses and citizens of the town, in order to bring in the level of income required via sponsorship and gate money, to allow us to compete at a decent level. As others have pointed out in their posts, that means being able to at least match Junior Club wages and even more importantly a commitment to establishing a proper youth system.' Another post establishes what we all honestly think as it states –'Managing a football club is a very fickle business whether you have millions to play with or not. Don't think HH deserves any personal attacks but it does look like its time for a change - however the players have got to raise the bar as well. It is time that we got it sorted out one way or the other so we can get behind the club while we still have one'. Strong words but this time honesty prevails from those who really care!

'Time Gentlemen please!' it's a curse, another manager is gone. This morning I listened to the news on Radio Scotland, being an hour ahead, it was possibly a bit early. It was reported on Radio Tay that the Montrose manager Henry Hall had left by mutual consent but I only found out as it was a case of one shall tell another and he shall tell his friend. A text from Gareth took not only me by surprise but most of my colleagues in an open plan office as the mobile croaked! As I read 'Hall leaves by mutual consent', my colleagues ridicule my choice of text alert.

The news of Henry's parting is on the back page of 'The Courier' but not on the DC Thomson web site. Maybe just as well, as the paper reports that losing top scorer Scott Michie had played a big part in results. The fact that Michie had in fact left the club prior to season 2004/05 somehow has slipped the sports writer's mind.

The news had also not reached the North East as the P&J failed to headline. The BBC web site however posted a short report. It read – Hall parts company with Montrose. Chairman John Paton said: 'The parting is mutual. There is no animosity, but after talking things over it was felt this is the correct time for change.' Assistant Ian Gilzean will take training in the interim until a new manager is found.

Last night the Board took the decision, whether it was right or wrong to delay, they now have to make it work and fans must now give the Board and the team their full support and not bemoan the choice of manager.

I have worked on many projects where people have been replaced as milestones must be met and if you don't meet these milestones you won't be there. It is a hazard of being contract, as you can be there one day and not the next. It's part of business, a continuous probation period for the incumbant as you are only as good as your last job.

For Henry Hall, the first quarter milestone had not been met in terms of points accumulated. Results have been poor since, and games that Montrose should have won were lost or drawn. Injuries had played a large part, but it is all about managing the situation and forming a winning team. Anything less is not acceptable, as any client will tell you - when buying a racehorse they don't expect to receive a tortoise.

Henry Hall can be proud of his achievements in turning the side around in season 2004 – 2005 during which Montrose possibly played some of their best football. I wish him well.

Last season one in three mangers lost their jobs. Success is a sign of the times. Rangers manager Alec McLeish won the Scottish Premier title last season but this term Rangers are currently in fourth position and a substantial number of points adrift which has put his tenure at Ibrox in jeopardy. Alex Ferguson has brought success to Manchester United but with recent results people say it is time he moved on. Success lifts expectations to a different level and it is then that fans expect even more. It is a no win situation for any manager!

Speculation abounds, who wants who, journalists putting more names down on paper and an interview process for the Board, if the vacant position is advertised. Different pairing's spring to mind, Jim Duffy and Gerry Britton giving us a striker, Baikie, then there's the old brigade of Terry Christie, Alex Smith and Ian Wilson. There are also the relatively young team managers, of Brian Irvine and Bobby Geddes and Highland League favourites of Shearer, Patterson and John Gardiner. If I had to choose I would go for a player manager, Billy Dodds, Graeme Jones, Gerry Britton or Stephen Glass, but again it is not my choice. The message boards seem firmly set on Eddie Wolecki. He is young and ambitious, has new ideas and has got a reputation for player fitness and preparation.

I think the question regarding a managerial appointment will depend on money, which will rule out a lot of the candidates. There are a lot of rumblings about the lack of youth development at the club, as well as board members concerns too, especially regarding the future and well-being of the club. The lowest bidder is not always the best tender applicant and can put the Board in a no win situation with the fans-is it worth the hassle? You can please some of the people some of the time but not all of the people all of the time.

We look forward, not back, it's another new start. The process of looking for a new manager coincides with our appointment period of finding a general management contractor for our Breda project. The process is the same as we produce a bid list and invite potential candidates. Some are interested, some not and some will not make final selection. Interviews are held and the scope of the project is discussed. Tender documents are issued and submissions are received for the work to be carried out. Further interviews define and sort out final legal details before the contract award is made. Upon appointment the contractor mobilises. Not too dissimilar to the Board's task except that it is important to make a quick appointment. So who is on the Board's bid list?

As the third casualty of Angus team managers bites the dust in a season barely four months old the media select their front runners. Former Dundee United and Celtic player David Hannah who currently plies his trade with St. Johnstone has shown an interest in the vacant managerial position and St Johnstone have indicated that they will not stand in his way but there are more experienced candidates in the running for the job. Eddie Wolecki and Brechin striker Paul Ritchie have also been linked to the position but there are others who are worth approaching. We need a good strong manager to lift the club.

Montrose Chairman John Paton had indicated that the appointment process had begun however he states that ideally he would like a player-manager which could mean delaying until the January transfer window in order for the right player to take the management role. I somehow think that a quick appointment will be made, let's hope it is one of the following.

1. Dave Baikie – successful with Junior outfit Tayport and has also had a successful senior management career with Arbroath and Cowdenbeath, leaving the latter for personal reasons. Baikie has just recently taken the reigns at Bo'ness but may relish the Links Park challenge. He is a manager who demonstrates grit and an attacking system of 4-3-3. If he was appointed I personally think that he would be a good choice to fill the vacant position. His previous experience in

bringing Cowdenbeath from a below mid-league position to just failing to make promotion, along with setting youth development structures is a distinct advantage.

2. Paul Ritchie – an experienced striker of many clubs who has an eye for goal. Currently back with neighbours Brechin, Paul would be a good addition to the forward line and would give a managerial presence on the field. Still to learn his managerial skills Paul would be a good assistant to the likes of Dave Baikie.

3. Eddie Wolecki – an ex-Montrose player and young enthusiastic manager with modern methods who is studying 'Sports Coaching and Development' at Abertay University. Currently managing Junior club Lochee, he has built a successful side who compete in the Junior Super League. Wolecki would, like Baikie, be a good choice but whether the Board are willing to invest in this young manager's methods are yet to be seen.

4. John Gardiner – currently manager of Highland League side Inverurie Loco's and has had previous playing experience at a senior level with Dundee United and Aberdeen. The ex-goalkeeper has won the Highland League Championship with both Loco's and Huntly as a manager and knows the Aberdeenshire soccer league's potential for playing staff.

I have just watched the highlights from Sunday's fixtures in the Dutch League. Successful sides play a 4-3-3 system; AZ, Feyenoord and PSV have a constant attacking threat on their opponent's goal. It's a great debate but one that needs to be settled before the managerial position is filled as an attack minded manager is a must. Sadly Utrecht's fine victory over Ajax is over-shadowed a few days later as one of their players dies in his sleep aged twenty-six. The Netherlands is shocked by this young death.

It's not over till it's over as the *Montrose Review* reports the now ex-managers thoughts at the close of play. The Montrose headline reads 'Hall's reign over – Victory for Boo Boys'. I have witnessed this, not just this season but also towards the end of last season and to Henry's son Euan. Henry feels that the chairman was put under pressure from the support and in particular from a few in a section of the crowd. But it does mean that those who did the shouting have won. He leaves with no animosity, just regret, as two or three supporters forced the chairman's hand.

The Board have indicated that they are looking to appoint a new manager prior to facing Alloa in the Scottish Cup. A quick appointment indeed, so they must have someone in mind. Chairman John Paton states that it may be time for a player manager and lists leadership on the park as being the main problem for results. Let's hope that it wasn't Paul Ritchie that he had in mind! According to today's *Courier* Brechin City's Paul Ritchie has declined to be interviewed for the vacant post. Montrose had asked to speak to the striker but his loyalties lie with Brechin. So that is one potential candidate, who is out of the frame.

The *Daily Record* publishes news that East Stirling manager Dennis Newall has parted company with the club. The Record instantly links him with the Links Park job- typical west coast journalism.

The media amaze me, one minute there are no reports and no interest in the club and the next, when your manager leaves, there is constant interest to the point of harassment. The *Courier* reports today, eager not to miss any pending appointment, that last night Chairman John Paton said "We will probably draw up a short list tomorrow night and start interviewing over the weekend, in the hope that we will be able to appoint someone early next week." Like the media, the message boards are inundated with posts and there is no surprise to what the topic is after Henry's parting comments!

Posts range from 'Now that Henry has gone, let's see if the 'Boo Boys' are happy with his successor' to 'Henry Hall doesn't deserve the personal insults.' One post states 'He tried his best' and reminds the support how well he started off. More posts come to the defence of son Euan asking to give the lad a break and he is also congratulated by one fan for giving one hundred percent of what he has to give in every game.

However there is a suspicion of guilt from one contributor as he say's, 'let's hope the three Boo Boys get behind the team now', but confirms his guilt as he continues to say 'along with the other three hundred who were after his head'. Ironically as stated before it is individuals who do the slagging, there is no need to toe the party line; you are entitled to your opinion – whether or not that opinion is held by the organisation that you are part of. Where have we heard that before, remember what goes around comes around! I remember that when Montrose was a winning team under John Holt, these same 'Boo Boys' were still shouting for the manager's head.

Who's next for the thankless task? Just who do the 'Boo Boys' want? Allegedly it's not Dave Baikie but if he was appointed then he would be judged on results! It is rumoured that ex-Peterhead management team Ian Wilson and Allan Lyons have thrown their hats into the ring along with ex-Montrose player Mark Bennett to make up the numbers. I doubt if they will make the short list as they are hardly player-managers.

The *P&J* reports 'Black-out at Elgin' as the Blacks' take-over bid of the club is gazumped at the final hurdle, after extra shares were 'discovered'. Elgin City's main sponsor has purchased a major shareholding in the club of 55 % which was accepted by the City Board. Kenny Black resigned as assistant manager forthwith and manager David Robertson has since followed suit.

The vision that the Blacks had for the club was too good to be true as they sought to establish a full youth development programme. Their departure has thrown the club into turmoil as no fixed plans seem in place. Not only do they have to go through the recruiting phase for a manager, the skill-seekers programme is in jeopardy, there is no coaching staff and wages have yet to be paid for November. The future of the club looks bleak but I hope they get things sorted out for the sake of the young lads who gave up education to join the skill-seekers, their fans and the loyalty that they have shown in the past.

It's been a troublesome week as three Third Division sides have lost their managers, which brings the tally to five so early in the season with only fifteen games having been played. Gone are the days of job security, which I myself found out, but things do move on and other opportunities will see their skills re-employed.

It's the start of December and its back to full League business for this weekend's matches. The top two meet at Shielfield with Berwick still taking medication for their Scottish Cup exit to Spartans. Stenhousemuir on the other hand are still smirking from scoring 6! Albion Rovers visit Cowdenbeath and Arbroath travel to manager-less Elgin where a potential players strike might cause the match to be postponed. East Stirling may just surprise East Fife at Firs Park with greetings of glad tidings as Gordon Wylde takes temporary charge of the basement club.

Manager-less we travel to Hampden. No time for preparations and no time for a new manager to take the reigns. Not the position I thought we would be in going into today's match. It will be an uphill struggle, limited money will be available for the January transfer window and the new manager will require the right connections to attract players to Links Park. However the show must go on and the players have already been called upon by the Chairman to raise their game for this match. If you can't play football at Hampden, the national stadium then you shouldn't be there. It is a spacious park and will suit the likes of Martyn Fotheringham who returns to the side from suspension. I am really looking for the players to prove that they can get a result and that means three points-not a draw. With almost a full squad to pick from with the exception of Martin and Ferguson, Ian Gilzean, who has taken interim charge, can be a hero for one game and leave on a high. It will be interesting to see his choice of line-up and I wouldn't be surprised if Jim Butter made a start in goal behind Donnachie, Doyle, Stephen and Dodds. With Kerrigan returning from injury I would expect him to line up alongside Webster, Fotheringham and Fraser. Henslee and McLean are the front runners and will rely on Webster making runs down either flank. The bench would see Reid, McKenzie, Hall, Russell and Watson as replacements. A win is what we need and it is not impossible.

Queen's had been unbeaten in November, having beaten Elgin, East Fife and Albion Rovers. It will be a tight match and again like the last encounter, the odd goal could win the day.

It's a sad weekend, as the Dutch League teams remember their Utrecht colleague who died suddenly midweek at the age of twenty-six, and George Best, possibly one of the most talented players that we have been privileged to see, makes that final journey in his home city of Belfast to his resting place.

In the lead up to today's match the *Courier* has Gilly (Ian Gilzean) in the lime-light as he informs the media that it has been a difficult task to rally the troops. He goes on to say that the mood in the camp is decidedly subdued and that the lads have been quiet although the spirit is good. After last week's 6-2, defeat and Henry's departure, he says that the best thing that the players can do is to go out, play well and obtain a result. Gilzean finishes by saying that he is confident that the team will raise their game and perform on the day. As always in the *Courier* you get the good news first before finding out that there is a doubt on Henslee as he has been feeling under par with a skin rash. With the possibility of being one striker down, reality settles in when also informed that Duncan McLean took a knock last week and is also doubtful. Salt is further rubbed into the wound as Willie Martin is definitely a non starter. On the plus side Steve Kerrigan is fully fit and will play. Not the easiest of weeks but the players' own professional pride should ensure they want to win the game!

A win for Gilzean today may just put him on the Board's short-list as he has indicated that he would like to make the managers position his. The message board reveals ('Mori-pole'- who else, although he has been quiet lately) that Gilzean would bring in Robbie Raeside as player/ assistant manager. Raeside is ex-Dundee and is currently with Peterhead. According to the latest 'mori-pole' there are three serious contenders, the Wilson / Lyons partnership, Dave Baikie and Eddie Wolecki, so take you're pick-obviously a man in the know or one who is clutching at straws!

As I leave *'Surf and Talk'* the score is all square at half-time with neither side having hit the net. I remember thinking to myself that games against Queen's Park were always close affairs and then I remembered my trip to Hampden in season 1990/91. It was the year we were promoted as runners-up to Stirling Albion. Big Doug Rougvie was player manager, the league was nip and tuck and we had to win against Queen's who were also vying for the promotion place. Montrose that day recorded a 3-0 win which set them up for the final day celebrations at Dumfries. Having reviewed Gilly's team selection on the internet I was relieved to see that Henslee was fit and playing. As thought, Jim Butter replaced Andy Reid in goal but the young goalkeeper had taken a knock in training and didn't even make the bench as Michael Hankinson was listed. In defence Stephen was recalled as he lined up with Donnachie, Doyle and Smith. Kerrigan also made his return to midfield joining up with Webster, Fraser and Euan Hall. Upfront we had Henslee and Martyn Fotheringham. Watson, Cargill, Dodds and McKenzie were the outfield subs.

I made my way home through the throng of Christmas shoppers, a busy weekend here as the Dutch day for presents is the 5th and 'Mandag'. Joy! What a present I received as the vidi-printer reflected a 3-0 score-line and what looks to be a good win for the team.

Dec 3rd. QUEEN'S PARK, Away - report and teams
A Steve Kerrigan strike and a brace from Martyn Fotheringham, who today repaid the fans for his moment of madness at Arbroath, was more than enough to win the match with no reply from Queen's. An impressive win after what seemed a sticky start in a match during which Queen's Park had substantial possession. The difference was that Queen's seldom threatened and found it hard to make any breakthrough. On the other-hand Montrose took full advantage of the few opportunities handed to them by finishing in style. Gilzean also showed that he is his own man by changing formation to a 4-4-1-1 system and it worked as Fotheringham supplied the spark between the midfield and Henslee. In a goalless first period Montrose defended well considering last weeks sieve and held the opening period. Jim Butter competently dealt with what little threat there was to the Montrose goal.

The second half was barely 7 minutes old when Kerrigan bulleted a superb header into the Queen's net from a Stephen Fraser corner. All of a sudden Montrose were in the driving seat as heads went down for Queen's, having been caught cold. Montrose supplemented midfield by bringing Dodds on for Fraser in 67 minutes, possibly looking to hang on to their one goal lead, which is a dangerous game. Fortunately a second goal was scored in 72 minutes when Fotheringham received the ball, striding forward before driving home from twenty-five yards. With barely time for Watson to replace

Henslee, Fotheringham scored his second and Montrose's third. As so many times before this season, the free-kick specialist curled the ball around the Queen's wall for another spectacular goal.

Highlights – Fotheringham redeemed himself in the eyes of the support (possibly five travelled) with two great goals and a fine overall performance. His only blemish this afternoon was another booking after clashing with his opposite midfield number Kettlewell who was also booked for his part. It was good to see Steve Kerrigan, who has been sorely missed, on the score-sheet back in his midfield role. The defence recorded a clean-sheet which is a plus point and the win puts the Alloa Cup tie in a different light and is a confidence booster.

In a post match interview Gilly stated that it was a great result but admitted that it took the side time to settle. Hopeful of the job, it will be up to the Chairman.

When John Sheran left the club as manager, Henry Hall was his number two and Ian Gilzean was player coach. Henry assumed interim charge while the Board looked at possible replacements. Under Henry's guidance the team rallied and picked up points and some creditable wins made the managerial position his. With one win already under his belt will Gilly be given the same chance by the Board to prove he is the man for the job or is a new broom required to bring some structure and commitment to the club? John Paton had said that an early appointment will be made but will Saturday's 3-0 win change the goalposts!

For the first time this season there is a change in League leadership as Stenhousemuir go top having beaten Berwick 2-0 at Shielfield. It is amazing the change in teams who are manager-less, as Elgin also record a home 2-0 victory against Arbroath, and East Stirling who faltered late in the game with East Fife narrowly beat them 2-1 after the Shire had led early on in the game. Cowdenbeath also disposed of Albion Rovers in a tight 2-1 score-line.

A confirmed short-list is not likely, although chairman, John Paton had indicated there were six good candidates. More names appear, it may be media speculation, who knows, as ex-Dundee United player Gary Bollan and John Clark show interest in the vacancy. David Robertson who resigned from Elgin is also looking to be interviewed.

Saturday's good result has taken a back seat as fans are more concerned about who is and who isn't getting the managers job. Interviewing started yesterday (Sunday) and will be ongoing today. The plan is for the new manager to take training on Tuesday and Thursday prior to going into

Saturday's Cup tie. After interviews are completed tonight a decision will have to be made. It could be a late call before we see white smoke at Links Park!

- and, so to plan 'B', as it is revealed the fire is yet to be lit and fans now fear the Board's plan is recovery after Ian Gilzean's guided win at Hampden. Hall's successor will not be announced until after the Alloa Cup-tie. A statement will be issued at the beginning of next week. It seems that the Board have a difficult choice! Impatience sets in on the message boards and it is not long before the booing starts as the Chairman and Board are accused of pleasing themselves yet again. It's dammed if you do and dammed if you don't!

Let's get back to football and focus on a third round place by giving Gilly and the players support for Saturday.

Cowdenbeath tonight catch up on a league postponement as they play Arbroath. Three points for the Fifers would see them take second place on goal difference. Cowdenbeath beat a ten-man Arbroath 3-2. It has been a bad week for Berwick as they drop to third place.

Two league matches have been arranged for this weekend. Berwick take on Albion Rovers and Elgin are down to play at home against East Stirling. It is appropriate too that the teams take advantage of this weekend, as they would otherwise have a vacant Saturday, having been knocked out in the first round of the Cup.

Here we go again! Friday night and the World Cup draw is televised. There is local interest here in Breda as the name of the Netherlands is in the second pot. Unfortunately the commentary is one sided as the focus is solely on England. The draw doesn't matter as the media report a replay of 1966 with Germany once again beaten finalists. There is also talk from one radio station of knighthoods for the team and manager. It's a bit premature, believe me, don't count you're chickens -our league position is testimony to that!

Recreation Park stands between Montrose and a potential money spinning 3rd round Cup tie against a Premier League outfit. It is a return to familiar surroundings for goalkeeper Jim Butter as he returns to his ex-club Alloa with Scottish Cup memories of their fourth round tie at Ibrox Park against Rangers. The cup match gives the players a break from League duties but that does not mean that the pressure is off, as fans expect a result from this match and that the name of Montrose is in the bowl for the 3rd round draw. Alloa currently sit bottom of League Division Two with ten points and have lost forty six goals to date. Last week saw Ayr score four at

Recreation Park with no reply, the gulf between the Leagues are less than in previous years and we must look at this tie positively, as it is there to be won.

Dec 10th. ALLOA, Away – report and team

It's over for another year, Montrose are out! No 3rd round tie for the Links Parkers as Alloa go through after a narrow 1-0 win. What might have been was a home tie reward against Premier League side Livingston, a repeat clash of last season. Only two sides are left in the Scottish Cup to represent the 3rd Division with Arbroath and Queen's Park making it into the next round.

Montrose made one change to their line-up from last week's squad. Gilly kept the same starting eleven and Duncan McLean replaced Cargill on the bench. As in the previous week Montrose had to weather the storm for much of the first period. In 23 minutes Alloa hit Montrose on the counter attack. Having had the advantage of being awarded a corner Alloa broke with Hamilton supplying the pass for Stevenson to drive in off the post from twenty-two yards. In 33 minutes Jim Butter came to the rescue saving from Hamilton and denying Alloa a second goal.

The second half saw Montrose positively step up the pace, passing smartly and moving forward. Alloa keeper McGlynn produced a couple of saves from half-chances and also came to the rescue in saving a 90th minute header from Neil Stephen. Gilzean changed things around by introducing McLean, Dodds and Watson for Fraser, Webster and Hall but it was not to be as 3rd round hopes disappeared with the final whistle.

Highlights – The defence is given credit and in particular Barry Donnachie who was singled out for his performance. The Club web site summed up today's game with the quote – "Montrose created very few chances throughout the match and can have little complaint about the result." In the two League matches that were played Berwick slumped yet again dropping three points by losing at home to Albion Rovers by one goal. Elgin fought out a 1-1 draw with East Stirling at Borough Briggs to share the points.

With this game now out of the way the media returns its focus to the manager's position. Further interviews are rumoured but it is expected that an announcement will be made early this week and that a new manager will be in place for Saturday's visit of Berwick.

The Board have had a difficult task, I should know as today I sat at a meeting discussing tender submissions, positives and negatives, and can we be one hundred percent sure in our choice? The answer is no. The more we talk the more we go around in circles and the less convinced we seem ultimately ending back at square one and a delayed decision. We deviate, not convinced as re-assurances are sought, further interviews may clarify the situation before making that final decision. More time is required.

I know what my decision would be, but you still have to go through the process to justify it!

The new manager is revealed, the selection process is over as firm favourite Eddie Wolecki takes over at the helm of the good ship Montrose!

The news of the appointment filters through to Breda, courtesy of Radio Scotland breakfast news. Wolecki a former player in the days of managers Rougvie and Holt takes up his position with immediate effect. Tonight he and his coach Ewan Peacock will meet the players as they take training for the first time. Chairman John Paton's statement to the press was fairly upbeat as he confirmed the news. Paton stated in 'The Courier' that "Eddie has a new approach to the whole game and we hope it will bear fruit". He continued by saying "He knows the Junior and Senior leagues well, and is a good disciplinarian and we have high hopes that he will turn the corner for us". Wolecki's credentials have seen him guide Lochee to the East Super League championship and his youth coaching experience at Brechin, Arbroath and Dundee United should see youth development back at Links Park. We wish Eddie well in his new position, but we must not forget to thank Ian Gilzean, who has spent two years as Henry's assistant, for his past efforts in team matters too.

East Stirling and Queen's Park finally get their postponed league match played at Firs Park. Convincingly Queen's demolish the Shire with fours goals without reply to secure three points and move into fourth place with East Fife dropping to fifth.

They say that honesty is the best policy! The P&J headline a question and answer article – 'Wolecki: There's work to be done but Montrose have potential to progress.' Quite simply Eddie's aim is to put a winning side on the park and he follows up by saying that if we can get that right then the rest will follow. He knows that he is facing a big challenge but is encouraged by previous results achieved by the players at Berwick and Hampden which shows Montrose are capable of competing with teams pushing for promotion.

Throughout the article Wolecki is positive and continually refers to the word we, obviously a team player as he brings with him a team of certificated specialist coaches, his coach Peacock, Mark Murray, goalkeeping coach and Malcolm McFadyen a clinical psychologist, all from Lochee. This allows him to delegate and lets him to do what a manger should be doing. When asked what long term ambitions he had for Montrose, he stated that every manager should have a goal and that his was to take the Club through the divisions.

He also realises that within the Junior ranks there is a wealth of talent and he has the contacts. Already with the January transfer window coming up the message board is giving advice on who to sign at Junior level. Even at Junior level players cost money but it may be that a more localised squad will be formed and that some players will be released who travel a distance. There looks as if there could be changes and one could be that training will be increased to three nights, which I whole-heartedly endorse. Fitness is only one area for improvement and I believe we will see many more as the management team settle down to carry out their duties.

Finally Wolecki is asked "What will your approach be for Saturday's match against Berwick?"
"No wholesale changes as the players who have been in the team will be given the chance to impress and stake their claim for the jersey."

Today, Friday, it's the turn of '*The Courier*' to interview the manager as they speak of his plans for the Club. Every day something else is revealed, hopes are high as exciting times lie ahead as the club is restructured. Wolecki speaks of community involvement and a team of which the town can be proud. The key to Eddie's plans is team ethic and improvement through attention to players specific needs. His match preparation plans range from energy systems, hydration and nutrition, to self-confidence and tactics, which he sees as the key to good management. It's an all encompassing approach to the game, based on thorough research, and is tried and tested having borne results during his term with Lochee, making them one of the top junior sides. Having encountered the same problems previously in coaching, Wolecki has already identified areas for improvement immediately at Montrose. The new manager has also confirmed that an offer is currently on the table to bring in an assistant manager who has local connections.

I had a chat with my son today, he coaches youth football, and he told me that at training last night there was great excitement among the youngsters, they were on a high. I don't know whether that it was just the lead up to Christmas or whether they were genuinely excited as they could not wait to tell him that Montrose had a Polish manager! In return they received a lecture and a lesson on Polish immigration from the History student and were saddened to find out that Eddie was born in Dundee. As one said-and there is always one – "Does that mean we do not have a Polish manager?" Disappointment – disappointment – disappointment!

Back to league business as first plays second this weekend with Stenhousemuir meeting Cowdenbeath at home. Elgin will look to add to their result against Arbroath as they travel to Bayview to meet East Fife. Arbroath take on Queen's Park and Albion Rovers are at home to East Stirling.

It's a home baptism for the new manager. Berwick are the opposition and with just two training sessions to see what he has to work with, he will have to make his first team selection. Fans will be looking for instant success and a win, thus setting the standard for future games. From Berwick we can hope for a Santa Claus act of generosity. Placed third, they have recently suffered a slump in form having lost their previous two League matches and a humiliating Cup exit at the hands of Spartans. After a good start to the season, their free scoring has come to an end and a goal drought has hit the club. Let's hope that it continues today! In this match Wolecki has to get the best out of the players and the players must impress the manager if they want to be in his future plans. Effort from all quarters is key to a positive result.

Dec 17th. BERWICK, Home - report and teams

Great, snow has fallen and my Christmas wish comes true – match and Wolecki baptism postponed! That means instead of seeing two matches when I am home, it could be three as three dates for the re-scheduled match spring to mind. It could be played this coming Tuesday, the 20th in the evening of the day I travel home for the Christmas break or next Saturday the 24th or most probably Saturday 7th of January, the day before I return as both teams are out of the Cup. Let's hope so! The *Review* reported that the manager had mixed feelings at the Berwick call-off. The players had been looking forward to the match and were disappointed that they were not in action. According to the *Review*, the manager has also set a fourth place League play-off position as a target but qualifies the position by stating that fifty six points are required. Montrose have twenty matches left, giving a possible sixty point maximum and need to accumulate a further forty points to their current total of sixteen points. It's a tall order, which only allows for 7 defeats!

One match survived the weekend weather conditions as Stenhousemuir retained top place by beating Cowdenbeath 2-0 at home.

I'm home and there is a game tonight as Eddie Wolecki has arranged his first glamour tie. Our opponents are Montrose Roselea, the town's other football side. He said that he would involve the community and this is a good first step. In his first few days he has certainly been very busy as already he has spoken to Montrose Youth, Roselea and organised an open day, inviting fans to training on Christmas Eve. Young fans will be able to join the squad in different exercises and take part in passing and shooting. It may be late in the day for parents to exchange a Rangers or Celtic jersey for the blue of Montrose but this is the encouragement that youngsters need to be able to support the team. I hope that this parent and kids day is a success but I have one problem, how do I disguise a twenty-three year old, after all, we are father and son!

Montrose secured a 2-0 victory in the bounce game against Roselea. McLean and Fotheringham were the scorers but the match was organised for Wolecki to see the full squad he had inherited, including players farmed out to Junior clubs. It was also interesting to see that Montrose were playing an attacking system as they lined up in a 3-4-3 formation. McLean, Watson and Fotheringham started off up front. Fraser wearing the number 3 shirt, Henslee, Kerrigan and Hall filled midfield and Doyle, Stephen and Donnachie were in defence in front of Jim Butter. With Montrose 2-0 up at half-time the second period saw many changes. Marc Connelly in his ten-minute stint looked as if he could be a good prospect as he made space and shot on sight of goal. Four players did not feature, Andy Reid and Kevin Webster are both were sidelined by injury and Martin and Ferguson are long term injury victims. The sad news is that goalkeeper Reid could be out for a minimum of four week's with a thigh problem.

It's good to be home for Christmas, seeing friends and family, catching up on news and who's doing what or going where. For a couple of years now I have been meaning to meet my good friend Bob. We met the first day on a project in Andover, near Boston, a fellow Scot and Dundonian and a project controls colleague. What a project that was, two Scot's with an accent as broad as Wallace's sword and a bunch of crazy Texan's who couldn't decipher the code. Meeting Bob helped me settle quickly and we have been friends ever since. Bob now works for another friend of mine in Rhode Island. It's a small world out there but you don't realise just how small it really is. Where ever I go I fly the flag. Some people laugh, you don't support Montrose F.C., do you. Others haven't a clue who Montrose are, when they look at the pennant pinned up for all to see. Yes, on full view.

I was sitting in the office one day and accountants from Canada were due for a tour of the unfinished plant. They arrived- nothing to do with me but Bob was involved. As they were walking through the office one gentleman stopped in his tracks, startled to see a Montrose pennant. He introduced himself, the gentleman in question turned out to be Scott Carnegie, at that time chairman of Dundee United Football Club. Little did he realise that Bob is a Dundee supporter!

I must tell you this! It's from my time with Bob at Andover. Americans can be so gullible at times. We were in a restaurant waiting to order at the bar, and there was a couple sitting listening to our funny Scot's accents. They were inquisitive, the usual, "My line traces back to the McGregor's. Do you know them?" Suddenly the woman asked,

"Is your wife here while you are on business?" Quick as a flash, with pan face, Bob replied,

"No I lost my wives in rather tragic circumstances."

" Oh", said the woman highly embarrassed that she had asked the question, "You poor thing!". Her inquisitive side came to the fore once more,

"What happened, were you married twice?" Bob started to tell the tale and I looked at him, knowing that it was not true. I could hear the woman saying

"That's just dreadful" and to her husband, "John do you hear this! "
He was reeling them in hook line and sinker. The pauses were unbearable as the tale unfolded and they came back for more!
"My first wife and I had decided to go camping in the woods;
 it was the first time we had done anything like that. She died that day."
"You poor thing, what happened?"
"She ate some mushrooms that I had found in the forest and they were poisonous." Patting Bob's hand she said
" That is so sad." .There was a tear in my eye as well, but it was a laughter tear. I was thinking, edging away, and saying to myself, get your-self out of this one Bob. But after a long pause and like any fish coming up for air she was still hooked to the bait.
"And your second wife, you said you lost her also."
"Yes, a few years back."
"How awful," Pause.
"I really didn't think lightning could strike twice" said Bob shaking his head. "So, what happened?"
"It's terrible really. I didn't want to go camping after what had happened with my first wife, but my second wife was the outdoors type. Anyway she eventually talked me round and we set off this weekend and tragedy struck once again"
 There was silence, Bob lifted his beer and took a steadying sip and placed it back down on the counter. It was time to net. So after a while the words came,
"And how did she die?"
"She was hit on the head with a spade."
"A spade? "

"Yes, you know a shovel."
"A shovel! John, John, do you hear this!" She needed details,
"How did she get hit by a shovel." As cool as you like the answer came back
"She wouldn't eat the mushrooms!! " You could hear a pin drop. Tell an American a joke on a Monday and like a second class stamp, it arrives a week later. Needless to say we didn't stay for our meal.

We look forward to a festive Christmas and a feast of matches over the holiday period. It's a chance for bigger attendances. People who don't normally find themselves at games will attend with family and friends creating a great friendly atmosphere. One away, two home - three matches within seven days. The first of the festive fixtures are featured on Boxing Day, Albion Rovers against Arbroath, while East Fife entertain Berwick and East Stirling are at home to Cowdenbeath. Match of the day is at Hampden where Queen's take on Stenhousemuir. For the Montrose support a lengthy trip to Elgin ensues, a trip that will not be relished by the Glasgow and Edinburgh based players.

Elgin are awaiting the transfer window, as speculation suggests an influx of five or six players to the playing squad. Thankfully we meet them today prior to the January transfer window. Stand-in manager and club captain Jamie McKenzie (26 years old) takes charge as a successor for David Robertson has not been made by the new Board. The club is still unsettled, there is a mixed response in the community after the Blacks' failed in their takeover bid. Since then the skill-seekers youth development programme has been abandoned, rumours are rife that top scorer Martin Johnstone is leaving the club in the January transfer window and players' futures are in the balance. Just when things were looking positive at Borough Briggs, all now seems doom and gloom.

Doom and gloom or not Montrose must guard against a repeat of the start of the season and their first league match when we just scraped a point thanks to Andy Reid. Having been unbeaten in their last 4 matches a win for Elgin would see the Morayshire side move into a berth above Montrose in the League. With the Berwick match postponed, Eddie Wolecki has had time to assess things and generally work out his playing system and team strategy having had a few more training sessions under his belt. The players now know what is expected of them and that means that their work rate will be increased to meet the managers expectations of 3 points in what is his first competitive league match.

Boxing Day match reviews from the press are sketchy, possibly because nobody works on Christmas Day. Like wee boys we are waiting for newspaper shops to open as we queue outside for written articles which are cobbled together from previous statements and press releases, going over old ground, telling you absolutely zilch!

We already know that Willie Martin has a back injury (although that was a tremendous flying save that you made in training Willie!) and then there is long term absentee Stuart Ferguson who has been out all season. We know that Andy Reid is injured and that Webster has a groin problem. The only bit of news is that Dodds stood on a rusty nail! Positively, Wolecki states "We do not have our problems to seek" and that there is no point complaining as every team has its problems. We just have to embrace them and get on with it!

Dec 26th. ELGIN, Away - report and teams
No major changes in team selection but a significant change in work-rate in what was an evenly matched game, the only difference was Elgin finished on one occasion. A striker must be a priority come the January transfer window! Montrose lined up 4-3-1-2 with Butter in goal behind Donnachie, Doyle, Stephen and Elliot Smith. Hall, Kerrigan and Henslee in midfield with Fotheringham sitting just in behind strikers McLean and Watson. Hankinson, McKenzie, Fraser, Cargill and Dodds filled the bench.

At the end of the day all that separated the two sides was a 56 minute winner for Martin Johnston as Elgin grabbed the lead with Johnston heading home from close-range. The match kicked-off with Montrose immediately on the defensive as Elgin's number eleven sent a shot just clear of the crossbar. Montrose replied a few minutes later when a Watson lay-off was deflected for a corner from a Fotheringham shot. From the resultant corner a Kerrigan header could not be forced over the line by the waiting Watson. Goalmouth action in the opening stages amounted to long-range efforts from Elgin, shooting from a distance. Watson then created a further two chances, the first was deflected wide and Renton saved what was a weak shot. The best first half effort from Montrose was a Steve Kerrigan header but goalkeeper Renton was well placed to collect. Then from a Renton kick-out, Elgin's McKenzie got the better of Neil Stephen to crash a drive just wide of Butter's upright. Elgin began to take control and Butter spilled a long-range shot from Johnstone, followed by dropping a cross after colliding with his defender. The resultant chip from Nelson hit the underside of the bar and was cleared to safety by the Montrose defence.

No changes at half-time and it was Elgin who finally broke the deadlock. A cross by Cumming from the right was met with the head of Martin Johnstone whose looping header found the back of the net. After the restart Montrose immediately stepped the pace up a gear and in 68 minutes were denied the equaliser. Calum Watson's fierce drive was superbly saved by keeper Renton, the keeper turning the ball away. Montrose then freshened things up with Cargill replacing McLean who had had a quiet match. A foul on Cargill resulted in a Fotheringham free kick being headed into the path of the onrushing Henslee. Henslee's shot was well saved by the Elgin keeper. Further substitutions saw Dodds on for Donnachie and McKenzie taking Hall's place in a bid to take a point from the game. With time running out Kerrigan fired wide from a corner and in the closing minute the Elgin defence cleared McKenzie's free kick.

Highlights – So there was no fairytale winning start for the manager, but he did acknowledge that if the players can give the same effort and commitment to matches and training then the corner can be turned. Today Watson worked tirelessly, Kerrigan put in his usual good shift and the team's play seemed to have more width than usual. Neither team deserved to lose but the main difference was that Elgin *did* score. Like a cat with nine lives, Montrose see another one slip away as three points diminish in their plight for a fourth place finish and the fifty six points target that Wolecki believes is required.

The remainder of the Boxing Day matches saw the weather take effect with postponements due to frost bound grounds at Firs Park and Cliftonhill. However there were no problems at Hampden with the match going on due to the under soil heating at the National Stadium. Queen's Park scored a goal in both halves to beat league toppers Stenhousemuir who obviously missed the services of Cramb and McGrillen. In the other match of the day there was another surprise for Berwick, who lost out to an 89th minute winner by East Fife's Paliczka.

Today's *Courier* headlined "No surprises for new Montrose boss, Boxing Day defeat at Elgin served to reinforce Eddie Wolecki's assessment of his squad." He knows where the problems are as his main priority since taking over has been organisation of specific areas but it will take time. One area that has received Wolecki's attention is the defence, as he wants them to play in such a way that the backline will be difficult to breakdown. He states ".. once you have that right you can start to work on other things". Having firstly worked on the defensive set-up he was not surprised that the thrust of the attack did not cut mustard at Elgin but you can tell that this will be addressed in training this week. Once again Wolecki praised the players' efforts and noted that they were keen to play for their places in the team.

For the first time the manager speaks about four players being out of contract in January. Goalkeepers Butter and Hankinson, Andy Cargill plus Duncan McLean. In my opinion only McLean may be offered another contract to the end of the season to prove that he wants to play for the club. From 'The Courier' Wolecki quotes "It doesn't take a genius to work out that we need to get a more balanced squad", and he is only one of the managers of clubs waiting for the transfer window to open. The manager is looking for left sided players to fit his game plan and to give the team the balance that they lack. Looking forward, Wolecki has already called up delayed signings James Russell and Robert Smith from East Craigie stating that the young players have been given till the end of the season to figure in the manager's future plans.

It's the end of the second quarter of fixtures, the halfway mark, what can I say? It has been a turbulent period both on and off the pitch. As they say expect the unexpected!

Seven points from the first three matches, disaster at Arbroath and it was downhill from then on with Henry Hall's finale a humiliating defeat at Ochilview. When you are down, you are down and you don't expect a manager less team to draw the rabbit out of the hat by taking three points at Hampden- but they did. Then with a new manager in place, Wolecki took the team to Elgin hoping for his first three points but the quarters tally still stood at 10 points and an accumulative total of sixteen points.

Wolecki's appointment by the Board on December 12th has seen a transformation in training routines, positive press coverage and a marked improvement in community relations and communication, although there is still much to do. In the few days since his appointment there has been a wave of optimism, which will hopefully turn into momentum in terms of crowd numbers that will increase during the festive period of matches.

The hurricane (Eddie Wolecki) that has swept through the club will not dissipate as the club restructures itself, both within the club and out in the community during the next period. A new manager means new ideas and a new enthusiasm to match, which he has already demonstrated. The transfer window of January also gives the opportunity to stamp his look on the team.

Quarter Two

POS		P	W	L	D	F	A	GD	PTS
1	Stenhousemuir	18	13	3	2	38	17	21	41
2	Cowdenbeath	17	12	5	0	32	13	19	39
3	Berwick	18	11	4	3	30	17	13	37
4	Queen's Park	17	8	6	3	27	18	9	27
5	East Fife	17	8	7	2	23	27	-4	26
6	Arbroath	17	5	8	4	26	28	-2	19
7	Elgin	18	4	8	6	19	28	-9	18
8	Montrose	17	4	9	4	17	24	-7	16
9	Albion Rovers	16	3	8	5	17	29	-12	14
10	East Stirling	17	2	12	3	17	45	-28	9

We have a lot to look forward too, including the ins and outs of January, after all our league position of eighth is better than ninth!

Hat-trick – HENNER!

Chapter 6

3rd. Quarter (Winter of Discontent)

Frost bound pitches, snow, the thaw and a meteorological forecast of the worst winter conditions for many years, as global warming takes it effect. The gloom and doom merchants have got it wrong before but this time it seems to be for real. It is a period when clubs feel the pinch as postponements take effect on revenue and training sessions are cancelled. A back-log of fixtures results in teams playing three times in the space of a week when the thaw sets in. It is then that injuries are picked up and bookings increase, as heavy ground conditions take toll on form.

The January transfer window gives opportunity for teams to change things around and in some cases to add to their existing squads as they make a concerted effort to be in a position for a top four finish.

For Montrose, the new manager will hope to be able to bring in a few fresh faces to balance the squad and for that to happen some players will be moved on. The loan period of Jamie McKenzie from Hibernian is also up in January, with him returning to Easter Road. Andy (Chins) Cargill looks bound to move to his home town of Arbroath as his six month contract ends, and Montrose also has no need for three goalkeepers on the books.
Another period of change as we enter a New Year!

Before a first-foot can cross the threshold of Links Park, or before the Bells can sound, there is a departure! The club website revealed that summer signing Willie Martin has been released. Manager Eddie Wolecki pulls no punches in the issued statement, as it serves as a stark warning to others. The statement read –"In view of his lack of commitment to training, it was felt that it was in the best interest of both Willie Martin and Montrose F.C. that he moves on and finds another club, nearer to home." Wolecki went on to say "While I am managing Montrose, players will be under no illusions as to what is expected from them, with regard to training." If that doesn't spell it out, what does? He also finalises the statement by saying "In any case, it's my intention to build my team around locally based players."

The Glasgow based striker was signed from Elgin City in pre-season by Henry Hall for a fee rumoured to be £3,000 pounds, but has been plagued by injury during his short time at Links Park. Four goals in pre-season raised the fans hopes of things to come. Willie also scored at Ross County on the opening day before becoming hero for the day in that memorable 1-0 win over Arbroath, having scored in 19 minutes.

The departure of Martin from the strike department highlights Wolecki's intentions in an area that was already depleted. We could see not just one but two additions to bolster the front-line.

One addition that we won't see is that of Jake Ferrier as the current Carnoustie manager has turned down Eddie Wolecki's offer of joining him as assistant manager. Wolecki has said in the past that he will wait to get his man and if that means the end of the season then he is willing to wait.

It would be good to end the year on a high note and begin 2006 the way we mean to continue. Three home matches give the club the chance to close the gap on East Fife and Queen's Park and the opportunity to move towards that fourth place spot. Who would have believed it!

Quarter Three - League campaign

Dec 3first.	East Fife	Home
Jan second.	Arbroath	Home
Jan seventh.	Berwick (re-scheduled from Dec 1seventh.)	Home
Jan 1fourth.	East Stirling	Away
Jan 2first.	Cowdenbeath	Away
Jan 2eighth.	Stenhousemuir	Home
Feb fourth.	Berwick	Away
Feb 11th.	Queen's Park	Home
Feb 1eighth.	Albion Rovers	Home
Feb 2fifth.	East Fife	Away

We start and end the quarter to East Fife home and away respectively. Having grabbed a last gasp winner on Boxing Day, Jim Moffat's team is hit with injury and suspensions. John Martin was shown a straight red in the Berwick match and is automatically suspended for today's match. Ex-Montrose player Craig Smart is currently serving a three match ban and is also unavailable. On top of that manager Moffat has a growing injury list with Brash being the latest casualty. Down to a much depleted squad, Moffat maintains that the remaining players are capable of taking all three points.

Montrose on the other hand will have some say in the matter of the points returning to Bayview. We could see some changes today tactically with Wolecki opting to play a 3-5-2 formation, which could mean a start for Dodds and Fraser in the line up. New squadies Russell and Robert Smith are also added to Wolecki's plans for tomorrow's game.

There are doubts as to whether the game will be played as the past few days have seen snow, freezing fog and rain. The rise in temperature today may be too late for tomorrow morning's inspection before fans travel. Protection covers had been laid at the centre circle and in both goal-mouths during the adverse weather conditions but that may be to no avail as the Hogmanay match kicks-off earlier than normal at 2 p.m.

The match survives as the weather changed late on Thursday night and saw a milder front. Unfortunately that milder front didn't extend to the car park at Links Park as the match day announcer, obviously in a hurry, could not understand that a car with reversing lights on is going to reverse. After a few hand gestures he parked hastily and at speed made his way to the microphone. It's a pity he hadn't remembered that it was a two o'clock kick-off.

Dec 31st. EAST FIFE, Home - report and teams

It has been seven weeks since the last home match at Links Park and the defeat by Cowdenbeath. In a hectic period today's match sees a new caretaker in place as we see off the old and welcome the new. Wolecki's home baptism could not have been better as the team come from a goal down to record a 3-1 well earned victory. Changes were made to the side that took the field at Borough Briggs on Boxing Day. Butter retained his place between the sticks, Donnachie dropped to the bench with Dodds taking his place. Doyle, Stephen and Elliott Smith kept their places. Midfield saw a bit of a revamp with only Hall and Henslee keeping their spots. Young James Russell made his first start for the club on the right and Stephen 'Chippy' Fraser took the berth on the left. McLean partnered Watson upfront giving Wolecki another chance to assess McLean's future as his contract is up in January. The listed substitutes had Hankinson, Robert Smith who had recently been called up from the Juniors, Donnachie and Martyn Fotheringham. The fifth member of the bench was a trialist signed earlier in the week from Scone Amateurs and given until the end of the season to secure his future. A name for the future, a striker, the name is that of Kevin Don. There was no sign of Steve Kerrigan (flu) who featured against Elgin. Today shows just how thin on the ground we are and I can see a flurry of signing activity early in January to bolster the squad. The opening exchanges were scrappy, Russell shot over the bar and Henslee saw his strike turned around the post by Dodds in the East Fife goal. Montrose were let off the hook when Butter tipped a Paliczka chip onto the bar with Doyle making the final clearance. Panic had set in, the back four were at sixes and sevens and it wasn't long before the Fifers were on the attack once again. Stephen was booked for an innocuous looking foul and before the kick was taken Doyle's name followed into Referee Hornby's book for allegedly kicking the ball away.

The referee's incessant whistling and inconsistent decisions affected Montrose more than East Fife to such an extent that the players would think that there was a vendetta against them as Hall was next to be booked for a timid challenge. Another attack by Russell, again the winger outpaced Lumsden on the right, finding Watson with his pass who then won the corner. The resultant corner saw Henslee's shot cleared off the line. Russell then fired in a shot, which the East Fife keeper held at full stretch under the bar. It was then Butter's turn to have the save of the match as he blocked a shot at close range before it was cleared to safety by a Fife forward as he scooped it over the bar. Another let off, with half-time minutes away.

No changes at halftime and no score but East Fife took the lead in 52 minutes from the penalty spot. This time Russell who had had a good game was the villain. Hall failed to head clear, Russell back-tracked and caught Paliczka with a tackle that only a forward would make. Referee Hornby had no doubt in the award but then proceeded to make a meal of the take with a song and dance routine. Kelly duly slotted the ball into the net sending the keeper the wrong way. Montrose were in shock and struggled to take control. Stephen limped off to be replaced by Donnachie with Dodds moving inside to replace the centre half. Donnachie was barely on the park a few minutes when Referee Hornby stopped proceedings to speak to the substitute. It's good to see that Barry has not lost his charm on the 'Knoll'!

Montrose equalised on the 65th minute mark. Russell chased a Donnachie through ball to the bye-line hitting a first-time cross to the lurking Henslee, who volleyed home for his eighth goal of the season. A few minutes later Fotheringham replaced a quiet McLean upfront. The substitution seemed to bring life to the attack as Montrose regained control of the match. Russell was causing problems with surging runs down the right, Smith and Henslee linked well on the left with Fraser. Another Russell cross was parried by keeper Dodds before finding Fraser and as the midfielder made in-roads in the Fife box, Kelly made that fatal challenge for yet another penalty award. Fotheringham slotted the ball down the middle past Dodds, after a lengthy stoppage for referee Hornby's encore. It was all Montrose, Fotheringham and then Watson drove past before Wolecki made his final substitution introducing Kevin Don-who signed after the match- for the tiring Watson who had a fine performance. With time running out Russell finalised his debut with a ninety-minute goal. Good work from Fraser feeding Russell, the winger beat two players to crash the ball past Dodds for Montrose's third goal.

The chance of the match fell to Euan Hall who had what looked to be the simplest of tasks to slip the ball past Dodds in a one to one with the keeper. Hall's finish was sent straight at the keeper but by that time the game was over just awaiting Hornby's final whistle.

Highlights – A good way to finish the year and a heart warming performance with the team coming from behind. Man of the match by a long shot was young debutant James Russell as he played a part in all four goals. Hero and villain of the peace, Russell showed great skill and good pace down the right. He was eventually rewarded for his efforts by scoring the third goal. His pinpoint crosses and willingness to shoot first time will surely secure him a run in the team. It was a team performance that finally won the day, Dodds played well when asked to fill in for Stephen. Donnachie's distribution of the ball changed the match as he worked well with Russell giving encouragement to the youngster. Imagine- Barry!-a role model! Henslee, Watson and Fraser played hard and were rewarded for their contributions.

A Happy New Year – well done lads.

Eddie Wolecki signed his first player tonight, capturing tall forward Kevin Don from Scone Amateurs. Kevin will join up with Montrose after playing one final game for Scone, next weekend. Twenty five year old Kevin, based in Perth, has spent his career so far in the amateur scene in Scotland, having played previously for Bridge of Earn amateurs, as well as a season playing at First Division level in New Zealand. He has been a member of the Scone Amateurs squad which has remained unbeaten in all competitions so far this season. Montrose boss Eddie Wolecki said: "I'm very pleased to have signed Kevin. I saw him play at a trial game in Perth the other week. He's raw, but he offers us height, pace, and aggression in attack. He's here to learn and develop, and we'll see what he can do for us."

Three other matches had been pencilled in for this weekend, the first, Cowdenbeath's Friday night encounter with Elgin, fell to the weather. Berwick's visit of Queen's Park and Stenhousemuir's home tie with Albion Rovers both had early morning inspections and suffered the same fate.

Although I am home word still filters through from the Netherlands as NAC Breda dispense with the services of their manager and coaching staff after gaining just three points from the last ten matches. With the club in freefall drastic action had been taken. Manager Tom Lokhoff still had eighteen months of his contract to run but has paid the price for his side's failings.

Monday will see the return of the "Battle of Fife" with East Fife at home to Cowdenbeath, Queen's play Albion Rovers and Stenhousemuir have home advantage over East Stirling. The match of the day is undoubtedly Scotland's answer to the "Ice Cream Wars" or was it the "Milan Derby" and it's at Links Park! The biggest derby outside the SPL? I don't think so, as not even Mo or Lichtie fans would claim that. But it generates a bit of interest in our small corner of the world and a good crowd is expected as the segregation barriers are put in place.

Today's performance brought hope-what a way to end the year and like any New Year we look forward, a restoration of faith but with this new found optimism there is always hint of uncertainty!

The bell tolls, the curfew sounds, a New Year and new resolutions. We all manage to resolve but never keep them. The manager resolves to do his best and focuses on a fourth place finish. Optimistic but you have to have a goal and a target to aim at. If he doesn't make it, it won't be for trying as his enthusiasm so far has spoken volumes. But for some of us resolutions will be broken within a few days.

15.00 hours January 2nd 2006 and that all important derby match with our fondest of neighbours, Arbroath, which seems to bring out the very worst in our supporters. It wouldn't be so bad if the support would concentrate their energies in getting behind the team by giving encouragement to every move but it seems one wrong move or loose ball or even worse condemnation in conceding a goal and it is then that the "grim-reaper" arrives.

"All blame is a waste of time. No matter how much fault you find with another, and regardless of how much you blame him it will not change you."
Quote - Dr.Wayne Dyer

We are where we are!

"You cannot change the circumstances, the SEASON or the wind, but you can change yourself."
Quote – Jim Rohn

I look for that change today and a positive reaction from the support by giving Eddie Wolecki and his management team their full backing. 'Boo-boys' please note! For once the MFC web site is being updated on a more regular basis. It reports that boss Eddie Wolecki was a happy man after seeing his side come from a goal behind, to beat East Fife 3-1 at Links Park on Hogmanay. "I was delighted with the second half performance" said Wolecki.

"I felt that we were unfortunate to go behind, after a bit of naïve defending from James Russell, but he will learn from that. It was certainly an eventful debut for James and he showed a great deal of character to fight back and have a hand in all of our goals, after the penalty incident." The manager continued: "However, I'm not one for singling out individuals. I felt that it was a very good performance from the whole team. We couldn't have asked much more from the team at this stage. I'd like to congratulate them all, substitutes and backroom staff too, as the whole team must take credit for the win." Wolecki's thoughts now turn to Monday's derby clash with Arbroath. "We're all well aware of the importance of the Arbroath game to our fans, and we're all looking forward to it- there's a good atmosphere in the dressing room at the moment."

Meanwhile the BBC report Eddie Wolecki recorded his first win as Montrose manager against East Fife on Saturday and he wants another one quickly against Arbroath. An under-statement, to say the least!

The Red Lichties have not been in competitive action since December tenth as their matches against Queen's Park and Albion Rovers have both suffered postponement due to the weather. Arbroath boss John McGlashan will be without defenders Paul Watson and Ian Dobbins who are serving one-match suspensions.

Jan 2nd. ARBROATH, Home - report and teams.
Today's match pulled a good crowd (1,402), pity about the football. It's always the same, as derby matches are close fought encounters. This one was no different. Montrose however were given the advantage with Arbroath being reduced to ten men and again after Arbroath took the lead the referee saw fit to award a soft penalty, but once again Montrose did not take the advantage. Arbroath were the team that wanted to win more and they did!

Injuries forced team changes once again, Stephen is out with a thigh knock, Kerrigan is still suffering the effects of flu and Wolecki had to call on the services of Cargill and McKenzie. Butter took his place in goal after a good display the previous Saturday. Donnachie started alongside Doyle, McKenzie and Elliott Smith in the back four. Russell, Henslee, Cargill and Fraser filled the midfield of the 4-4-2 formation. Watson and Fotheringham took the front-line positions. Hankinson, Smith, Hall, Dodds and Don were on the bench. Duncan McLean did not feature.

The match started at pace and with it vendetta's peppered the first half. The opening exchanges saw Russell taking a snap shot at goal with the goalkeeper turning the ball narrowly wide of the post. Next up Butter had to look lively when he tipped a strike from Millar just over the bar. Passes were going astray, there were no flowing movements and it wasn't long before Barry Donnachie and Jay Stein tangled, with Donnachie fairly making his presence felt after Stein initiated the foul. A 'legend' at work finally pleading his innocence with the referee but it was a feud that continued until Stein was substituted late in the second half and at one time the linesman intervened as Stein took a sly kick at the full-back with play taking place up-field. Brazil was booked for dissent and was fortunate to remain on the field as he committed a further act of dissent by throwing the ball down in front of the referee. Then just before half-time Arbroath were reduced to ten when Brazil was shown a straight red card for a rash challenge on Jamie McKenzie. The referee had no hesitation in sending the Arbroath player off. The half-time whistle sounded and the support looked for changes to be made at half-time if not in personnel, then in formation to take advantage of the ten men. The first half saw more entertainment on the terraces than on the field of play with some spirited banter from a hung-over crowd.

Wolecki saw fit not to make any changes as the team returned to the park for the second period. Arbroath's goal came in 63 minutes when Jay Stein outstripped his marker and lobbed the advancing Butter. As usual Arbroath score and there is an instant reaction from the support or should I say those who you never see at a game. It is incredible, they support the Old Firm and because they decide to turn up at Links Park for the day they think that it gives them the right to slate Wolecki. Up till then everything was hunky dory! The mood changed momentarily when Montrose were awarded a penalty for a push on McKenzie in the box. A soft award but a welcome lifeline was handed to Montrose. Fotheringham had dispatched Saturday's penalty and duly stepped up to take the kick sending it high into the rafters of the enclosure. Instant guffaw's from the Arbroath fans and a stunned silence engulfed the Wellington Street end. Heads went down, had we scored then it would have lifted the team to possibly collect all three points. Changes were then made but it was left too late. A double substitution took place Hall and Dodds replaced Russell and Fraser before Don came on for Cargill. In the dying minutes a golden chance fell to Jamie McKenzie. With the goal gaping, he swivelled, blazing the ball over the bar.

A busy day for the referee as he also added Montrose's Henslee, Fotheringham, Watson and substitute Hall to his book. Cook, Rennie and McMullen followed for Arbroath along with the red carding of Brazil. That brings the tally of discipline for the 3 derbies to 19 yellows and 2 reds. Not a good record!

Highlights – A day best forgotten, we could have played until the coos cam hame (all day) and not scored, it was one of these games. Arbroath closed things down quickly and broke up moves with ease. Players under performed, we only saw flashes of James Russell, Henslee worked hard with little effect and Watson made heavy weather upfront to the extent that we only had one direct shot on goal in either half. On many occasions today, Montrose also put themselves under unnecessary pressure, Jim Butter's kicking of the dead-ball was truly awful today and as the game went on it got worse as his confidence deteriorated. A Jekyll and Hyde performance compared to the demolition of East Fife. We need to stay positive, new faces will arrive, the manager knows what is required and team selections will eventually see a settled side, but it is going to take time.

East Fife won the Fife derby with the disposal of Cowdenbeath 2-0. Stenhousemuir scored five, McGrillen scoring a hat-trick in the process, against East Stirling. Queen's Park and Albion Rovers slogged out a 1-1 draw.

NAC Breda have been quick off the mark in securing the services of Cees Lok who had resigned from NEC Nijmegen last month. The Dutchman takes up his appointment immediately. It is an interesting selection and one of surprise to NAC fans. The new manager has already shown the door to Breda's full-back by terminating his contract for lack of commitment to the club. Another will be released in the summer and will join ADO den Haag.

It is strange how things develop; circumstances are mirrored at home and away as we re-build the pieces of the jig-saw in this double life.

Sobering thoughts as Wolecki offers no excuses in his match post mortem, believing that wounds were self-inflicted. He stated, " We caused our own problems. Everyone has to take blame from the coaching staff all the way through."

It is also a sobering thought when you read the message board as posts appear already declaring that Wolecki will only change Montrose into a Junior team. There is no appreciation of the manager, his team or players from fans; it's nice just once in a while to support what is being done.

Oh ye of little faith, especially when the same punter was telling the board that Wolecki was the man to take over from Henry Hall. Eddie has had three games to assess things, already he has implemented many changes for the benefit of the club, but for some you could lose all the matches as long as you beat Arbroath. Too much emphasis is put on these games; they never turn out to be classics as they are played at one hundred miles an hour with the object of the game being to kick anything that moves. It's time for a reality check!

The month of January will see big changes and changes *are* coming, but I estimate that two months is required before we see the transformation that Eddie and his team are trying to achieve. Patience and understanding is required from the fans. If they can't see this or are not willing to give him time then I would say that they should stay away as negativity breeds negativity and we can do without that! Long-term injury victim Willie Martin released by Montrose last week has wasted no time in finding another club after signing for First Division Stranraer at the weekend. Stranraer training nights are held in Glasgow and will drastically cut down the travelling for the player. He made his debut in Monday's derby match against Queen of the South. Enough said!

Tie your shoe laces together and try to walk – you won't get too far. Sometimes you have to go backwards to advance. Last week Eddie called up both Russell and Smith from the Juniors and gave them six months to prove that they would be in his future plans. A week later and Wolecki obviously has seen the commitment he is looking for as he offers contracts to May 2008 to the pair. Long term thinking by the manager, as he looks to build a team around local lad Greg Henslee.

It's a strange world that we live in as we are given names for life but the ones that stick or that you remember are for some other milestone achievement in your life. I have worked with many characters but there are some who for reasons unknown are dubbed or blighted by their friends or colleagues. When working in Boston I remember three Native American Indians. They were steel erectors and well muscled. We all had radios to stay in touch and these guys used the same channel. Some of the conversations were classic as you would hear, "Come in Cornbread", "Is that you Chicken-Bone", or "Is Dog-Head with you?" These guys drove big pick-ups displaying not only gun racks but their names emblazoned across the windshield. In some neighbouring towns to Montrose you would expect to see the names of boy-racers, 'Burberry' and their co-pilot 'Chantelle' but this was 'Cornbread' and 'Chicken-Bone' with a 'Del-boy' horn for good measure. Just in case 'Cornbread' had an identity crisis at any time, the large tattooed letters down the length of both arms would let him know who he really was. A dead giveaway, but names do stick.

For my sins I was called 'The Count''. We would play dominoes at lunchtime, it's a game that you have to read and invariably somehow I always ended up with the double blank. Needless to say, most games ended with a count! These are the names that stick for life. Football is no different!

Why can't the BBC get our goalie's name right! Reporting is inconsistent, inaccurate and full of creative or not so creative journalism in some cases. 'Fingers' (Jim Butter) is the man in question, not Butters, Buttery or Butler. Having come back into the team and saving our bacon in the past two games the veteran's name has appeared on more than just the team list after his performances. Rumours, message boards, 'Heard it Here First'', unconfirmed, Jim Butter has left the club!

The January sales have just started or should I say 'transfer window'. Eddie Wolecki has made his decision, it is confirmed in the press, out with the old and in with the new. Jim Butter's departure is no real surprise as he also held the position of goalkeeping coach and with Mark Murray coming in as part of the Wolecki team he is surplus to requirements. As the manager says "By releasing Jim, I've freed up a space to perhaps bring a player in on loan." There is a mixed reaction from the fans. The 'I-told-you-so's have started already, three games under Eddie and there is dissent in the ranks of the supporters. Just what do they want? Wolecki wouldn't be here if Henry and his squad had been up to it! Comments range from "He doesn't know how to handle older players" to "Ed's mind games won't work". Realistically someone had to go, as we have too many keepers on the books. Others take the positive view by stating that Wolecki is trying to rebuild a team. If Montrose are to improve it's quite simple, players will have to leave the club. 'You can't make an omelette without breaking eggs' is an analogy on one post that rings so true. There is speculation or is it just another rumour, but we don't have long to wait to find out as a press release hits the 'Courier' and the headline of 'Wolecki makes double swoop'. Two new signings are in place for today's match against Berwick. Auchenblae youngster, nineteen year-old goalkeeper, Sandy Wood has been signed on loan from Celtic. Sandy was a Montrose youth team product, (although he was on Aberdeen's books originally) as after he was released he played for Montrose under-eighteen side (that was when we had a youth development programme!). Having drawn Celtic in the BP Youth Cup and on the end of a drubbing, Celtic saw enough as he signed for the club at the age of 16. Although he did not make a first team debut at Parkhead he has been involved in playing reserve team football with the club. Sandy has been brought in to give Andy Reid some competition for the number one spot and could make his debut today as Reid is on the injury list. Wolecki has also secured a loan deal with Dundee which sees Graham Hay, a very promising central defender come to Links Park for the remainder of the season to gain some first team experience. Hay is a straight replacement for loan player Jamie McKenzie who returns to Easter Road.

The strategy of building a home-based team takes another step, but what I can't understand is that we have signed them on loan from their clubs and is it with the view that they will be released some time in the near future? As the '*Courier*' puts it, it is an audacious transfer swoop and fantastic signings for the club. Meanwhile Montrose are willing to listen to offers for third choice goalkeeper Michael Hankinson and striker Duncan McLean.

The third match at home in the space of a week and another chance to change things around by getting back to football on the deck. Today's rearranged match sees Berwick fans journeying to Links Park for the first time, since their Scottish Cup exit at the hands of Montrose several years ago. Kevin Webster, the man they love to hate, is injured, and will not have to endure the taunts of their support. Webster scored in the 1-1 draw in October at Shielfield and will be missed today, as he always seems to be a thorn in the little Rangers' flesh. Maybe James Russell can be that thorn today. New signings Wood and Hay are both in contention for a start today. Steve Kerrigan could also return after missing the last two games, having recovered from flu. There is also good news about long-term injury victim Stuart Ferguson who is in training and this time things are looking good for him, although he is someway off match fitness.

Berwick have a few players out, first choice goalkeeper Coyle, there are doubts over striker Gareth Hutchison- but he might make the bench- and Connolly is still not fit to take a place in the side. The wee Rangers have been going through a sticky patch after a great start to the season and have since slipped to third spot in the league but are still a force to be reckoned with. A result for Montrose of any kind today will be an achievement as new players try to find their feet!

This is a bonus match for me before my Sunday flight to Amsterdam and my journey down to Breda ready to start work on Monday. I will miss all the goings- on, having to resort to the web sites to keep me updated, back to the frustrations of not knowing and back to the Saturday ritual of '*Surf and Talk*', vide-printers and text messages. Welcome back!

Jan 7th. BERWICK, Home - report and teams.
On a cold, grey dank day with both teams subjected to 'smirrin' rain, it really wasn't a day for silky football but they did their best. Berwick's small band of followers should be commended for making the journey on a day like

this and further commended as they would make the long road back after the scoreless draw encounter.

With the departure of Butter, and the tag of 'open to offers' which is hanging over Hankinson it was no surprise that on-loan Sandy Wood made his debut in the Montrose goal. Donnachie and Elliot Smith filled the defensive flanks with new boy Graham Hay in central defence along with Paul Doyle. Midfield comprised of Russell, Hall, Kerrigan and Fraser. Fotheringham sat in the hole between front-runner Watson and the midfield. The listed subs were Hankinson, Dodds, Robert Smith, Don and Andy Cargill who for some reason did not take part in the warm-up. Absentee Greg Henslee will be missed today and one can only assume that he is injured.

The match started with the Berwick support really getting behind their team. Berwick are a tall side with physical strength and you could see that from the kick-off, Montrose would have problems with that in midfield. We simply did not compare in stature, today showed both Fraser and Hall as light weights as they did not have the degree of strength required in the tackle and were too easily knocked off the ball. In saying this, it was the defence that looked firm as they dealt with the Berwick forwards, closing them down at every turn as they reverted to shooting at long range. Early stages saw Wood the busier keeper as he saved from a McGarty free-kick. Goalkeeper O'Connor was in fine form at the other end as he turned a James Russell attempt just over. Then Wood had a fine save as he beat out a cut-back from the line.

The second period started as before as players set about their tasks in keeping things tight. Montrose came close in 55 minutes when Martyn Fotheringham spotted O'Connor off his line, but the resultant twenty yard chip came back off the bar. However it was Berwick who had the ball in the net first, only for the strike to be cancelled out for an offside decision. Wolecki made his first substitution by introducing Kerr Dodds for Russell who had had a quiet second half except for a good run into the Berwick box with no help available to pass too. Don then replaced Fotheringham and a minute later Montrose were awarded a free kick. Sod's law, the free-kick expert had just been substituted and Doyle then went on to orbit the resultant kick. In the closing stages a few chances fell to Montrose, they were either mis-cued or bounced just the wrong way on the heavily sanded pitch. Three players were booked, Watson, Fotheringham and for some reason Hall picked up his third yellow in three matches for a challenge! Thankfully the referee called time and as we trudged out of the park we found that Division Three representation in the Scottish Cup had been obliterated. Hibs had dealt with our neighbours, knocking them for six and Spartans carved the name of

Queen's Park on their door post of conquests coming out on top by three goals to two. The journey back to Berwick for their fans wouldn't be quite as bad now!

Highlights – The defence today looked competent, Wood's sharpness, experience and full-time training at a Premier team showed. Both Donnachie and Elliot Smith dealt with strong players and held their own. Hay was steady at the centre of defence and slotted in well with Doyle. Wolecki will be pleased with the progress of the defence as he has always said that sorting the defence was his main priority. With the return of Fergie in the not too distant future, Stephen, Dodds and young Robert Smith, the future looks good. I felt sorry for Calum Watson today, he got himself into some good positions but could not finish. He is a player who is trying so hard in the strike role, maybe too hard, and things just won't fall for him. I believe if he did get a goal then it would take some of the pressure off him. Looking around when the players were warming up, you can see that Wolecki's fitness regime is starting to kick in, as weight loss is evident. The goalkeepers are given a rigorous workout and everyone is involved whether playing or not. All that remains is getting the attack on track, and for that I would expect to see a few signings this coming week to replace Martin, and the out of favour McLean.

We are going through a phase of transition, things are not going to be right or perfect, Rome was not built in a day or four games and the fans young, middle-aged and old need to realise that. Due to the inclement weather today I stood where I once congregated with others when I first went to Links. It only reminded me of why I changed my terracing location. On one side I was treated to Waldorf from the 'Muppets' who criticised everything that Wolecki had so far achieved and to the south, the echoes of, "Get him off". No such thing as well done or hard lines, after all we did get a point for which the players fought hard. This wasn't a bad game, as far as no score draws go. If we could take anything from today's game it is how to support your team. The encouragement shown by the Berwick fans to their team who have been going through a bad patch was good to hear including cheering them at the final whistle. What did we get – "That's me lads, I'll see you next season!"

Two other Division Three matches were played this afternoon. Elgin recorded an away victory, 2 - 1 at Methil. East Fife really are a Jekyll and Hyde side, having beaten Cowdenbeath a few days earlier, or does it just show that there is no great differences between side in the league? Albion Rovers took three points from our next opponents, the Shire in a 4 – 2 home win.

Back at work, it's great. I have recruited a new supporter. Hang a Montrose pennant in your office and you soon get questions and before long they are telling you the MONTROSE SCORE!

When I left for Aberdeen yesterday, Gable End Graffiti had yet to put up his match report and with it his views of what had transpired giving this ex-pat the desired lifeline. Today the site had been updated and headlined – '**An Announcement**' but not the announcement that I had expected, no news of a striker or for that fact any signing, but it did announce the virtual end of the Blog!

I know how he feels, work commitments, travel, a book to write and complete for publishing and not enough hours in the day to do it. Something has to give and unfortunately it is the reliable Blog. Reports that are written for the match programme will still be posted but this will be the cleaned up version, no more verbose ramblings from its author '*Steeplejack*'. A standing ovation is the order of the day for this enjoyable blog, written from the heart for the love of Montrose Football Club, and I for one will sorely miss the updates.

Wolecki viewed Saturday's game a success, as the '*Courier*' reported that Montrose's defence could not be meaner. Wood and Hay were singled out as completing fine debuts, but the whole defence were committed and concentration in particular was kept for the full ninety minute period.

By keeping a blank sheet, Eddie stated that there might have been a chance of grabbing a winner. He recognises that work now has to be done going forward and this will be sorted out in training. An injection of pace is required upfront and the likelihood of some fresh faces could be as imminent as this week, and in place for the East Stirling game.

Elgin City are in the news again as they now have a shortlist of three for the vacant managerial job. In the frame are Brian Irvine, Ian Wilson and current club captain Jamie McKenzie who has had interim charge. It's not a straight forward choice, nothing is that easy at Borough Briggs as the ghost of Christmas past hovers around the proceedings. The Board are undecided as Steve Patterson could also be in the running. Elgin's dilemma is two-fold- appoint a long term manager now, or let McKenzie who has rejuvenated the side take charge till the end of the season. The latter may see Paterson installed, once Forres Mechanics complete their Highland League campaign. Otherwise it is perm one from three!

Another exciting weekend for me here in Breda and a Division Three card that pairs second against third as Berwick visit Cowdenbeath. Stenhousemuir have a tricky match at Gayfield against Arbroath and Elgin are looking to extend their good run at home to Queen's Park. Albion Rovers and East Fife are matched at Coatbridge and there's a 'Happy Bus' going to Firs Park to shout on the MO! One person I hope is not on the bus is post 'Disgruntled Mo Man'. We can do without his type of support as he has upset most of the fan base with his comments. 'Dave Larter's 'Tache' is spot on as he retorts – "Unbelievable!" and - "For once, just once, wasn't it nice to read something POSITIVE in the press about the Mo, rather than the same old 'injuries, suspensions robbed us' scenario."

He's right, why should the manager who has worked wonders in such a short space of time take this flack. Eddie Wolecki needs time- like any manager he has set targets, one being a fourth place finish. An aspiration rather than a pledge but for some this is not good enough. I think that this kind of negativity harms the club; it affects the morale of the players and is not what you would expect from a so-called supporter of the club, or is he an impostor or wind-up merchant? Anyway, if success is not instant then we must build on positives to gain that success in what ever time it takes. Eddie Wolecki and his team are the men to do it, just give them a chance! Negotiations are taking place concerning a striker, as Eddie Wolecki vies for the signature of ex-Montrose player Scott Taylor after his release from Forfar. The striker has received much attention from other clubs and has also interested East Fife, Arbroath and Junior club Carnoustie. Here's hoping!

For once it is good news at Elgin and it's not the appointment of a new manager, but it is the first time that an Elgin manager has collected the 'Bells' Manager of the Month Award for Division Three. Caretaker player-manager Jamie McKenzie, at twenty-six, is the youngest Senior manager in British football and consequently, McKenzie has become not only the club's first monthly award winner, but the youngest. All that is left to take place is for the traditional curse from this award to strike tomorrow with a win for Queen's Park!

It's imminent! Where have I heard that before, a standard reply for design consultants and one that irritates me, as in this business they try to evade the question. But on this occasion, if it's on the 'Courier' web site then it's got to be right. More press for Montrose as Eddie Wolecki is set to announce the name of his assistant today. It's may be just me putting two and two together and getting five, but it is possible that it could be Kenny Black who had failed with his take-over bid at Elgin. Kenny Black is interested in youth development and ran the skill-seekers programme at Elgin. Then again it might be someone more local. The manager also reports that he is in talks with a striker and midfielder and that he hopes to secure their signatures by the weekend. Training has been increased this week from the usual two sessions by adding a bounce game against Junior side Coupar Angus (5 – 2 Montrose). It has given players who had not been playing regularly a chance to show the manager what they can do and that also goes for five young local trialists who are on 'Skill seeker' contracts at Elgin, who will be released at the end of January. Eddie Wolecki had previously stated that he hopes to have an under-19 team in place for next season to give a development path for home-grown youth into the Senior arena. As part of his vision for Montrose, he sees the importance of home-grown talent and that it is the way ahead to have a relatively young side with a few experienced players in key positions. Things are definitely moving forward in the right direction, but will the support see this!

This really is a depressing time of the year, its dark when you go to work and it's dark when you return, but since my return to Breda, I feel as if the roof has fallen in. First the 'Blog' is reduced to a limited update, now Euro Sport teletext has changed and not for the better. Interference, to 'Radio Scotland' from a local radio station makes me wonder where it is all going to end, as all I need now is for somebody to let my bicycle tyres down!

Doing time when working away is hard enough, no home comforts, family, cut-off from things and limited company but it's the small things that matter and that you appreciate, like watching 'Dad's Army', 'Taggart' with Dutch sub-titles and 'friets!'. I saw an article, a study by a sociologist pleading the plight of footballers and the life they have to lead. Many are on the move having been transferred to teams and places that they don't know. They are away from home and family as their wives cannot yet be with them. A year here, six months there, big money, but they have short careers – poor souls. I'm not going to go on as obviously the sociologist has not met the ex-pat!

Sometimes it's best not to plan anything, and then nothing can go wrong. Last night I watched the opening of FC Groningen's new stadium by Arjen Robben (Chelsea). In the match that followed, Groningen played hosts to SC Heerenveen.. A big occasion for FC Groningen, capacity crowd, mainly home support and a run on scarves and 'Erik the Viking' Nevland hats from the club shop. What a pay day and terrific atmosphere as the game is played end to end at one hundred miles an hour and it is that man Nevland who opens the Groningen account at the new stadium.

It is often said that the Dutch are masters of the game, but it is the structure not just for football but sport as a whole that gives kids the encouragement to take part. The facilities, the coaches, the community support are all there and that's what makes the difference. Winter is not a deterrent as all facilities are floodlit and it is not just one facility per town as each housing area has one. I think at times we are short changed as they pay in Euros what we would pay in Pounds. We are taxed to the hilt and are nowhere near competing with our Dutch counterparts. You don't see youths hanging about street corners or kids in bus shelters, as the youngsters of this country are being developed by the structure set in sport. A lesson for us all and I can see where Eddie Wolecki's ideas are coming from. May he succeed!

January sales, 70% off, and where am I? I am in *'Surf and Talk'*. It's the joys of Saturday once again as I sit down to sift the internet, news sites and message boards.

During my time in *'Surf and Talk'* I started to realise that the changes being made are not just at playing level as the Board have also been very busy. It was on the Club web site 'Montrose Football Club – Customers / Supporters Charter plus Anti-Discrimination Policy' and it is that which caught my eye. Discrimination, the words – or general behaviour, stood out and at last it seems the Board are going to act against those 'Boo-Boys'. If it gives Eddie a chance, this is one welcome change and a massive step by the Club. Those who think that because they pay their money, they are entitled to abuse players, management, Board and Arbroath Football Club will now be caught in the realms of this policy and a possible order banning them from Links Park. As the Board say "We are committed to challenging and dismantling all forms of discrimination in our Club". Yet another step forward!

No news of Eddie's assistant, or a midfielder or a striker. We just can't score at present as the day's events eventually reveal three points for East Stirling and a win for newly appointed manager Gordon Wylde.

Wolecki points out that this week's training was the first opportunity to start working on attacking play. It will however take time, weeks, months, before we see the benefits in set pieces, counter attacks and open play.

For today's match, Eddie reports that Kevin Don is unavailable, Neil Stephen is back from injury and Henslee has taken light training after an ankle knock. Both could be in contention today as the emphasis and concentration is on youth.

Jan 14th. EAST STIRLING, Away - report and teams

As expected Montrose field a very young side against the Shire. Hankinson was a surprise inclusion as he took his place in goal replacing Sandy Wood who injured an ankle during training with Celtic. Almost a new back four of Donnachie, Stephen, Hay and Robert Smith defended Hankinson. The midfield also took a new look of Russell, Hall, Henslee and Elliot Smith with this week's front-runners Watson and Kerrigan. It is evident that Eddie is building a team for next season as he relegates the non-locals to the subs-bench. Doyle, Dodds, Fotheringham and Fraser filled the sidelines along with a trialist.

It's amazing what a new manager will do as East Stirling turned in their best performance of the season so far under new charge hand Gordon Wylde. The first forty-five was poor with not much going to plan, as passing moves went astray. Within the first two minutes Barry Donnachie came to the rescue by clearing an Oates shot off the goal-line. It was then the turn of Hankinson to turn a Dymock drive with a spectacular save. Deadlock however was soon broken as East Stirling opened the scoring in 20 minutes through Dymock. Brand provided a cross into the box for a Thywissen header, which was blocked on the goal-line and Dymock despatched the rebound. Montrose soon replied as shots from Henslee and Kerrigan flashed past the uprights but that was little to show in an effortless first period.

Half-time brought a change with Doyle replacing Hay who was suffering from flu. In an improved second half, Montrose took control of the midfield but lacked finishing power with the best chances falling to Euan Hall and Martyn Fotheringham. Hall missed from point-blank range and Fotheringham's shot was superbly saved by Jackson in the Shire goal.

Fotheringham had come on as a substitute for young Robert Smith who was making his debut. Wolecki's final substitution saw Hall being replaced by a Trialist striker Michel Lombard who had experienced football with Aberdeen and Ross County, but this was to no avail.

Highlights – Statistically we had a poor day with Barry Donnachie possibly the best player on the field although Hankinson should also be mentioned as he pulled off some good saves. With only six goal attempts on target and four off it shows that we failed to capitalise on play. It's never easy being beaten, but it hurts even more when it's the club at the bottom of the table, and it will be hard for the fans to accept, but we need to stick with the policy of youth as it is the only way forward. Yes we are going to take a few hits, but better now as we build a future. There are always lessons learned and from this match we carried no threat going forward. As did Henry Hall, Eddie is doing his best to bring in new faces on the strike front, but to bring in the new some have to first move out. With one or two players considering offers from other clubs we may see some movement in the squad if these deals work out. Wolecki has several irons in the fire at present and is committed to bringing young talent with ambition to the club to further their careers, but for now as Eddie say's "We need to work hard in training". After today's match, Tuesday's 'Meet the Manager' could be interesting as supporters put their questions to Eddie, but as always he will have done his homework and will be well prepared to answer any questions that are put to him.

A Brazil like performance saw the striker score two in Arbroath's 3-2 win against league leaders Stenhousemuir. Cowden and Berwick share a one all draw and Albion rovers put East Fife to the sword with a 3-1 victory. The 'Manager of the Month Award' lived up to it's curse as Elgin lost at home to Queen's by a 2-1 margin.

These results may not mean a lot to some but having dropped one league position last week, we drop yet another this week. Yes, we are now back in ninth position!

NAC Breda were at home this weekend, as their fans welcomed their new manager in a game against Roda JC Kerkrade. All did not go well for the Breda debutant as Roda scored four with one goal destined for what could be the goal of the season. NAC have their problems as they slip further down the league and it's not just on the field, as fans are not willing to listen as they look for instant success. At today's game striker Pierre Van Hooijdonk was confronted by a fan when taking the field for the second-half , a slanging match evolved between the two, stewards were no where to be seen. It is not good for the game. Where is it all going to end, even Cowdenbeath and Berwick fans at Saturday's game are now calling for segregation after trouble flared between supporters for a second time this season. Stewarding is part of the problem. They have no real authority and see it as a couple of hours pin money. Some are too interested in watching the match to be bothered with fans antagonising each other. If the football authorities won't act by imposing penalties then clubs will have take the initiative in calming these situations. Why have a discrimination policy if you are not going to use it!

It may be the aftermath, but today's comments show that Saturday's defeat has clearly hurt Eddie Wolecki. Embarrassed that the league's bottom side passed us off the park, he makes no excuses. Again he emphasises that with a few new signings and hard work during the week, he is confident that things will begin to turn for the better as the season develops. At the Links Park 'Emergency Ward 10', Wolecki thinks that club captain Stuart Ferguson could make a playing return in four weeks time (mid-February) and stated that both Webster and Reid had dates for receiving surgery. Injuries have hampered the club from the outset of the league campaign, which in turn has given both managers selection headaches. Even on Saturday there was the injury picked up by Sandy Wood, and this affected the managers preferred team selection. A day or two later than advertised and Eddie Wolecki reveals his new assistant manager as being Scott Kopel and yes two and two did make five as I got it wrong!!! The son of former Manchester United, Blackburn and Dundee United player Frank Kopel, Scott was a one time Jim McLean prodigy and has played at both Senior and Junior levels. He has also been heavily involved in coaching and youth development in the Dundee area and will have his finger on the pulse regarding possible outlets for bringing youth players to Montrose. To compliment this, we need someone covering the Aberdeen and Grampian area and a scout could be the answer. Introduction of Kopel to the players and coaching staff took place at Monday's training session.

He's a busy man but Eddie Wolecki made time to answer questions at a 'Meet the Manager' forum that the Montrose Supporters Club had arranged. I have just read the minutes from last night's session. It seems to have been an excellent communication with the Supporters Club and very worthwhile. Eddie Wolecki gave good well thought-out answers and had obviously done a lot of preparation work before hand. It's good to see that his enthusiasm is rubbing off on others and that a structure is developing for the future. He is under no illusions with a five year development timescale clearly in the open and a target of First Division football at Links. Wolecki was eager to speak about youth development and his plan to have a 17 – 19's team in place for next season. He also has a coach on board to work with a 14 – 16's group and has made huge steps in putting this in place.

Training has been changed to Monday (Links) and Wednesday (Dundee) and is now very specific as they use the ball in everything to develop the use of the same muscles used in a game. He also stated that everyone has to play for the jersey, be prepared to work in training and give the required commitment to the club or lose the jersey. There was no news on the signing front, but he is looking to have a squad of twenty-two to draw on for selection purposes. In the past we have lost players at the end of the season as contracts have expired. Eddie hopes to remedy this by putting an end to the days of Peterhead raiding our resources. Most players at the club have one year contracts that will be up at the end of the season and it is his aim to address this now, in the January window. Players will be spoken to over the next few weeks and futures will be decided as Wolecki is of the opinion that if they don't want to commit to the club then they are as well going in January as May. It will benefit the club in the long term as the right attitude is required. He also addressed my question now that Scott Kopel is on board, and that is what about coverage of the Aberdeen and Grampian areas? His reply is that there is a person who knows the area well and has been able to attract some of the best young players in recent years. Let's hope they come our way.

It's going to be a long haul to get it right and we will get results like last Saturday because the management team are changing things, but Eddie is adamant that we will have a successful team on the park and we will be competitive in the longer term. Good communication has been a problem in the past, but not now, as it has been given priority in many ways. The Supporter's Club should be commended in the way that they have handled themselves in organising this event early in the management change. It is one thing running the event, it is another communicating to the fans, whether they are members or not, before Chinese whispers start on the rumour mill. To this end a four- page minute brief was out in double quick time before we were able to wake. The Supporter's Club is doing everything possible to give Eddie the support that he needs and it's time that others followed suit! The challenge now for the fans is to start thinking outside the box and to move on from 'God-help-us-ness' and parochialism as the future is round the corner. The support have to embrace this more business like approach, from the Board, down through the management structure to the grass roots of this development hub. That is the future!

There are still a few 'doom and gloom' merchants on the message board; it looks as if we are in for a 'winter of discontent' as supporters are split in their views over the club's policy. At last nights meeting the Manager's view was clear-cut!

Focus is becoming apparent on the World Cup; the build up has started to the finals in June. I had spoken before about ill-feeling, hurt that still exists here in the Netherlands from the war years. The Dutch Football Association like their English counterparts are on tender hooks as both sets of supporters do have a history with Germany and are eager they refrain from referring to the war. It is not surprising that the Dutch Association is less than happy with a company's merchandising of orange coloured German war helmets. There are many ways that you can make a joke but this is not one of them. This type of irresponsibility incites trouble between supporters and the Dutch authorities must act to have them withdrawn from the market before the invasion in June.

It's the end of an era, may it rest in peace, 'Gable End Graffiti' is dead. The site is closed, the link is no longer, as the pseudonym of '*Steeplejack*' is no more. I for one will miss his ramblings!

A midfielder arrives at Links and Elliott Smith departs in the opposite direction in a swap deal for East Fife's natural left-sided player Kris Brash. No fee was involved for Brash who had spent a loan period at Montrose from Dundee a few seasons ago. No sign of a striker yet as Scott Taylor opts to sign for Arbroath and completes John McGlashan's plans in pushing for fourth place.

At last, Duncan McLean out and Gary Middleton in, striker for striker but there is a fee as Wolecki does a deal with Super League Junior club, Tayport. There was no news on the '*Courier*' web site and since there is no reliable blog I had heard nothing. There was a one liner in the '*Record*' – Montrose have signed striker Gary Middleton from Tayport. It was only when I received a phone call from home that I was informed that we had signed a striker and that it was in the '*Courier*' -but the article hadn't made the web site. Some are still not happy and as one post put it – 'If you want immediate success, go and watch Montrose Roselea. They're going not bad!'

Two new faces for Eddie Wolecki to consider for Saturday's league fixture at Central Park. It's anyone's guess what the team selection will be. The park is tight, and as long as we can put what has been emphasised in training to good use then we can keep a clean sheet. Can we score? This is an area that work has been done on in training this week. A point would be a good result but as we have not scored for a few games, today could be the day to break that duck. Here's hoping, but Wolecki has warned fans not to expect a sudden improvement, there no magic wand as confidence comes through winning. The manager realises that the team have been shot-shy but hopes that they will rise to the occasion against promotion chasing Cowdenbeath. Cowdenbeath have a couple of injuries but are boosted by the addition of Irish Internationalist Michael O'Neill who has taken the post of Assistant Manager.

"McDonald's, McDonald's, Kentucky Fried Chicken and a Pizza Hut, McDonald's, McDonald's, Kentucky Fried Chicken and a Pizza Hut!"

It's like having a Dutch bout of Y.M.C.A., as there are even dance actions to the song. Who ever thought it up obviously had a lot of time on their hands or just loved 'fine' dining! Certain songs, they hit a spot. Why is it we always end up with the same CD's when we travel, every ex-pat is the same, it's like 'Dessert Island Discs' as we have that feeling of desertion, an outcast marooned on an island in this small world. There are lows and highs like any occupation. January and February can be bad months as sometimes we feel sorry for ourselves as we lack support at hand, but it is the simple things that lift our spirits in this up and down life as we look for assurances. What gets you through? It could be as simple as Dougie McLean's song 'Caledonia'. Homesickness affects some more than others, but it is common for some to just pack it all in, give up, jack it, and yet there are others, "The what am I doing here brigade?", who manage to bridge the days with their target of going home as they strike-off the days. Once home, withdrawal symptoms start to kick-in, as they know nothing else.

In some circumstances, isolated so far away from home, it is left to others to deal with issues, as we are powerless to do anything. A cause for anxiety, it can be a terrible feeling, kid's being ill, parents sick, and you bottle it up, but a few words from 'The Who' and things are back into perspective. 'Can't Explain" but I can recommend it!

Today started early, it had been a busy week working with figures for cash flows, different currencies and a calculator that had been battered to death. I needed to clear my head, do something different, so I did my usual and started to walk in a direction I did not know! I would do this in Kazakhstan, but I would have company, as it was safer in numbers. Today I was on my own. It can be strange as you don't know where you are going but somehow you end up at a place that is of interest. That's what happened today as I found my self standing outside Baronie, one of the Junior clubs of Breda. It's like a feeder club, Montrose Youth to Roselea, but the main difference was the young age that both boys and girls were encouraged to play. Ten o'clock and I had already missed most of three matches. The complex has seven large parks, all sectioned off, giving coaches a couple of metres to patrol the touchlines without interference from parents who cannot give instructions to their off-spring. There was a '14's' match that was just starting and what struck me was the 4-3-3 line-ups; even at an early age this is installed in kids as the Dutch structure. The other noticeable fact was the teams were tall at the back, winners in midfield and had pace and height up front. Just what Eddie Wolecki has been saying all this time. There was a nice touch of sportsmanship by the referee as both sides shook hands before the game started, it was similar to scenes from the Champion's League.

A good youth development set-up, and as well as there being changing rooms for the teams there were also cafeteria facilities for parents giving the club some income. Youth development systems don't run on fresh air and facilities like this require sponsorship not just for jerseys but from the community. A simple board stood tall at the entrance to the facilities, it held three columns of plates the size of car registration numbers with the names of sponsors. Fifty pounds here, fifty pounds there, it all mounts up, it gives smaller firms and shops a chance to contribute and in return receive some prominent advertising as they can't all afford the large billboards that surround some grounds. We can learn from this, revenue will be needed for youth development; a sponsor's make-over at affordable prices is just one of many ideas that could be initiated.

Jan 21st. COWDENBEATH, Away - report and teams

It is the first time under Eddie Wolecki that we have leaked more than one goal but we held it late until seven minutes to the end against a ten-man Cowdenbeath. According to reports Montrose did play with aggression today and were unfortunate not to take a point. On the other hand we did not score and were the only Third Division side not to do so. A late Friday night swoop into the transfer market sealed Wolecki's eighth signing in a short spell. Midfielder Hugh Davidson moved up the coast for a small fee from neighbours Arbroath.

In a changed team list, Brash, Davidson and Middleton all made their debuts. Montrose lined-up: Wood in goal, Donnachie, Doyle, Hay and Brash in the back-four, Davidson, Kerrigan, Fotheringham and Fraser in midfield with Gary Middleton wearing the number nine shirt alongside Watson upfront. Hankinson, Hall, Stephen, Robert Smith and Russell were the bench select.

The match started as it did on November 12th when we last met, with a carbon copy goal in 3 minutes, the only exception was that on-loan signing McKenna on this occasion was at hand to slot home a cross from Markus Paatelainen. Montrose battled hard in midfield, keeping their shape and put together some good passing combinations. In 39 minutes Darren McGregor was shown the yellow card for a push on an opponent and within 3 minutes the utility player found himself in further trouble as he was shown a straight red card for lashing out at Hugh Davidson. As with the match against Arbroath, the opposition were reduced to ten men for the entire second period. We found it hard against Arbroath and today was no different as I think it can be harder playing against ten than taking the advantage. In between times Kerrigan who had picked up an ankle knock earlier in the match had to be withdrawn and was replaced by James Russell with Davidson moving inside. With this change Montrose lost some of their rhythm but had completed an improved first half performance.

The second period saw Cowdenbeath still continuing to make chances, this time it was the turn of brother, Mikko Paatelainen to head over and for Wood to save another effort from the Finn. Montrose did have their chances with a Kris Brash drive going close and a volley clipping the crossbar. The match was finally brought to a close in eighty-three minutes when substitute Buchannan chipped over Sandy Wood as the keeper advanced. Montrose had kept it tight to the last ten minutes but pushed forward to try and salvage something from the match and cannot be faulted for their effort.

Highlights – A good ninety minutes from the newcomers. Hugh Davidson, who earned a booking, is a physical player and has height and pace. Brash added aggression down the left side and Middleton provided some good touches and pace upfront. An upbeat Manager this morning is starting to see his team's effort bear fruit as he praises performance and positive attitude. He stated that we had kept the ball well and never lost shape as the team battled to recover from losing the early goal. Wolecki hopes that the fans will have seen the real qualities that the new signings have brought to the side. Cowdenbeath are a good side and in the coming weeks we play the League's first and second placed teams which will be a good test of our strengths but will also show any weaknesses in our play. Keeping fitness in mind and the fact that so many new faces have arrived at Links Park, Eddie has arranged a bounce match against Brechin Vics this evening. It will serve to build from Saturday and also give confidence providing we win!

Another round of results, Berwick stay in second spot as they beat Arbroath 2 – 1 to take all three points at Shielfield. Elgin battled from a goal down to win 2 – 1 to Albion Rovers. Stenny left it late to finally win 4 - 2 and Queen's scored 3-1 against East Fife and East Stirling respectively.

As I read the message board this morning I could hear myself saying 'welcome to the club' as one post replied to – "How are things in foreign parts"! I am glad I am not the only one, as I read – 'Like the rest of you I have not had much to cheer me up on a Saturday night of late. Watching the BBC web page, refreshing every two minutes (allegedly) isn't a lot of fun at 22.40.' He goes on - 'I have to say that watching 1-0 confirmed as a full-time result against Arbroath earlier in the season, in an internet café in Kota Kinabaula, Borneo at 23.49, while hardly qualifying as witnessing a great sporting moment, was a flicker of light.'

Radio Scotland commentaries from the SPL are only available free in the UK; Gable End Graffiti is gone and is a big miss. Welcome to the world of the ex-pat, but at least I can count myself lucky as I did see that 1-0 victory!

At the club the emphasis is on change, new people coming in. Likewise at work, now that we are in a construction phase we are dealing with new people and heading in different directions. Travel, early morning meetings, new routines and destination Eindhoven, home of the mighty PSV and the sight of another stadium.

'Start as you mean to go on'. A lesson in life that we should all acknowledge. Back to basics, setting the foundations for success, scheduling what has to be done within a timescale and budget. If we don't get it right at the start then it's going to be a rocky journey. You can tell if things are right by the set-up, first impressions are important. The meeting room walls are adorned with pictures, previous conquests, projects undertaken, show-piece installations, and pride of place goes to the 'Phillip's Stadium' here in Eindhoven. It is a magnificent stadium and PSV are very lucky to have such a wealthy sponsor as Phillips to support them and must be the envy of the Dutch league sides.

Goalkeeper Jim Butter is back in business having left the club. After a few matches turning out as a trialist, Butter has sign for East Super League Junior side Carnoustie Panmure till the end of the season.

It's a tough test this weekend for Montrose, when we play against league leaders, Stenhousemuir. Having suffered a 3-0 home defeat and a humiliating 6-2 defeat at Ochilview we are in for a difficult day. This is the type of team that we have to be able to compete against and must show a physical assertiveness from kick-off, as we have been over-run time and time again by the Warriors. Backs will be to the wall on Saturday, but if we are to start building a team for next season what better stage than at Links Park and I am not talking about damage limitation as anything we win now can be looked on as doing other clubs a favour in their quest for fourth place.

Talking of building a team, there is movement in the transfer market once again before the window closes on Tuesday. St Johnstone midfield man Stevie McManus and Dundee North End's Ian MacLeod are signed to strengthen the squad. In the deal for MacLeod, a six foot two striker, Robert Smith and Kevin Don are farmed out to North End till the end of the season on delayed signings. Wolecki emphasises that the two will be back at the start of the close season as he wants Smith and Don to use this time to gain experience so that they can make a claim on a first team jersey at the start of next season. In the meantime however they will still train with Montrose and play for North End on match days.

Elgin, after a stormy period of Board changes, has finally named their new manager. It is former Aberdeen player Brian Irvine, who had been acting as Youth Development Coach at Ross County. The first priority for Irvine is to re-instate the 'Skill seeker' programme and to have it up and running for next season. Another Board, seeking to be a community based club, a new manager with ambition who hopes his new charges have what it takes.

Do we have what it takes? The World Cup finals are in June, there is no Scotland and today as the European Championship groups for the 2008 finals are drawn, we receive a tough draw. Paired n Group 'B' with France, Italy, Ukraine, Lithuania, Georgia, and the dreaded Faroe Islands, a team we always struggle against. The group couldn't be tougher but it will give the much travelled *'Tartan Army'* a few interesting journeys into the unknown.

As midfielder McManus arrives at Links Park, Andy Cargill whose contract is up this weekend will depart a free agent. These are not the only decisions required as the window starts to close. We still have three goalkeepers on the books; Reid is currently awaiting an operation and will be out for a few weeks yet. Wolecki was willing to listen to offers for third choice keeper Michael Hankinson thus freeing up a wage. It's a bit of a lottery, do we need a sub keeper on the bench while we wait for Reid to recover or do we risk it and release Hankinson before the window closes as I dare say Dodds would stand-in as he seems able to cover every other position. Eddie has also said that he would be speaking to others whose contracts are up in the summer to see if they are will to commit to the clubs future. The other area which requires attention is that of Elgin's current bunch of 'skill seekers' who are due for release from the club on Tuesday the 31st. We won't be the only club with interest in these lads and will surely have competition for their signatures. The window of opportunity closes but not quite yet!

In his pre-match comments Wolecki sums up the visitors by saying that there is no denying their strengths, Stenhousemuir are a very good side, but Montrose can give a good account of themselves today as it is the perfect opportunity to show that they can compete at the top of the table. Injuries rule out Henslee and Kerrigan, who will be out for a few weeks. Martyn Fotheringham finds himself serving suspension and is also unavailable for selection. All clubs have injuries and suspensions as Wolecki prefers to focus on the positives and in particular performance. If performance is right then results will come. The good news is that club captain Stuart Ferguson played in Monday's bounce match with Brechin Vics. It is the first step towards recovery and a place in the first team. This coming Monday, Eddie has arranged a challenge match against Peterhead at Links Park. He certainly believes in match fitness and working with the ball.

You can't even spend a peaceful day looking for a birthday present without your 'ozone' space being inhabited by decibels from the mobile phone. I was back to my childhood as I browsed in a shop selling *Airfix* models. The shop was full of middle-aged men with child-like looks upon their faces, reliving their past, interrupted by the arrival of '*Starsky and Hutch*'! At first I thought it was a car out on the street due to the volume as it blasted out 'Oh I wish I was in the land of cotton'. Heads turned, looking towards the doorway of the shop only for some cretin to pull out a mobile phone and announce "Hoy!" the traditional Dutch greeting. What an embarrassment, at least when my mobile sounded a few minutes later it was a frog croaking and of course a text message, but not what I expected. No, we are not one down, oh ye of little faith, but we have lost Neil Stephen as the big centre half is sold to Peterhead. Never mind he will be back on Monday night as he lines up with his ex-Montrose brothers of Gibson, Michie, Sharp and Wood. It is better to have sold him now rather than to see him leave in the summer and having a tribunal deciding a pittance of a transfer fee. Having been the player of the year last season, the fans may see this as a backward step for Montrose, but the money will finance a few more faces in order for Eddie to make his squad of twenty-two. It could be an unconfirmed rumour but Monday's *P&J* confirms the first signing of the January transfer window for the Peterhead manager. The fee is undisclosed.

The mobile sounds once more, no we haven't sold another player but we are one down!

Jan 28th. STENHOUSEMUIR, Home - report and teams
Like last week, signs of a revival, and despite losing a goal in twenty minutes we were still in the match until a dubious penalty for hand ball five minutes from the end pulled the carpet out from under our feet. There was no change in the defensive set-up of Wood, Donnachie, Doyle, Hay and Brash. In a changed midfield due to injury and suspension, Davidson moved inside to replace Kerrigan and young McManus made his debut in place of Fotheringham. Russell and Fraser patrolled the flanks with Middleton and McLeod leading the strike force. Hankinson, Hall, Watson, Dodds and Stuart Ferguson sat on the bench (that's if they could find a seat).The starting eleven contained only three survivors from the Henry Hall era, Donnachie, Doyle and Fraser. McManus and MacLeod made their debuts; Stenhousemuir's vintage strike trio of McGrillen, Cramb and Diack with the support of Andy Gibson indicated that we would be in for a day of bombardment from their front line. An envious look at their substitute's bench with the talented John Paul McBride, Mercer and the young David Templeton also showed there was much in reserve if reinforcements were needed.

The game kicked off and Montrose passed the ball well in the first twenty minutes. Middleton was unlucky in 8 minutes as he saw his header tipped over by the Stenny keeper Willie McCulloch. Stenhousemuir opened their account in 16 minutes when Andy Gibson turned young Hay to play a ball though to Diack who finished clinically from fifteen yards. Diack celebrated his goal in style and was duly booked for leaving the field of play as he celebrated with fans on the terracing behind the goal. Donnachie was then added to the referee's book for bringing Cramb down to earth and Brash soon followed for a poor tackle. At the other end McCulloch came to the rescue blocking a close-range Brash effort. Wood then saved from Cramb and Diack to go in at the break one down.

Wolecki made a half-time change in midfield, withdrawing Fraser who had not been in the match, replacing him with Euan Hall for the start of the second period. Five minutes into the second half and Montrose were forced to make a further change after Brash clashed with McCulloch as he dived at the feet of the left side player. Watson replaced Brash as the player was stretchered off the field from the collision. Stenny were in the driving seat as shots from Sinclair and Diack flashed past Wood's goal. Templeton replaced Diack, MacLeod headed wide from six yards after Hall's cross and Templeton had a goal ruled off-side, shortly after he came on. Wolecki made his final substitution in 72 minutes with Stuart Ferguson receiving a warm welcome from the Montrose support as he made a welcome return from injury, his first appearance this season. Doyle had to look lively in clearing a Templeton shot from the line with the Montrose goal under siege. In 85 minutes Stenhousemuir were awarded a dubious penalty after a shot from close range struck Russell who was unable to get out of the way. McBride, who had replaced McGrillen, sent Wood the wrong way from the spot to put the warriors two in front. The referee completed his day with two late bookings, Middleton from Montrose and Stenhousemuir's Mercer.

Highlights – Stenhousemuir were made to work hard for their victory before sealing the points late on. It's a time of transition for Montrose; you just need to look at the team lines today to see that. Results in the coming weeks will come as the effort and commitment is there. Wood and Davidson were singled out for their performance in goal and midfield. On the plus side it was good to see the return of Stuart Ferguson earlier than expected. Ferguson will be playing in tomorrow night's friendly with Peterhead and it is hoped that he will come through the ninety minutes. There is a lot going on at present, the scene is changing, give the manager time and support, as now is not the time to get cold feet. This is only the tip of the iceberg, it's what is submerged that is the basis of the future of the club and that has yet to be revealed.

Score of the day goes to Arbroath, as Cowdenbeath plotted their own downfall. Having lost the services of McGregor due to last week's sending off,

Baxter and Mauchlan followed suit this week reducing Cowdenbeath to nine men. The final score–line of 4 – 1 somewhat flatters the home side with 3 goals in a frantic last two minutes, never the less a good win for the Red Lichties. An 8ninth minute penalty was enough for Queen's Park to take all three points at Bayview. Queen's who are in fourth place are now trailing third placed Cowdenbeath by three points. New manager Brian Irvine saw his Elgin troops score 2 at the Shire to take the points, whilst Berwick recorded a 1-0 win at Cliftonhill.

The clock is ticking, midnight and the transfer window is closed. However, Neil Stephen's transfer to Peterhead was not the last piece of business to take place at Links. The side is beginning to take shape as fans look from the terracing for survivors from the wreckage in this winter of discontent. Glasgow commuter Paul Doyle and Edinburgh based Kerr Dodds are released from the club. The release of utility player Dodds is a surprise to me and it now looks as if third choice keeper Michael Hankinson will be kept till the end of the season. Wolecki quite rightly points out that both Doyle and Dodds are good players but highlights the difficulty of training with the squad for Central belt players. The decision has been made now rather than later as the travellers have gone and Wolecki is left with local based players. As the January transfer window closes, there is no sentiment expressed as people move on, the fans interest is only in who has signed for their club. An unbelievable ten new faces at Links Park with nine moving on, but there has also been movement elsewhere in the Division as teams bolster their squads to push for a top four place.

Stenhousemuir have added that 'man of many clubs' and prolific goal-scorer Ian Diack and have also signed Andy Gibson and Paul Cassidy from Partick and have Neil Scally from Falkirk on loan. Cowdenbeath have secured the services of Elgin's Pat Scullion, Darren Thomson from Alloa and loan signings McKenna from St.Mirren, Stuart Boyd from Ayr and yet another Paatelainen brother who is playing-out the Finnish winter close-down. Arbroath have enlisted the services of Robbie Raeside, no surprise there, as he teams up with his long time friend- Manager John McGlashan. Gavin Swankie has also made a return to his former club on loan after a £20,000 transfer to Dundee and former Forfar striker Scott Taylor has been added to the squad. East Fife have added front runner Joe Savage from Stenhousemuir, Kevin Gordon from Berwick, plus Elliott Smith from our good selves and extended Marco Pelosi's loan period from Hearts till the end of the season. Berwick have taken two young forwards Mark Ramsay and Stephen Manson on-loan from Falkirk. Sean Peliczka has also signed from East Fife for the Borderers. Martin Lauchlan after his departure from Stenhousemuir has made his way to Elgin City. East Stirling boss Gordon Wylde took no time in signing Mark Malloy from Barry Town in Wales and striker Alan Patrick from the Motherwell Amateur league. Queen's Park signed that other man of many clubs, goalkeeper Mark Cairns after his release from Arbroath and also bring in a striker, Kartan Finnbogason from Celtic on loan.

Wolecki's ins and outs!

Players - IN	Players - OUT	On the MOVE
James Russell – called up	Willie Martin - Freed	Jamie McKenzie – returned to Hibs after loan period & was released
Robert Smith – called up	Jim Butter - Freed	Robert Smith – delayed transfer (Dundee NE)
Kevin Don – Scone Amateurs	Andy Cargill - Freed	Kevin Don – delayed transfer (Dundee NE)
Sandy Wood – ex Celtic	Elliott Smith – East Fife	
Graham Hay – loan Dundee	Duncan McLean - Tayport	
Kris Brash – East Fife	Neil Stephen - Peterhead	
Gary Middleton - Tayport	Paul Doyle - Freed	
Hugh Davidson - Arbroath	Kerr Dodds - Freed	
Stevie McManus – St Johnstone		
Ian MacLeod – Dundee NE		

There are times in this job that you think that you have heard it all-but then again! Open plan offices are fine but sometimes there are phone calls that you wish nobody could hear. You wonder are people really this stupid or are they winding me up, as other people also listen in!

It was a simple enough question, "Can you give me your Company's mailing address", my colleague was asked and it was second nature for my colleague to rhyme it off ending with 'The Netherlands'.

Answers inevitably raise further questions as the reply came, "The Netherlands"?
"Yes, Holland."
"Is that in Brabant (an area of Holland)?"
"No, Holland. The Netherlands is the country. The Netherlands is Holland."
"Where is it?"
"It's next to Germany."
"Germany?"
"Yes, Germany and Belgium. It's in Europe."
"Europe?"
Still no further forward the call was ended.
There is only one place I know of that does not have a clue about geography and it didn't take a lot of working out. The call was from New York,

Yankee's don't even know where the state of New Jersey is and it's on their doorstep! Enough said, as it is a sad fact that only 19 % of Americans have a passport and have travelled further than their home state. If there ever is a war with the US and Europe, then we will be safe as they will bomb the country of Brussels thinking that they have hit the city of Belgium!

On-loan youngster Graham Hay has signed a deal to the end of next season with his club Dundee. It means that there is no chance he will be released from Dundee at the end of the season and no chance that Montrose could secure his signature as is sometimes hoped with loan signings. He is quite clearly here for first team experience before being blooded at a higher level. However there is hope as Elgin City's 'skill-seekers' are freed to move after coming to an agreement to terminate their contracts. With several clubs interested, it allows them to move on as free agents. Competition however will be stiff if we are to secure any of these youngsters for our youth development policy.

Before the transfer deadline, it was rumoured that Montrose had made a bid to bring Chris Tawse to Links from Eddie Wolecki's previous side Lochee United. Having failed in the bid, the player's contract is however out at the end of the season and would then be free to move from his present club. Watch this space! Paul Doyle's release has been East Fife's gain as the ex-Montrose player signs for the Fife outfit. A few days later Kerr Dodds appears for the Fifers as a substitute at Elgin.

Berwick this week, two draws previously and we always save our best performance for the Borderers. There have been so many comings and goings, but can we field a team? We still have three goalkeepers, one injured, four defenders, one injured and one on comeback. Nine midfielders, three injured, and three forwards, all available. No problem we can play 1-2-5-3, a squad of nineteen will clearly not do but a point would suffice! Montrose failed to score in January but I fancy we can break that duck today at Shielfield despite the sceptics on the message board. Second in the league, away from home and injures. Let's not write ourselves off before the match as you never know the pitch might just fail the referee's inspection. A victory for us then!

It's a bit alarming, fans want instant success. Six weeks have passed, the strategy has been explained time and time again and still there are some who undermine the Board, manager and players. For some, radical change has taken place too quickly; they can't see the wood for the trees or get their head around the long term concept. Come back in three years, don't post meantime and accept the long term solution as it isn't going to happen in six weeks!

Yes! – A point for us and the duck is broken as we scored our first goal in 2006! A Gary Middleton goal was enough to take another point from Berwick, the third this season. The team can take confidence from this result as they now have two home matches against Queen's Park and Albion Rovers before going to Bayview. This is the time to put a bit of a run together as a few results will strengthen the character of the team.

Feb 4th. BERWICK, away - report and teams

As thought, a bit of a make shift team and walking wounded on the bench as injures and suspension take their toll. The team lined up with Wood in goal, Donnachie, Hay, and Ferguson being able to take the captaincy role for the first time this season as he took his place in defence. Stephen Fraser filled in at left back. Russell, Davidson, McManus and Hall linked up in midfield. Middleton and a fit Henslee slotted in upfront. Fit substitutes, Hankinson, Trialist one and Trialist two. Injured players, Kris Brash and keeper Andy Reid filled the last two vacancies. The trialists were possibly from Elgin's release of 'Skill seekers'. Next week we will also be without the services of Barry Donnachie, but I will tell you about that later when the red mist clears! Montrose had a decidedly shaky start, the new look defence took time to find their feet on a heavy pitch. Berwick's Haynes missed two glaring chances in the first half with the striker failing to convert. Passing was inconsistent and that basically summed up a rather tepid opening period.

The second half was barely 9 minutes old and Berwick opened the scoring. On the 54 minute mark Danny Swanson drove a cross in for Kevin Haynes and this time at his third attempt the big striker did not miss as he headed in. Having struggled to score in January things were not looking good. Six minutes later and we were level through a well worked move involving McManus as he slotted the ball through for Gary Middleton to finish. The goal gave Montrose the incentive that they needed as they enjoyed a good period of pressure forcing corner after corner. A string of chances went a-begging, due to a mixture of inexperience and the inability to finish. It will all come good in one match, wait and see. Despite the pressure Berwick scored and fortune shone for once as goalkeeper Sandy Wood was judged to have been fouled from the corner. A let off, but we deserved it. The game raged from end to end with Wood making some timely saves, Berwick giving away a series of fouls and then there was the sending off, of Barry Donnachie or Bonnachie (the BBC can never get it quite right). Referees never get it quite right either and seem to end up punishing the innocent party due to their own lack of consistency. With only two substitutes available 'A' replaced Russell in 61 minutes and 'B' got 8 minutes for Henslee although the match did go on well past stoppage time. I now look forward to next weeks match to see for myself for the first time, the new charges.

Highlights – Remarkable spirit in taking a point from this match especially when we were one down. A lesson was also learned today as the manager has always said that if we are able to defend then there is opportunity to score. How right his approach has been. Today was a tough match against a big and strong physical team but we were able to hold our own by all accounts. It is good to see Stuart Ferguson back doing a full ninety minutes and also the return of Greg Henslee to the side. Gary Middleton scored his first goal for the club in three starts since stepping up from the Juniors. I hope this is the first of many for the striker as he settles into the team. Stephen Fraser played in the unaccustomed position of left back and deserves a mention as he put in a good shift. That red card! True to form Barry gave the referee his best civil engineering of the English language after receiving a shocking two footed tackle which went unpunished. It must have been something he said or the referee misinterpreted! Guaranteed suspension next week reduces the number of defenders available yet again and will give Wolecki selection problems. One part of me thinks that I will be glad when this season is over but the other part says that we must use this time wisely and build for tomorrow a team that is capable of performing consistently and getting results.

Number one in the League played third at Central Park and the spoils were shared one a piece in a 1-1 draw. Stenhousemuir led through a McBride penalty before Buchanan equalised just before half-time. Keen on a fourth place spot, Arbroath travelled to Hampden looking to take the points in an effort to gain ground on Queen's. On this occasion however both teams played out a 0-0 draw that was riddled with poor refereeing decisions. Arbroath's striker Ally Brazil suffered a broken leg, in a 50-50 challenge. An under strength Elgin team let rip by scoring 5, giving Brian Irvine the home managerial win he wished for. In an 8 goal thriller the Elgin support at last had something to cheer as they demolished East Fife in a second half goal flurry. East Stirling added to their points tally at the expense of Albion Rovers with Ure scoring early on in a 1-0 home win.

Rumours of a take-over hit the street, 1990 saw Aberdeen business man, owner of Bon Accord Glass, Bryan Keith take over at the Club. This time the interested party quoted is Kenny Black who recently failed in his bid at Elgin. Black's plans at Borough Briggs were scuppered at the last minute as he sought to invest in the club, by taking youth development facilities to a new level.

It was previously said that the club had someone who knew the Grampian area well concerning young players. There is no doubting Black's experience in running the skill seekers programme and it may just be the injection of cash that is required for Montrose to kick-start their development programme in return for a stake in the club. Interesting times!

Today's '*Courier*' reported that Eddie Wolecki was pleased at taking a point at Shielfield. Wolecki stated that with eight players unavailable he had asked the team to show some resilience as he was not looking for excuses. He was particularly encouraged by the character and determination shown by all, after the team were reduced to ten men, as the team were able to hold their own. There is a sense of clam in the dressing room now that the transfer window is closed, players can settle down and get back to concentrating on playing as the squad is settled for the remainder of the season. Wolecki hopes that trialists Calum Rae and Phillip Reid from Elgin will become part of the Montrose youth set-up. The manager is also waiting for international clearance for a Frenchman who has been training with the Links Park squad. Gael Corre a student studying at Dundee University is the person in question that he hopes to sign. Striker Gael scored a hat-trick in the bounce match against Brechin Vics. This could be the signing that could improve Barry's 'French'!

Jim Moffat takes the score to six after being dismissed in the aftermath of East Fife's defeat at Elgin. Barely a week after the transfer window closes and the manager who persuaded you to sign is gone. I feel sorry for the likes of Elliot Smith, Paul Doyle and Kerr Dodds who signed for the club after leaving Montrose. Greg Shaw takes interim charge while the post is advertised.

'*Sailing*', a Rod Stewart hit, but for me the sight of the road and rail bridges in the Forth was to be a welcome view as it meant that I was home except for the drive up to Montrose from Rosyth, after a horrendous journey in a force 12 gale. A change of transport for my homeward journey and twenty hours after leaving Breda I am back in Scotland and as green as a Celtic supporter's football top due to conditions. No matter where you end up you can have a few horrendous journeys as you travel back and forth to wherever next. For instance sitting at airports waiting and waiting and waiting, it's no fun. People think it must be great but you can go from meeting to meeting, airport to airport and see nothing of the country you are in.

On one Christmas break travelling home from Boston and returning in the New Year, everything that could possibly happen, happened, from booking in at the airport to interstate chaos on my return.

With 9/11, paranoia had set in. It seemed a straight forward procedure when booking in at Logan Airport, tickets were issued to Heathrow and for my onward journey to Aberdeen, baggage had been tagged, but before I could say "You have a nice day!" I was escorted to a side room. Passport and visa's were examined, holdalls were opened, emptied and swab tested for explosives. They found nothing, did not have the courtesy to reinstate my belongings to the bag and left the room saying to take my bag back to the airline for re-tagging when I was ready. No sooner had I done this and I was approached and stopped by the National Guard for 'twenty questions'. It was clearly not my day, but the same could be said about the next day and the day after that, in an epic forty-nine hour journey, which ended in my return to Aberdeen with no luggage and none of the Christmas presents I had bought. Nobody knew where it was, but I was assured that it would be delivered to my home as soon as they found it! My return to Boston was no better. After three false starts to catch red-eye flights out of Aberdeen, I finally embarrassed the airline into transferring me onto Dutch Airlines on the fourth day. There is no excuse for poor service and that is what you get-No excuse!

Since this instance I have declined to travel with this "Best of British" airline and it is only recently, due to circumstances, that I had no option but to travel with them. Once again they surpassed themselves with delays and catering problems, but there was no reduction in fare price for this level of service.

I remember one pit-stop in Kiev to de-ice the wings of the plane and the KGB hospitality that we received as they insisted that we vacate while this was done. Freezing conditions, no coats or explanation what was happening as we were 'held hostage' on a bus on the runway until the job was done.

Travelling by ferry and rough crossings can be an experience as sea conditions can change dramatically. One trip from Swansea to Cork was touch and go, severe weather warnings were not heeded which resulted in the ship sheltering for hours off the Irish coast unable to go anywhere. Another trip saw the cancellation of all fast ferries, so I was on the slow boat to China (Cairnryan to Larne). The journey, a lot longer than normal was bad enough, but on arrival the weather was too bad to dock for disembarkation and returning to Larne was the favoured option.

Today's trip was hit by bad weather; let's hope Saturday's match is on, and that it beats the weather for us, to take all 3 points. The gong for manager of the month goes to Billy Stark the Queen's Park manager and hopefully with the jinx that follows. Queen's are one of the most consistent teams in the league having lost only one match in the last four months.

However Wolecki is confident as he states that we are improving technically, physically and psychologically. In the short term we have taken some knocks, but it will lead to longer term benefits. The manager highlights retention of the ball, as without it you cannot exploit the weaknesses of the opposition. Since Wolecki has taken charge there have been many changes and this week saw a first for the manager as he fielded an eleven a side practice match during a training session. That is the benefit of local based players!

Fotheringham returns from a three match ban, MacLeod is free from the birthing duties of an expectant father, Brash has recovered from injury and Watson from tonsillitis. Kerrigan has undergone training this week but is not one hundred percent and Webster having undergone an operation for a groin problem has only started light training. Things are improving but Donnachie will be missing as he starts the first of a three match ban.

Feb 11th. QUEEN'S PARK, Home - report and teams.
Another good point today from a no score draw against a side technically the best in the league. Queen's play football, a quick passing game to build their attacks, where as Stenny have the physical presence that wins games. Today it was like a who's who as I stood on the 'knoll' trying to identify the few recognisable faces. We have a lack of defenders and no more than today as the Montrose line up confirmed. The announcer proceeded to educate the uninitiated who was who! Montrose fielded Wood in goal, appropriately Euan Hall, daytime apprentice for Barry Donnachie, filled the right full back position for his suspended boss. Hay, Ferguson and Fraser made up the back four with all the full back places filled by midfielders. The midfield saw Fotheringham returning from suspension along side Davidson, McManus and Henslee. Middleton played up front with MacLeod wide left. The substitute's bench looked a bit better this week, and reflected less of the walking wounded. Hankinson, Brash, Russell and Watson were fit to make a start and the injured Kerrigan took the final spot to make up the numbers.

The match kicked-off and it was honours even for the opening 10 minutes before Queen's surging runs started to take effect. In 13 minutes the back four were caught on the back foot and Ferry shot over with Wood to beat. It was then the turn of Quinn to shoot over from the edge of the box after a good one-two set the player up. In between times Davidson of Montrose drove low and hard on target but keeper Crawford gathered. In 36 minutes Hall played a great ball in from the right but the pace of the ball beat Middleton and Crawford was there for the pick-up. Queen's then created another couple of chances but woeful finishing saw them fail to open their account.

Montrose made a change at half-time with Brash taking the place of McManus. The second period saw Montrose back on the ropes at times as they withstood the storm. Respite only came when Fraser moved up the left to knock a ball across Crawford's goal but there were no takers to stick Montrose one in front. 55 minutes and captain Stuart Ferguson had to go off after picking up a groin strain. Russell took his place playing on the left side of midfield and the defence reshuffled with Fraser playing alongside Hay and Brash taking over at left back.

A long range Davidson effort on the hour had Crawford guarding his right-hand post as the ball flashed wide. Queen's freshened things up by making a double substitution within minutes and Fotheringham also made way for Watson. With five minutes to go Russell's name went into the referee's book after tussling with Trouten. It was never a dirty game as play flowed from end to end with very few stoppages, those only usually for an offside decision. In the final minutes Montrose required a goal-line clearance from Brash to keep their goal intact as the defender headed clear.

Highlights – You can see a bit of belief, as we defended well and at the same time led a charmed life. The main thing is that we never gave up as we chased everything, even lost causes. It was a make shift side, especially in defence. Montrose have suffered more than their fair share of bad luck this season but have ground out with the aid of hard work a result of sorts. Today was no different. Stephen Fraser started at left back for a second week, but moved inside to the centre of defence after Stuart Ferguson had to be replaced. Fraser adapted well to both positions and would receive my vote for man of the match as he put in an outstanding solid performance. Davidson and Hay made crucial tackles when it mattered and Wood produced vital saves when under pressure. Wolecki must be happy with a point from the match and the effort as players kept focused on the task to the end.

This week first played second with Paul Murphy's second half strike separating the teams at the final whistle with Stenhousemuir taking all three points. After a 1-0 half-time score line Rovers not only gave up their lead but fell to a hat-trick of goals from the Cowden midfield masters. A late winner for Elgin saw neighbours Arbroath fail to capitalise on home advantage. Finally, manager less East Fife found their home tie against East Stirling to be a coupon buster as they allowed the 'Shire to record an unaccustomed away victory. Second half goals from Dymock and Tyrell secured the points as Pelosi could only reply from the spot before being subjected to a red card. Today's win for the 'Shire puts them within four points of Montrose which is too close for comfort. Today's result sees Montrose move from ninth to eighth position over Albion Rovers, setting up a must win scenario next week at Links Park as we take on the Coatbridge outfit.

Lochee defender Chris Tawse has walked out on the Dundee Junior club. Having signed a pre-contract agreement the player is dismayed that his club rejected approaches from Montrose during the transfer window. Tawse will be a free agent come June having been released from his contract.

If you can't beat them, join them! I don't know if I am wise but I have decided to take a bicycle back with me for the summer. Yes I know what I had previously said, but it is the way to travel and the way of life in the Netherlands as it cuts down on parking costs or as someone once told me at a meeting, the Dutch only <u>think</u> they are mean but the Scot's <u>are</u>. 'Dutchified'- all I need now is the bright orange polo shirt and pink trousers.

After the dust had settled, Wolecki reflected that all that was missing was a telling final ball into the box. It was no surprise to the manager that the match ended goalless, as he stated that "We have frustrated teams in our recent run of difficult fixtures". With the team only being together for a couple of weeks, they are already a hard side to break down. The fact that opposing managers find us frustrating tells you that the manager is on the right track. Wolecki states that now we have to work on the cutting edge, attacking play and being able to become a hard side to resist as an attacking side too.

It always amazes me, when you are out for a meal and your wife asks for the bill. Why then, does the waiter place the bill in front of you? The waiter must have seen the expression on my face as I didn't make a move. Suddenly he informed me 'pants pay for skirts', "Well they did in my day" he stated. Embarrassed, I let the moth out my wallet for air. It just proves that the Dutch can get blood out of a stone!

It's an encouraging result from this weeks bounce match against Forfar as Montrose record a 3-0 win. A Russell double and a McManus strike was all that was required.

Just when you think that the transfer window is closed and that the squad is fixed till the season end, Montrose sign four and release one. All four signings come from Elgin City's released skill seekers. First to sign was striker Philip Reid who had already appeared as a trialist against Berwick. Also appearing against Berwick was sixteen year-old Calum Rae and he too has signed for the club. Wolecki completes the quartet by signing Darryn Kelly and Jamie Ralph, two young central defenders as he builds for the longer term. The four youngsters are local based and were pushing for places in the Elgin first team and will not only play a part in the Montrose youth set-up but will be important for Montrose teams of the future. Wolecki confirms his belief in the signing of these youngsters by stating that one, possibly two will be part of his plans for tomorrow's clash against Albion Rovers and that they will be included in the team selection. Doubts for the match are defender Stuart Ferguson who has a groin strain and Gary Middleton who has been unable to train this week. One player who will not feature is Kevin Don as after signing from Scone Amateurs he has been released, having taken up a new job which will curtail training and playing opportunities.

It used to be Dial M for Murder but for the '*Record*' it was Montrose! The west coast press obviously had a slow news day or possibly ran out of things to print about Rangers and Celtic. No matter what, print a story they did as 'Cash strapped Montrose players are being forced to spend a chunk of their wages calling a premium rate telephone line to find out their training schedule'. Quotes of being charged 50p a minute from a mobile and the loss of a third of their basic wage is just bizarre! Yes, Eddie Wolecki implemented this system but not at peak rates. Players have to take responsibility for their own time keeping and it also gives the manager a check, as calls will be logged. It's called progress. I remember Alex Ferguson tracking his players on the eve of a match checking that they were tucked-up in bed at a reasonable hour before playing the next day. It's all about discipline. A phone line is not a bad thing, but for one player it has obviously stunted his Friday night dance routine at the 'Locarno' Ballroom!

Saturday and I am confident of some kind of result from today's game. No time to sit in 'Surf and Talk' as I decide to do some shopping in Dordrecht. After a short train journey I find myself lost, standing outside the train station and a busy road intersection. To cross here you would have to have eyes in the back of your head. My thoughts must have been the same as the local council as at the road edge I was met with a set of eyes and an arrow pointing in the direction that you would be knocked down from. Nice!

It's not everyday that you are twenty-one and it is a long time ago for me, but the object of the day was to get a birthday present for son number two, something different, something unusual, but what? I thought what would you get a Dutchman? Fortunately for me one of the first shops had what I was looking for, a unicycle!

So far, so good. I had just gone to spend a penny and disaster. My mobile croaked the information that I had received a text message. You wouldn't believe it; we have just kicked off, hardly time to sit on a stand-side seat, message reads' 0 – 2 Rovers'. In disbelief I text back, wondering if

Gareth was winding me up, only to receive the words in return, '2 free headers'! What a bad start, but ever hopeful I listened intently, hopeful of another message, hopeful of good news. '1-2, MacLeod, a screamer', another message on 40 minutes. It is times like this you wish you were there. Two goals in the second half, can we do it! 45 minutes can be long, especially when you are waiting for a text. I had actually given up, I was back in Breda, I was just home, I had just put BBC final score on, Montrose 2, Albion Rovers 2, and the first vide-printer text revealed Davidson had equalised in 85 minutes. A minute later the next text was irrelevant as it only confirmed the final score. Another point, a third consecutive draw, and another match undefeated.

Feb 18th. ALBION ROVERS, Home - report and teams
The manager had indicated changes in the line-up for today's match, as he had said, one possibly two youngsters would make their full debuts. Wolecki brought in Darryn Kelly to replace Stuart Ferguson in the back four as Wood retained his place in goal. The defence lined-up Hall, Hay, Kelly and Fraser with a midfield of Russell, Davidson, Fotheringham and Henslee. Phillip Reid was blooded upfront and took his place alongside Ian MacLeod in the strike force. Hankinson, Brash, Kerrigan, Watson and McManus looked for a start from the bench. The match kicked-off and in 2 minutes Montrose conceded a free-kick as Albion Rovers looked the hungrier side. Doyle's resultant kick saw Chisholm rise to freely head home past a stranded Wood. With 4 minutes on the clock, Montrose looked dead and buried. A long kick-out from keeper McGlynn found Donachy on the edge of the box, the striker was given time to control the ball and to drill home. Caught cold on two occasions and an uphill struggle then proceeded to take place as Montrose tried to redeem themselves. Montrose fought back but it took till the 37th minute. A telling pass from Fotheringham found McLeod on the left with the striker volleying an unstoppable shot past keeper McGlynn to pull one goal back. The goal gave some hope for the second half.

Philip Reid was replaced during the interval after a tough 45 minutes with Kris Brash taking his place for the second period. Chisholm of Rovers wasted a great chance in 49 minutes to clinch the match as he put his shot well over the bar. Wolecki then replaced Fotheringham with Watson before pulling young debutant Kelly for Kerrigan as he joined the front-line in a final push. The longer the second half went on the more Montrose had come into the game, putting pressure on the Rovers goal with McGlynn making several saves. Pressure finally paid off when Hugh Davidson met a Calum Watson lay-off at the edge of the box to level the match. Lennon then joined Bonnar in the referee's book for time wasting as Rovers held on. Controversy however followed as birthday boy Watson scored at the death, but he was adjudged by the referee to have bundled the keeper over the goal-line when it looked as if McGlynn had knocked the ball into his own net. The innocent Watson earned a booking for his trouble.

In the end a draw was a fair result from a heartening display by Montrose, of "Never, say Die" football.

Highlights - After a disastrous start, Eddie Wolecki was a relieved boss to see his side fight-back to earn a point. In his post match view he stated that the team are competitive and that he was glad that we had salvaged something from the match. On the Watson incident Wolecki was quoted as saying "I didn't think it was a foul on the goalkeeper, but to be honest if we had won that game it would have been theft." The manager praised the efforts of the team and was also happy with youngsters Kelly and Reid, who went off after a first half knock.

Sunday's newspaper up 40 cents, it's a lot for a Scotsman- not the newspaper, but the national. If you want to know what's going on there's a price to pay for the little limited information that Scottish football receives from the international printed rags. It's not that I grudge the price increase- well it is- it is just that there is more information on the side of a Scottish Bluebell matchbox.

The gap closes at the top of the League as Stenny drop all three points to Elgin who eye fourth spot. Elgin who won 2-1 are now within three points of fourth place Queen's Park who were soundly beaten after being hit for six with no reply by Cowdenbeath. A shock result as Queen's are a tight-knit side who never give away many goals far less six. Berwick had a narrow 1-0 victory against the Shire and Arbroath took the points as East Fife suffered another 2-1 defeat on consecutive Saturdays.

A bit of news on the youth development front. Montrose now has an Under 17 youth side playing in the Aberdeenshire league on a Saturday. Undefeated, having played two matches, it is yet another piece to Wolecki's jig-saw puzzle with February still not at an end. Attitudes are changing amongst fans with positive vibes from the support. Impressed by the commitment of the team too, fans now recognise that constant encouragement by the players of each other builds a sustained pressure. Just think what the same encouragement by supporters would build! Other fan comments reflect a Montrose side which would not give up, fought to the end and were justly rewarded with a point. There was a sense of pride in what he had written and a pride in the management and players. Now that *is* encouraging!

Albion Rovers have scrapped their youth development set-up. The board and directors have decided to call it a day, as losses are no longer sustainable. Despite funding from the Scottish Executive and SFA, there has still been a financial shortfall for the past few years. It's difficult; to develop you have to spend money and when you spend money there is no guarantee of a return. As stated before we <u>will</u> need financial support for our youth development.

East Fife have confirmed that that they are unlikely to appoint a manager before Saturday's match against Montrose. Numerous names have been touted by the press, including ex-Montrose manager Henry Hall, for the managerial job, but Dave Baikie must be favourite to fill the vacant spot.

Who needs the transfer window as Montrose finally sign up French striker and student Gael Corre? A good bit of business by Wolecki as Corre has played at a high standard having played in the French and Dutch leagues. The manager stated that Gael is technically very good and can play up front and through the middle, out wide and in midfield. Having excelled in bounce matches Wolecki may find a place on the bench for the twenty-five year-old striker who could make his debut at Bayview. Eddie has also offered Stephen Fraser an extension to his contract having signed the player for a further two-year commitment. Wolecki stated that Stephen had worked hard in training and deserves a new contract as he is obviously committed to the club.

A new 'Blog', *MONTROSE DYNAMO* gives support for the Wolecki revolution, long live comrade Eddie! Out of the BLUE, I can't explain but a new blog takes the lime-light and a new life-line for an ex-pat!

It begins, 'Nine weeks after the revolution began, it's been a '*White Knuckle Ride'*, a player transfusion and a great leap forward has taken place.' As the Blog say's – 'So on paper, we're still struggling, and in the bottom three of an utterly atrocious league. But those who aren't faint hearted and can see the massive changes that the club have undergone in just nine weeks, in their totality, can at last begin to see that we are turning the Montrose super-tanker in the right direction!'

At Breda, progress can only be described as being on schedule. We are where we are and that is down to hard work. No, it is down to teamwork!

There is satisfaction in seeing end results to a challenge, but early on it was identified that the only way to get results was to play as a team, after all if one fails we all fail. We set targets to achieve our goals and we achieve our goals by working for each other.

After giving ourselves a difficult task last week with a disastrous start, you can rest assured that the foundations of the defence shook during training this week for their careless actions. In previous weeks the defence has looked solid and has given little away and I would think that they will be forgiven after an encouraging fight-back with the players showing both commitment and an appetite for the game. In this weekend's match against East Fife, the manager is hopeful of including both Kelly and Philip Reid once again. Ferguson and Middleton will also be available for selection and there is an outside chance that Kevin Webster could be on the bench as he makes his return from injury. The manager less Fifers have a large contingent of ex-Montrose players, some of whom may have a point to prove after being released by Wolecki. Recent poor results saw the dismissal of manager Jim Moffat, boycotts and demonstrations to the Board, as supporters showed their displeasure. A new manager is yet to be appointed. If Montrose expend the same effort as last week then an away win could be on the card at Bayview. Kerrigan is out for Saturday after picking up an injury in a bounce match against Dundee earlier in the week.

Freak injuries happen and usually when you least expect them. I remember our project manager ('Ace') returning home, his daughter was getting married and it was a big day for him as he would be leading her down the aisle. Like all men he had been warned to be on his best behaviour. As usual when you return home this or that needs mending, some are small jobs and some are irritating the neighbours. It was the day of the wedding, the dog had been finding a way into the neighbour's garden and the fence had to be fixed before the wedding as the neighbours would be there. It was a simple enough repair as a new plank was all that was required, but first the old piece of timber had to be removed. Ace pulled on the claw hammer, the nail head shattered and blood rained down. Black and blue, nose busted and taped in place, he did give his daughter away that afternoon. Two things I remember, one, he daren't sneeze and two - Not a lot could be said about the wedding pictures!

It's 'CARNAVAL' – a four day celebration in the run up to Lent! A time where adults become kids again. You wouldn't believe the costumes; families dressed as devils and angels, brick walls with trailing plants for head gear and Oompah bands dressed in pink! There are floats that tower above the lamp standards and Royalty dancing in the streets as everyone takes part in the celebrations.

(Is this the way to Amarillo !)

Well almost everyone, as Scotland's victory on the rugby field over England had my Welsh boss saying that it was a good day all round but for me the exception was the MONTROSE SCORE!

Feb 25th. EAST FIFE, Away - report and teams
A 4-0 defeat and an atrocious performance what can you say? Not a lot really but I'm not the manager! Wolecki did not miss the target, it is a team game and the team came in for criticism from the manager. Nothing positive was taken from the match as the game was shaped by two things, an early East Fife goal and a missed Henslee penalty. Places are up for grabs for the derby match next Saturday after this showing. The manager warns that coaching staff and players can expect criticism from the support and finishes by saying "We deserve it!" The starting line-up put Wood in goal, Hall filled in at right back for possibly the last time as Donnachie completes a three match ban. Hay, Ferguson and Fraser completed the defence. Kerrigan was absent in midfield through injury as the places were taken by Davidson, Fotheringham, Henslee and MacLeod. Watson and Middleton were the strikers. In two minutes Wood had to look lively to save from Hampshire. A

few minutes later and East Fife won a free kick. Hampshire's direct shot penetrated the wall to open the scoring in 7 minutes. One down but not out as we are award a soft penalty from referee Boyd as MacLeod is brought down in the box by Lumsden. Penalty misses have been part of our season, Martin at East Stirling, Fotheringham against Arbroath and now Henslee at Bayview. A chance to equalise thrown away! It was one-way traffic as we went in at the break lucky to be one down as both Bradford and Fortune were denied a place on the score sheet.

For Wolecki half-time must have been a relief, a chance to put things right and a time to lift heads. No changes at the break but it did not take long for the manager to introduce debutant Gael Corre, for Fotheringham, in an attempt to instil some fight into the midfield. With 55 minutes gone things went from bad to worse as Gordon netted for the Fifers. Montrose goalkeeper, Wood, fumbled Gordon's low shot into the net to put them two in front. Unlike the week before, it was all over. Hampshire then shot wide before Gordon made it three in 58 minutes. Gordon's shot took a deflection off Ferguson which wrong footed the keeper before landing in the net. Bayview, home of East Fife is truly a bogey ground for Montrose. To make matters worse Joe Savage managed to waltz through the Montrose defence to make it four in 88 minutes to complete the scoring and a drubbing! Our only glimmer of hope in the second period came from Corre as the Frenchman almost gained a consolation goal but Dodds in the East Fife goal blocked his close-range shot. Only Davidson, Fraser and Corre received pass marks, we were second best in every department and must put this display behind us. We must remind ourselves that transition is taking place, there is no magic wand. All I ask is – GIVE THE MANAGER A CHANCE!

4-0 seems to have been the score of the day as Cowdenbeath and Arbroath recorded away victories at Elgin and East Stirling respectively. Stenhousemuir won by the odd goal after Albion Rovers had taken the lead at Coatbridge. Berwick defeated Queen's Park at Hampden 1-0. After Queen's Park's defeat today, fourth place is starting to get very interesting. Tuesdays match at Gayfield could see Arbroath come to within a point of the Spiders if the Red Lichties win.

Pierre to the rescue, a 70 minute strike by van Hoojdonk gives Feyenoord a point at FC Groningen. Out of favour with supporters and a new manager at Breda saw Pierre return to one of his former clubs. He couldn't have been local based!

Feb 28th. BRECHIN – Forfarshire Cup first. round

Montrose had arranged to play neighbours Brechin in the local Forfarshire Cup. The tie had been re-arranged after falling victim to frost in November. Tonight's match was to be played to a finish but is once more postponed, after the North of Scotland was hit with snow! Just when you think everything is past, and Spring is just around the corner the weather turns for the worse.

Tonight we also see the first of the postponed matches rescheduled. These are the matches that tend to change league positions and it is no different tonight. An Arbroath win closes the gap on fourth place; a Cowdenbeath win at East Stirling sees Berwick drop to third place and an Albion Rovers win at Ochilview would mean Montrose dropping to ninth place! Fortunately for us Albion Rovers lost to a McGrillen goal and the remaining two ties fell foul of the weather.

Forecasters got it wrong yet again, unless you were in the realms of the Soviet Union and in particular the city of Moscow (you can't count Tuesday's postponements). Games survived the weather, there was no mass back-log of fixtures and injures lessened. One thing that we did manage to forecast was the increase in suspensions as red cards were plentiful as red mist descended among players as they defended their corner.

Changes all round during the January transfer window and none more than at Montrose. January wasn't a good month for the team; hopes had been raised with a late demolition of East Fife the day December closed. A barren month ensued, goals having deserted the frontrunners. February and a turn of fortunes, three draws and one defeat setting the scene with 4th quarter hopes, kicking off at Gayfield!

Quarter Three

POS		P	W	L	D	F	A	GD	PTS
1	Stenhousemuir	27	19	5	3	57	26	31	60
2	Berwick	26	15	5	6	37	21	16	51
3	Cowdenbeath	25	16	7	2	51	22	29	50
4	Queen's Park	25	11	8	6	34	28	6	39
5	Elgin	26	10	10	6	34	40	-6	36
6	Arbroath	25	10	10	5	41	35	6	35
7	East Fife	27	10	15	2	39	50	-11	32
8	Montrose	27	5	14	8	23	38	-15	23
9	Albion Rovers	26	5	14	7	30	45	-15	22
10	East Stirling	26	5	18	3	24	65	-41	18

– A third quarter ends and with it a 'Winter of Discontent'.

Chapter 7

4th. Quarter (With Spring in Step)

With a spring in our step, Quarter 4 finds us on the last part of a journey after a disastrous end to February at New Bayview, having taken three points from the previous three matches.

At last a chance to salvage some pride from a season which has taken us from the highs of Henry putting together a potential championship winning squad, to thinking a derby win was the turning point. Then there was the October revival, to the lows of a poor season start, a September of inconsistency and finally November's managerial departure. December's Christmas present appointment had the rollercoaster picking up speed in January, out with the old and in with the new, in a turbulent month. February has seen the dust settle, a new look side and a management team working hard to achieve success as they go through a learning curve. It must be remembered that Wolecki and co. have started from square one. He is trying to build a team that <u>all</u> Montrose supporters can be proud off. Wolecki has the right idea in building from a grass roots nursery of local talent (ideally 90mins from Links Park), developing the youngsters to play at senior level. Fans however will have to remember that like rearing a beast; it will eventually be sold at market to provide funds for further investment in young calves to be fattened up.

Wolecki is a young manager, given a chance he will succeed. He cannot be judged on results just yet as he needs the rest of the season to set the standard of consistency in play that is required for the team to hold their own against any opponent. The season is not yet ended, not even for Montrose, but I am looking forward to the future and seeing how Eddie handles pre-season, the type of competitive fixture that he organises, to the regime of training sessions to sharpen reflexes. I am glad that the fans have finally accepted that there is only one way forward and that is to give team and manager their support by getting behind them!

Working away from home at times has its advantages, but I know that I don't really mean that, as win or lose you want to be there, see for yourself, and to go through the pain! As one message board poster puts it – "We can all play our part by turning out as often as we can at Links Park and by cheering them on. The more people who turn up at the gate, the more money is made available to invest in players. Negativity leads nowhere – Let's do our bit to break this vicious cycle once and for all!"

Beware the Ides of March!

It's not over until the "Fat Lady" sings! Stenhousemuir may be ten points in front of 3rd placed Cowdenbeath, but the Fife side have two matches in hand. It can be said Stenny have the points in the bag but if the Miners do win then the league title is once again open and up for grabs. Berwick could also be in the frame. Having surrendered top spot in a poor second quarter, the Borderers have fought back and sit in second place some nine points adrift. They have a match in hand and a win could close the gap. Berwick also have home advantage against their counterparts in this final quarter. An "April Fool's Day" clash between Stenhousemuir and Cowdenbeath followed by a Berwick- Stenny match a week later could decide the fate of the league. However all is not lost as the remaining two sides will take second and third spot play-off places and may live to fight another day!

Queen's Park, Elgin and Arbroath all eye the last play-off position. Queen's have a difficult run in as their remaining three matches are against the top three front runners. Sad to say Arbroath are the team to watch!

We kick-off our quest at Gayfield and a derby grudge match against neighbours Arbroath. Spoils so far this season are with the Red Lichties but there is a chance to level and preserve our honour. Too much can be expected from these matches, there are never a lot of goals as neither side gives much away. The remaining fixtures may seem meaningless but that is not the case on two accounts. Although a play-off place is out of the question, we can have a say in who takes the final places and a final league position is important as we build confidence for next season.

Mar 4th.	Arbroath	Away
Mar 11th.	East Stirling	Home
Mar 18th.	Cowdenbeath	Home
Mar 25th.	Stenhousemuir	Away
Apr 1st.	Berwick	Home
Apr 8th.	Queens Park	Away
Apr 15th.	Elgin	Home
Apr 22nd.	Albion Rovers	Away
Apr 29th.	East Fife	Home

The team is now on the right track despite the Fife defeat, local based and an expectation of hard honest graft. Fans and supporters alike are now reconciled, on-side and giving their full support realising that the future will take time to develop in the long term. This is a big step for the club and something that needs to be built on in the future. It is going to take substantial financial backing for a youth development system to be up and running, it is also a long term proposition, not just a one day wonder. The fans can play a part, but first, please let's not get hung-up on one game, let Gayfield pass!

Emergency lighting - The lights are back on after a Black-out at Elgin as the P&J headlines 'Skill seekers get sorted out'. The demise of Elgin City's skill seekers programme has benefited several clubs, one of which has been Montrose having signed four of the youths or is it five? Kenny Black has shown a sense of loyalty to the young players having been responsible for taking them to Elgin. He has made a point of seeing that their futures are secure as some would go part-time and would require day jobs. Reid, Rae, Kelly and Ralph, all signed for Montrose. Kyle McKendrick? News to me. The plan unfolds as two former Elgin youth coaches, Bob Scott and John Wood have also joined the coaching set-up at Links Park. They both currently look after the new under-nineteen youth team and their workload will increase next season when an under-seventeen side will be in place. Both teams will compete in the national leagues run by the Scottish League.

"If players can't motivate themselves for a derby match such as the one against Arbroath, they shouldn't be playing for us at all." A parting shot from the manager after last weeks dispirited performance. Montrose now have to regroup for Saturday's match against Arbroath, but will it beat the weather?

Mar 4th. ARBROATH, Away - report and teams
A severe overnight frost, more snow, A90 and A92 coast road are closed, there is no way north and all Division Three games are wiped out!

Who was it that said the weather forecasters got it wrong!

A call from home confirms this, possibly I spoke too soon, casting doubt over the Met Office forecast or was it Breda's winter sun that deluded me. After all, it is Spring! There must also be doubts whether rescheduled matches for Tuesday will be played as the forecast for the rest of the weekend is not good. I am scheduled to be home this coming weekend; I just hope Links Park will be playable as it may be my last chance to see the team play this term.

The derby match with closest friends and neighbours Arbroath has been re-scheduled by the Scottish League, for Tuesday, March 21st.

It's Tuesday, there is a bit of a thaw which gives tonight's matches a 50% chance of being on. True to form two games survive the weather and matches at Cowdenbeath and the Shire are called off after the referee's inspection. Berwick's loss was Queen's Parks gain as they went down 2 – 1 at home. Arbroath hard on the heels of Queen's Park for fourth place took the points at Coatbridge with a 2 – 0 win. Tonight's results set up an interesting few fixtures on Saturday. Berwick take on Cowdenbeath and a win for the Fifers would enhance their chances of catching League leaders Stenhousemuir. Queen's could put paid to Elgin's hopes of a fourth place and set up a crucial game at Gayfield this coming Tuesday to take out Arbroath from the fourth place equation. It's all in the melting pot!

After a redundant Saturday, Montrose take on the Shire at home, honours are even, a draw earlier in the season and each team having won one game apiece since puts pride at stake for the final match. Wolecki, not one for a free Saturday to kick his heels beat the weather by organising fitness level tests for all the players at Abertay University so that individual development plans could be put in place. Training Monday and a bounce game at Kirriemuir on Wednesday, the manager has tried his best to regain lost ground after the Fife debacle as confidence building and three points is top of his agenda. The manager still has injury problems to deal with, Kerrigan and Webster are still on the road to recovery and Andy Reid has yet to have his operation but is continuing to train to retain fitness. Martyn Fotheringham will also be missing as he has picked up a groin strain and will sit the match out.

Mar 11th. EAST STIRLING, Home - report and teams
It was like being at the "Wheel Tappers and Shunters Club" with the MC reading out the teams over the PA, the microphone crackling with the intermittent team selection. Donnachie, Kelly and Henslee were at least playing and I did catch the names of substitutes Philip Reid and keeper Hankinson finalising the cabaret. Changes to the line-up had been made from New Bayview, Wood held onto the goalkeeping position, Donnachie returned to his duties after suspension alongside Kelly, Ferguson and Fraser. Russell, Davidson, Henslee and Brash filled the midfield berths with Middleton and Watson leading the front-line. Substitutes, Corre, Hall, and Macleod made up the bench along with the double-act of Hankinson and Reid.

In an impressive opening twenty minutes, Montrose played a good passing game, were first to every ball and were in total control. Henslee who had been a hat-trick hero in the previous meeting at Links Park was a constant threat from the kick-off and almost opened his account in 10 minutes. A Russell free kick found Henslee, his header bringing out the best in keeper Jackson. Four minutes later it was Henslee again firing in a ball from the left, this time keeper Jackson let it slip into the net as Middleton distracted the keeper. Montrose kept up the pressure and soon made it two with Henslee and Middleton combining once again to stretch their lead. A ball floated in from the left from Henslee was headed in at the back post by Gary Middleton with 19 minutes on the clock. East Stirling's first effort came with almost half an hour of the game gone, Wood holding a Thywissen header comfortably. Jackson then saved from a Russell free-kick as Montrose piled on the pressure looking to kill the match. They were almost rewarded in 38 minutes; Henslee again was the provider for Brash who crashed his shot against the post with Jackson beaten. Just before half-time Middleton was unlucky not to add to his tally when a through ball from Donnachie was taken by the striker on the turn, but he shot just wide.

The second period started with an improved East Stirling coming more into the game. Montrose had lost tempo allowing the Shire to move forward more but they were limited to shooting from a distance. With twenty minutes left Montrose regained control, Fraser set-up Watson who shot wide, Jackson then had to look lively, collecting at the feet of the striker. Wolecki started to freshen things up by introducing Philip Reid for Watson followed by MacLeod for Russell. In a final substitution Gael Corre made his home debut, replacing Brash. Finishing on top Montrose came close once again as Jackson fumbled a MacLeod shot.

Highlights – A comfortable win against a poor side but Montrose did show spirit and signs that a passing game was starting to take shape. Fraser, Davidson, Henslee and Middleton all looked sharp as training regimes are obviously increasing fitness levels. The development of strength and depth of the squad, especially upfront (despite the loss of target man Kevin Don) where there are now options (players who can double up from midfield) and permutations that reflect the variety and versatility of formations that the squad can now adapt to before and during a match. Wolecki must be pleased with the way things are developing, both on and off the park. There is still a long way to go and the summer may see a few strategic signings by the manager as he seeks the right balance of professionalism. Meanwhile next Saturdays match against Cowdenbeath will be yet another test of character!

A first half goal was enough for Berwick to regained favour with their support as they took the points at home to Cowdenbeath. Arbroath secured a point in a drab no-score encounter at Ochilview and Queen's Park snatched a last minute point from Elgin who had excelled in their performance at Hampden. A single East Fife goal recorded a home win at the expense of Albion Rovers.

Another manager bites the dust as the "full monty" is achieved in Angus. Brechin manager Ian Campbell fell on the sword after Saturdays 5-1 defeat to Clyde and was relieved of his duties by the Glebe Park Board. Messrs. Hall, Cairney and Fairley have all vacated managerial positions at the other Angus clubs in the past few months. Campbell's release finalises the quartet.

Two midweek games survived the weekend weather. Neighbours Arbroath drew 1-1 with Queen's Park. Both teams may rue the day over missed penalties which could have a bearing on the final say for fourth place. In the other match Elgin despite scoring first were eventually beaten at home 3-1 by Berwick. Cowdenbeath's game at East Stirling was postponed for a third time.

We face the high flying Miners of Cowdenbeath on Saturday as they seek to record a quartet of wins over the wounded. Markus Paatelainen wounded in the battle of Elgin weeks ago will be out for the remainder of the season having received emergency surgery caused by an injury sustained in the match. The talented Paatelainen was saved from missing out on a promising career with the Miners by the expertise of Edinburgh doctors as he underwent a series of operations on his injured leg, preventing amputation after a blood-clot had developed. Boss and elder brother meantime has signed former Partick Thistle striker Armand One to fill the void left by Markus. Short-term signing Mikko Paatelainen returned to Finland this week having played his last game for the club at Berwick. It may look as if Cowdenbeath will be under-strength for today's match, but that is not the case as they have possibly one of the best youth development set-ups in the lower leagues that they can call on!

Manager Wolecki meantime states "We're getting there" as he sees last weeks win giving a bit more confidence to the players as they go through a transition period. In training emphasis is on developing a style of play rather than stopping opponents. Wolecki holds no fears in facing Paatelainen's men as the pressure is on the Miners as they start to face a back-log of fixtures.

It's Friday and tonight's televised match is NAC Breda as they play Vitesse. Within minutes of the match starting, Breda's woes continue. The defence is caught cold by a simple ball in from the right and it was a matter of who was going to score! One down but not out as the goal proved a rude awakening for Breda as they chased and harried every ball. Their persistence finally paid off when Leonardo won the break of the ball in successive tackles taking him through on goal to shoot home for the equaliser. The goal turned the match. NAC dominated and looked a changed side but could not add to their tally before the interval as they squandered chance after chance.

Leonardo scored his and Breda's second goal straight from the kick-off, relief engulfed the stadium as fans had their sights on three much needed points to save the blushes of relegation play-offs. Like a lot of stories there was no fairytale ending, even with Vitesse reduced to ten men, disaster then struck. We are in injury time, seconds are left in the match and Vitesse are awarded a free-kick. With all hands to the deck a brilliant back-header from the Vitesse goalkeeper was enough for it to be bundled over the line for the equaliser. Tonight, poor making lost the game for Breda, it emphasises that you can't afford to give away free gifts, a lesson for all teams. The future for NAC Breda looks bleak as they face a tough run-in to the end of the season with thoughts of relegation play-offs now firmly in fans minds.

I've said it before, "Why me"! On taking a train to Eindhoven I was asked yet again for directions. The platform was crowded but in the distance I could see a man making his way though the crowd, there was only one target and that was me. But how could a blind man pick me out? Before I was developing a complex, now I definitely have one!

Mar 18th. COWDENBEATH, Home - report and teams
Manager Wolecki made two changes to the starting eleven that beat East Stirling. Graham Hay replaced young Darryn Kelly in defence and Iain MacLeod took the place of Watson who was on the substitutes bench. Both Kevin Webster and Fotheringham returned from injury finding a place among the subs.

Two late first half goals killed any chance of a Montrose revival. In an evenly fought first period Montrose matched their counter parts until the 40 minute mark. A Guy corner caused panic within the Montrose defence, Cowden's Buchannan headed against the bar and Innes Ritchie prodded the ball home. Montrose hit back through Middleton with the striker crashing his shot of goalkeepers Hay's post. In injury time, Ritchie put Cowdenbeath two in front with a close-range volley to stun a Montrose defence who were denied an offside decision. Other than a few minutes of madness Montrose played well enough but had given themselves an impossible second half task.

The second period started with heads firmly down, passes going astray and no headway whatsoever made in a uphill struggle. It didn't take Wolecki long to introduce Webster and Corre in a double substitution for Russell and Brash. Before the subs could settle Cowdenbeath went further ahead after Buchannan had his shot saved by Wood, but was able to net the follow-up. In the last 20 minutes Montrose improved, creating a few chances but it a little too late to save this match. Ferguson, Fraser and Middleton were booked by the referee for their day's work which rounded off a day best forgotten.

Highlights - Donnachie gained pass marks in defence, Henslee worked away and Middleton lacked support. Substitute Gael Corre for a second week showed some good touches and fine passing once introduced to the fray.

In his post match comments Eddie Wolecki stated "The five minutes before half-time virtually killed us off." Cowdenbeath had pace, organisation, power and strength. It is going to take time to put together a team with these qualities. The manager states that results have been up and down, a reflection of what is happening behind the scenes with so many changes taking place-short-term pain hopefully for long time gain. Not a lot more could be said but the manager now has the task of lifting team confidence for Tuesday's derby.

Interesting times as the gap at the top is closed to within one point. Stenhousemuir dropped three points this afternoon to East Fife with the Fifers running out 2-1 winners. Berwick took advantage by collecting all three points at Arbroath with a 2-0 win to put the pressure on Stenny and now sit within one point of top place. Queen's Park's fourth place offensive suffered a set back dropping two points at the Shire in a scoreless draw. Elgin secured the points at Cliftonhill wining 2-1.

It's not over yet as Tuesday is derby night!

More rescheduled matches and with it the gap could be closed for some teams.

> Cowden v East Fife
> Arbroath v Montrose
> Albion Rovers v Queen's Park
> East Stirling v Stenhousemuir

Its official- Spring is here, it's the start of Keukenhof (Bulbfields Festival) and time to reflect after Saturdays defeat. By all accounts we played alright in parts of the game but were in a generous mood in handing two goals to the Miners on a plate. We cannot afford to show that type of hospitality tonight as we travel to Gayfield. A 'Rock Steady' performance is required with 'Security' the key to sneak a win over our neighbours. How would you describe tonight's derby? It could be described as a "blood and guts" affair, a match that is all about commitment and not much football as it is played at one hundred miles per hour. In three matches to date the two sides have notched up nineteen bookings and two ordering offs. You can see from the figures there is no love lost between the two, a rivalry that has existed for many years. Wolecki is destined to make one or two changes for the match and could bring Martyn Fotheringham back into contention and Webster may be included from the start. One thing is for certain it won't be a game for the faint hearted.

Sure enough it wasn't! 15 minutes gone and no word. It's terrible clock watching, 25 minutes pass, is it still no score? Nine-fifteen in Breda, half-time, let's hope there is no injury time stun-gun to shock the Mo fans. It is too good to be true, as my messenger relays a 2-0 score-line, as hopes and dreams are dashed by a Swankie double. Worse was yet to come as unknown to me it wasn't even half-time as Swankie netted again in 36 minutes to complete his first-half hat-trick. The final score-line confirms we lose 3-0, a repeat of Saturday. The lesson is, NEVER ASSUME!

Mar 21st. ARBROATH, Away - report and teams
Only one change made to Saturday's team as Fotheringham takes Russell's number seven shirt. Donnachie, Hay, Ferguson and Fraser sat in front of goalkeeper Wood. Davidson, Fotheringham, Henslee and Brash were in midfield with Middleton and MacLeod up front.

Clad in their yellow away strip, there was no change of fortune for Montrose as we sold the game in the first half. The opening exchanges were fast and furious with Arbroath having the better start as they took the lead in 7minutes with Swankie skilfully dispatching a McMullen overhead flick. Davidson became the first Montrose player to be shown a yellow card for a foul on Swankie. Brash, Middleton, Henslee, Watson and Donnachie soon also followed the path of the yellow peril. Wood saved from Arbroath's Watson before two minutes of madness sealed the match for the home side.

In 34 minutes McMullen once again found an unmarked Swankie alone in space and the striker had an easy task and calmly slotted the ball past an unprotected Wood. Two minutes later and Swankie completed his hat-trick with a goal that killed the match as the defence stood still.

Wolecki made one change at half-time by substituting MacLeod and introducing Calum Watson. The start of the second period saw tempers flare, bookings, and the final tackle by Barry Donnachie on Swankie in 62 minutes. Having collected a first half booking for his elocution, Donnachie was shown red reducing Montrose to ten men. Davidson then escaped red when he was withdrawn for his own good. Russell then made an appearance for Middleton.

Highlights – A miserable night in which only a Henslee shot came anywhere close. Wood didn't have much cover in losing three goals, Henslee, Middleton and Watson when he came on all worked hard but it takes more than a few players to make a team! Poor communication is blamed for the defensive errors, but discipline must also be questioned. Twenty-seven bookings, three ordering offs in the four games played is not a good record for either team and as a result, Donnachie could miss the remainder of the season as he will face a lengthy ban for tonight's misdemeanours. Kerrigan is still out injured and is missed in midfield for his strength, timely tackles and distribution of the ball. He is an influential player to be missing from such a young side. Maybe his return will herald better times.

Tonight's other matches saw East Stirling suffer the back-lash of Stenhousemuir's recent loss of form as the Warriors scored seven. In the duel of the Kingdom of Fife, Cowdenbeath showed yet again their strength by dumping East Fife 4 – 1. The gentlemen of Queen's Park failed to make ground in their quest to secure fourth place by dropping all three points at Coatbridge. Albion Rovers have closed the gap on eighth placed Montrose and sit a point behind. Arbroath's win places the Angus side within two points of Queen's Park.

Finally we top the league at something- who said we couldn't do it-it is a tremendous achievement! This is how it's done – teamwork – as Andrew Stephen's editorial stewardship and his team of writers take the "Programme Monthly", Scottish football programme of the year award for Division Three. Well done to all! Success at last as we do deserve something from the season for our efforts.

Ochilview saw the axe fall on Henry Hall last time round. I hope the fans don't expect the same result this Saturday, as yet again the human factor kicks in. I said at the beginning of this quarter to let this game pass. Why do so many fans get so hung-up on this one match? It never does us any good as we inevitably lose to Arbroath and its 'Sack the Manager' as the sceptics give their verdict!

I can't see the team getting anything from Stenhousemuir this weekend but I will still give my support. It is still very early days, there are more pieces to the jig-saw and the full picture is not yet painted. Have patience and give it time. As the song goes "*Life is LIFE*"!

It's Saturday, it's Stenny and it's been relatively quiet apart from some moans and groans, but again people will complain about the smallest thing. For example, Montrose wore their yellow away strip to play Arbroath. Some questioned the action and could not understand why Montrose did not take to the park in their blue strip. What does it matter? We were away from home, so we played in our away strip, its no big deal. What matters is that we have to try to move forward but I have the feeling that it won't be this afternoon!

Sure as apples are apples BBC Final score confirms a 5-1 rout. However there was hope at the half-time interval as a 1-1 score-line reflected that we had held our own. The second period however opened the flood gates.

Mar 25th. STENHOUSEMUIR, Away - report and teams
Another case of don't assume as the 'Montrose Dynamo' web site indicates with the statement "It's not often that one can come back from a 1 – 5 pumping with several positives to take from the performance", but that was the case today. Donnachie was automatically suspended for today's match and his apprentice Euan Hall wasn't even on the bench as young Darryn Kelly took the number two shirt. The team lined-up Wood in goal, Kelly, Hay Ferguson and Fraser with a midfield of Webster, Davidson, Fotheringham and Henslee. Middleton and Watson were paired in the striking roles. McManus, Macleod, Corre, and Philip Reid filled the outfield substitution roles with Hankinson as back-up for Wood.

In the first half Montrose more than matched league pace-setters Stenhousemuir. With 11 minutes gone Fotheringham silenced the Warriors support as the jubilant "Links Park Four" (the travelling support) celebrated. The goal came from a Webster-Kelly overlap with the youngster firing in a cross from the right for Fotheringham to slot home past Fahey at the far post. Our lead however was short lived, 7 minutes to be precise, as we gave away yet another free header at a set piece corner. Sinclair rose unmarked to head past Sandy Wood to level the match. Montrose continued to make ground creating a few chances and pinning the Warriors back into their own half. On the thirty-five minute mark Stenny broke forward in numbers, the defence was caught cold, goalkeeper Wood sent Templeton crashing in a rash challenge. There was only one outcome as the referee pointed to the spot. Wood redeemed himself for his moment of inexperience as McBride's kick was palmed away from the top left-hand corner of the goal. At the other end Fahey thwarted Davidson at close range. Level at half-time Montrose had fought well and possibly played their best football all season.

No changes in personnel at half-time. The match tempo started where it had left off. In 55 minutes Montrose had a great chance to regain the lead. A good passing move in midfield led Webster on a run down the right and into the box to square to Middleton, who lifted the ball over Fahey's bar when it was easier to score. Wolecki then brought on Philip Reid for a tiring Webster. As happens, if you don't take your chances then they will come back to haunt you and haunt it did as a second penalty award went to Stenny. Dubious to say the least, yet again worthy of an equity card, Ferguson was penalised for allegedly tripping a maroon. Cramb slotted the spot-kick home. Sinclair made it three in 63 minutes, the flood gates had opened!

Middleton's miss had cost us dearly and this saw the striker's confidence dwindle and it was no surprise when Wolecki made the change with Gael Corre coming on to support Watson. The game was soon over as Diack crashed a Cramb cross home and McGrillen chipped the advancing Wood. Although heads did go down Montrose never gave up and created a few chances to gain a consolation goal. MacLeod was a final substitution but by this stage it was all over.

Highlights – You've got to give credit where credit is due, Stenhousemuir may have won this match but were only convincing in the later stages of the game as for 60 minutes Montrose had the upper hand. Some may think another drubbing and poor Montrose performance, but they would be wrong to judge, as the score-line did not reflect the closeness of the game. Davidson and Henslee worked hard in midfield breaking up moves and Kelly made a formidable debut on the right flank in the unaccustomed full-back position. The defence is very young but I think that through time it will bear fruit. It is a learning curve that the youngsters are going through, now is the time to do it as come next season things will have to be tight. They need the experience. Manager Wolecki was disappointed as statistics showed a balance of twelve attempts on target to Stenny's thirteen. The difference was obviously in finishing.

Berwick and Cowdenbeath continue their good form collecting home points by disposing of Albion Rovers and Arbroath. The match at Shielfield looked closer than it was with Rovers receiving a last minute penalty as Berwick won 2 -1. Cowdenbeath beat a ten-man Arbroath side 4 – 2. In the other matches Elgin score three first half goals against the Shire and Queen's Park and East Fife shared the points at Hampden in a 0-0 draw.

No changes in the top three league positions as Stenhousemuir hold the number one spot on sixty-seven points. Second placed Berwick are four points adrift and Cowdenbeath in third spot are on fifty-nine points but they have two matches in-hand, to East Stirling and Elgin. The next two Saturdays could see the league winners more or less decided. Will Cowdenbeath make April Fools out of Stenny and can the Borderers take the points at home from the Ochilview side the following week? The pressure is on the Warriors!

Another rescheduled match on Tuesday, this time Cowdenbeath taking on Elgin at Central Park. In a see-saw first half, Elgin took the lead on two occasions, only for Cowdenbeath to finally take control with a McKenna double on half-time seeing the home side go in 3-2.

The Miners added to their first half tally and ran out 5 -2 winners to set up a crucial Ochilview visit. Now on sixty-two points with a game in-hand next week against the Shire, Cowdenbeath have the opportunity to take over the league's number one spot. That's if they get a result at Stenhousemuir!

The effects of Saturday's result kick-in, true supporters would have been there to swell the numbers of the "Links Park Four" and realise the positive factors within the score-line. Again someone starts the thread of 'sack the manager' on the message board, before long negativity starts and before you know it there is a full scale riot. Not this time! Its like a game of cards, the response wasn't there so let's try another lead, let's try the Board! Maybe someone will show their hand. No takers once more, what about the 'Supporters Trust', again there is little response as the 'Dave Baikie' supporters club flog a dead horse. It is time to face facts, a reality check of where we are and the next step forward in this major re-construction of the club. It's only a few, but for them today we mourned the passing of a beloved old friend, Mr. Common Sense. He will be remembered as having cultivated valuable lessons such as 'knowing when to come in out of the rain' and that 'life isn't fair'. The obituary reads, Common Sense was preceded in death by his parents, Truth and Trust; his wife, Discretion; his daughter, Responsibility; and his Son; Reason. Not many attended the funeral, so few realised he was gone. Condolences go to those who remain, step-brothers; My Rights and Ima Whiner!

If you remember him there is still time, if not then join the minority and do NOTHING!

April Fools day starts the run-in to the end of the season and the finalisation of the play-off places. With second and third spots out of reach it looks down to the last four matches and four possible candidates for fourth spot. Queens Park, Elgin, Arbroath and East Fife vie for that spot with Montrose having a deciding factor in their run in to the season's closure. One way or another Montrose will play a part in who goes through.

	8/4/06	15/4/06	22/4/06	29/4/06
Arbroath	Elgin (A)	Albion Rov (H)	East Fife (A)	East Stirling (H)

East Fife	East Stirling (A)	Berwick (A)	Arbroath (H)	Montrose (A)
Elgin	Arbroath (H)	Montrose (A)	Stenhousemuir (H)	Cowdenbeath (A)
Q Park	Montrose (H)	Stenhousemuir (A)	Cowdenbeath (H)	Berwick (A)

It's a tough run-in for Queen's Park, Elgin also have matches against tough opposition to contend with and Arbroath must be wary of assuming that Albion Rovers and East Stirling will lie down. East Fife, are the only side to be away from home for three out of the four matches but first the Bayview side have today's hurdle of Elgin at home. Funnily enough the other two contenders meet this April Fool's day as Arbroath take on Queen's Park at Gayfield. Fourth place could be a last day scenario as it could go down to goal difference!

Here we go again, Berwick at home, if form or previous encounters have anything to go by then it will be a draw. Again, a fit Webster who has the knack of upsetting the Borderers could be the thorn in the Berwick side. Like a cat with nine lives, Barry Donnachie is available after serving a one match suspension after the sending off at Gayfield. A lengthy ban was forecast but Barry escaped the points threshold (only just) and is available for selection. With five games to go it may not be wise to risk Donnachie's inclusion as he has already been red carded at Berwick. It could be a lesson learned for the full-back; then again he could incur the wrath of the SFA once more sending him over the points threshold for a stiffer penalty. It would only take a booking for a rash challenge or a throw away comment to the referee, as he always has to have the last word. I for one would prefer to see him running down the "Knoll" touchline but young Kelly may have other ideas after putting in a good performance in Donnachie's absence. Wolecki calls for rearguard action as we have conceded eleven goals in the last three games. His first priority is to keep it tight at the back.

Before you can say boo to a ghost, we find ourselves one down in 6 minutes or as the text message said '1 – 0 Berwick – clearly offside' confirmed by Middleton's booking for dissent. (And I was worried about Barry!) The internet café 'Surf and Talk' confirmed 1 -0 half-time score-line and another text gave some hope '1 – 1 Foxy', followed by '2 – 1 Berwick, never defended a corner'. It was not over yet, with time to strike again for another draw with the Borderers but Aprils Fool's day was to strike first as

Fotheringham was sent off for a second bookable offence. 'Foxy off- 2nd booking, ref is a joke, gave the game to Berwick' It said it all!

An eventful day but even at this level there can be fairytale endings as Gretna who joined the Scottish leagues four years ago after playing in the northern leagues of England secure themselves a Scottish Cup Final spot after beating Dundee. Even if they lose in the final they stand a chance of representing Scotland in Europe.

Contrary to the long held theory that foreign players have weakened the Scottish Leagues, the fact is that the continued success of Gretna is a testament to the benefit of having foreign players. At least five of Gretna's players are "English"!

Accepted to Division Three for the start of season 2003/04 they gained promotion at a second attempt and this season have seen promotion to Division One. Good luck or possibly good fortune as they are bank-rolled by cash magnet Brooks Mileson.

A tremendous achievement by a team making progress!

The race is on! 4.45 confirmed a 2 -1 win to the Miners at Ochilview. League positions remain the same, Stenny, Berwick and Cowdenbeath, but only one point now separates the positions and the Miners have a game in hand to bottom markers East Stirling. Come Tuesday, we could have new league leaders. Wins for both Arbroath and Elgin brings both sides level with Queen's Park on forty-six points as they slog out for the scraps of fourth place. In the only other match Albion Rover's win against the Shire leap-frogs them into eighth place past Montrose!

Apr 1st. BERWICK, Home - report and teams
One change from last week's team sheet, with Hay dropping out of defence. The team read Wood, Donnachie, Kelly, Fraser and Ferguson, supported by a midfield of Webster, Davidson, Fotheringham and Henslee. Middleton and Watson were once again paired in the strike roles. Subs were the same as the Ochilview cardboard cut-outs. Berwick may have collected the points from this encounter but they were made to fight all the way to the final whistle. The game started with a burst and striker Haynes volleyed home a McLeish cross in six minutes. Claims for offside went unheard, the referee only seeing fit to book Middleton for dissent during discussions. Sometimes it's better to accept the referee's decision, as it is usually final, and can save a lot of grief including suspension for a silly booking. Montrose fought back with Berwick keeper O'Connor deflecting a Fotheringham shot and minutes later a

Watson shot went just wide of the target. At the other end, Fraser saved the day after Kelly was short with a header back to Wood. Wood then pulled off a tremendous save from Berwick's Little on the 30 minute mark. Still keeping to their task, Montrose worked hard to get back into the match but the sound of the half-time whistle stopped play.

After the re-start Henslee played Watson in and the strikers shot was tipped over by O'Connor. In 57 minutes the hard work finally paid off. A one-two between Henslee and Ferguson found Watson whose shot was once again saved by O'Connor but Fotheringham volleyed home the keeper's spill. A break-through, we were at last level and on the verge of a point. At this stage Montrose were the hungrier team but were stunned in 63 minutes when Haynes doubled his tally as he rose unmarked at a routine corner to head on. Minutes later the blonde striker was booked for dissent. In 68 minutes Fotheringham fell foul of the referee for a 50– 50 tackle picking up a booking. Watson soon followed him into the book for a tackle on Haynes and with the game starting to get out off control the referee produced a second yellow card for a Fotheringham touch-line tackle. Reduced to ten men, Wolecki brought on fresh legs with Philip Reid replacing Webster. Ten men or not Montrose played to the final whistle and did not throw in the towel!

Highlights – It could be said that Montrose were unlucky not to have taken something from the match and Wolecki reflected this in his post match report. Positive points- we worked hard and showed character to get a deserved equaliser against good opposition only to wipe-out the good work by poor marking at a corner. Another sending off today raises the question of poor discipline; we need to finish matches with the team intact and cannot afford to lose players to suspension.

The Under 19's played yesterday at Links Park, their opponents Arbroath and by all accounts it was a very good match. Some say better than the day before! The youngsters recorded a 2 – 1 victory over our neighbours in a match that saw Darryn Kelly play his second ninety minutes in two days having competed in the previous days game against Berwick.

Given the support, these youngsters are the future!

East Fife, are in the news as they hastily appoint Dave Baikie to the managerial seat, vacant since February. The weekend saw care-taker manager Greg Shaw resign his post as events off the field have taken a higher profile than results. Best summed up by the headline from the 'Courier'. 'Baikie calls for 'peace' at war torn New Bayview'. Fans have been unhappy for sometime and had demonstrated against the Board by boycotting matches. In the long running feud the appointment of Baikie is the first peace making step.

At last the twice postponed Forfarshire Cup tie with neighbours Brechin is played. It is the first match for newly appointed Michael O'Neill who has taken over the vacant Glebe Park managerial seat after Ian Campbell's departure. O'Neill assumes his duties after tonight's match, where he will see his charges for the first time as a spectator. Montrose manager Eddie Wolecki used the match to give fringe players a full ninety minutes which also saw the return of Steve Kerrigan from injury. The match ended in a Brechin 2 – 1 win. Montrose however took the lead in 7 minutes when James Russell sprinted clear, rounding the goalkeeper to fire home. Brechin equalised in 30 minutes with King sending a dipping shot over Hankinson. All square at half-time, it was not until the 80th minute that Brechin took advantage of hesitation in the Montrose defence as Byers squared the ball for Templeman to hammer the ball home.

Highlight of the night, the referee was Hornby!

East Stirling one, Cowdenbeath one, the Miners 'Blew Braziled' it! After having their chance to take over as league leaders they now require a big favour from Berwick if they are to have title hopes. Lying one point behind the leaders both Berwick and Cowdenbeath couldn't be closer. Berwick also have title hopes in their sights and Stenhousemuir need a win, anything else at Shielfield and Stenny fans may suffer a further bout of Saturday post match depression! Focus now changes for Stehousemuir fan's, they never thought there would be a possibility of play-offs and their main worry turns to the Division Two candidates, Dumbarton and Alloa. Goal difference separates the pair as both are on the same points. The two meet on the second last Saturday of the season, a match that could decide either team's fate of relegation or a chance for play-off survival.

For some players the opportunity to play at Hampden, Scotland's national stadium raises their performance no end. The large playing surface lends itself to a passing game but the bigger the surface the more ground there is to cover and open space to defend. Fitness will be a key factor and Montrose can also take confidence from the previous 3 – 0 win at Hampden in November. Given the space Wolecki may recall Russell or Kerrigan to fill the vacant midfield position left by Fotheringham's suspension. I would hope we can take something out of this match to regain our eighth place position from the Rovers.

Apr 8th. QUEENS PARK, Away - report and teams

Take something we did but not enough to step in front of the Rovers, but it is a good point especially coming back from a two down score-line. In a game of two halves, the first we could have quite easily been put to the sword, we had no answer. The second saw the shoe on the other foot and it could have been three points in our favour. How the tide changed!

We lined up with more or less the same faces but a change in formation with Hay coming in for the suspended Fotheringham. Wood took his usual place in goal surrounded by Kelly, Hay, Fraser, and Ferguson. Barry Donnachie played a role in front of Hay and Fraser in no man's land supporting both midfield and defence. The berths in midfield were filled by Webster, Davidson and Henslee with Middleton playing a left supporting role for the lonely Watson upfront. Subs saw the return of Kerrigan, Russell and Brash to the bench along with MacLeod and Hankinson.

Despite completely dominating the whole of the first half and having numerous chances Queen's Park could only show a one goal lead for their efforts. The goal came in 26 minutes from a Paul Harvey twenty-yard drive soaring in at the top left hand corner of Wood's goal. From then until half-time other chances fell to the Spider's but poor finishing kept the score-line down. Playing a system that clearly was not working and creating little going forward, fans expected changes and that support would be given to Watson who was ploughing a lone furrow. After the re-start, set in our ways, we continued and soon suffered the consequences. Weak defending in 51 minutes when we should have cleared our lines saw the Spider's number nine Felvus ram the ball into the net from ten-yards. Queen's second goal spurred change in the minds of the Montrose management team but before they could raise the substitution boards we had scored. Awarded a free-kick in the Queens half, Middleton swung the ball over for Henslee to net with a side footed volley past Cairns. The goal not only spurred change but also formation as Brash replaced Middleton and Kerrigan came on for Kelly with Montrose reverting to a 3-5-2 system. Donnachie played left-side of midfield; Kerrigan supported Watson upfront and had an immediate effect, causing consternation in the Queen's defence. A transformation took place, Henslee saw his shot well saved by Cairns, Brash then struck the woodwork with his effort. With 11 minutes to go the equaliser came. Following a corner, the Spider's defence failed to clear, Russell who had replaced Webster chipped in for Fraser to head home. From then on the Queen's Park goal endured increasing amounts of pressure as the winning goal eluded Montrose.

Oh, and Barry was booked!

Highlights – The team showed commitment in the second half against a good side and credit can only be given as they turned around a 2-0 deficit to gain a good point. Today we dealt a blow to Queen's Parks play-off hopes, Elgin is the next challenge, can we do the same at Links Park?

Another Saturday turns the table and the separation of one point becomes two. It is Berwick's turn to subject Stenny to defeat at Shielfield as the Ochilview club drop to third place. A few weeks ago after having suffered a 5 -1 defeat by Stenny the 'Montrose Dynamo' Blog stated that the engraver might as well get busy now on the Third Division trophy. Oh how things change! Berwick's emphatic 3-0 win did the damage against the Warriors as Cowdenbeath defended their league leader image with an unconvincing 2-1 win over Albion Rovers. Borough Briggs hosted fourth placed equals Elgin and Arbroath. A 4-1 outcome now gives Elgin the initiative. East Fife's troubles continued as the Shire collected the points at Firs Park giving new manager Dave Baikie an uphill Bayview task.

Down to the last three matches, whoever wins the Division Three title will be celebrating with their home fans on the final day as all three teams are scheduled to play at home. To the Scottish League, I say hold the engraver and book the helicopter now to hover over the Firth of Forth as this season is going to the wire. The common denominator for all three sides is Queen's Park. Fighting for the final play-off place, the Spider's will certainly not be a walkover in the run in. Elgin now in fourth place also travel to Ochilview and Central Park and will be looking for points.

Saturday night in Breda and finally I am able to get a ticket, not for the movies but to see NAC as they play NEC (Nijmegen). A seven–thirty kick-off, panic as the BBC web-site states 18.30 but I soon realised they were talking GMT as I made my way to the stadium.

It's not like Links Park, leave the house at ten to three, park the car, pay at the turn-style and emerge on the terracing for the referee's whistle to sound for kick-off. Timing is everything, for a start it is almost a sell-out, the crowd is in the region of 16,000 and it is down to a bar-code to whether you gain entry. Chalk and Dutch cheese!

Once again police were out in force monitoring the incoming crowd. Horses wore shin-guards and riot visors, ready as a back-line of defence. Boyfriend/girlfriend, husband/wife, grandfather/grandchild attend Breda's answer to Saturday night entertainment. Civilised, with the emphasis on family (maw, paw and the weans) and if you want a beer, you can get one but nae pies! Fans hang banners and flags from allocated railing space, a place set aside away from advertising boards. There is no risk of a pitch invasion as a ten foot high walkway surrounds the playing surface acting as a moat. I only really noticed when I saw the strand of razor wire.

The teams warmed up prior to the match, training routine much the same as our own. We must be doing something right. As the teams emerge from the depths of the moat ticker-tape explodes into the air littering the immaculate pitch with strands of yellow and gold paper streamers. I don't see the point of this as ground staff then proceed to use blowers to clear up the mess before the game starts. At the *'Tribute'* end of the stadium, flares engulfed the goal-mouth in a thick fog of smoke.

The match kicked off and with eighteen seconds on the clock NEC went one ahead, I didn't see the goal and neither did the keeper as the ball was lost in the flare fog! What a start, even we couldn't lose a goal in that time! NAC levelled in 14 minutes with a through ball being slotted beyond the NEC goalkeeper. Celebrations all round, enter the flag-boy like a school-kid on detention, his job, to run a circuit of the moat complete with Breda flag. The goal injected life into Breda with players breaking quickly upfront as a few inconclusive offside decisions went against them. Match officials in the Netherlands are no better than at home. During the warm-up period the fitness of the flagman (linesman) looked suspect and this was the case as he could not keep up with play. The words "stick" and "flag" are the same in the Dutch language as anywhere else, you just need to fill in the adjectives as fans vented their displeasure at his decisions.

Half-time1-1 and a rendition from Gerry Marsden and *'You'll Never Walk Alone'*. If someone would only record *'I Was Born Under a Gable End'* we could be famous and it would save us listening to *'Should I stay or Should I Go'*! No matter where you go the football chants are the same with the exception of *'I Was Born Under a Gable End'*, that is something special. It doesn't matter what the language is, you can still recognise the football song but *'Amarillo'* and *'Rivers of Babylon'* that's got me beat! The Breda fans sing *'We're from the B side'* (behind the goal), the *'Honorary'* side responds and so it goes on. I somehow wouldn't think that Wellington Street and Beach ends along with the "Knoll" at Links Park could even muster support to carryout a reply!

It is interesting, people are creatures of habit, they sit in the same seats and they know an interloper when they see one. At half-time I was approached by a supporter, something was said in Dutch,and I apologied indicating that I was from Scotland. "Ja so you are a scout. Who are you watching!" There's a lesson to be learned here, never ever go to a football match in a black coach's jacket with a pen and a piece of paper!

At the start of the second period NEC had a few chances but failed to capitalise on their efforts, but a goal did come in 55 minutes and the flag went around the moat once again. 2-1 Breda and the match started to get physical as clumsy challenges broke up play. NEC's Welshman, David Jones (on-loan from Man Utd) was spoken to by the referee (Come here good boy!) for a set-to down the line. The game then deteriorated further when NEC introduced substitute Bart for Romano, it could only be the sequel to the return of Mark Yardley. If this wasn't bad enough, NEC finally lost the plot and the game in a last man incident. The player involved (oddly enough it was number 2) instantly removed his shirt and headed for the changing room before the referee could produce the red card. Four minutes of injury time did not change the score-line as NAC collected three welcome points.

A few days later I decline the offer of a seat at the PSV v Feyenoord match as I am flying home to see the Mo play Elgin. There is no comparison!

Midweek and the manager publicises his intentions for next season in the way of squad size. It is the first time Wolecki has stated that he sees a squad of eighteen as being the optimal number. With three games remaining, the incentive for players is there. Take away two for goalkeepers, we already know that four new faces are coming in, twelve places are up for grabs which means players will move out and on!

This is where I came in, same time, same place but a year has since passed. Three pm., standing on the "Knoll" looking down the tunnel and we were playing Elgin! I remember the '*Proclaimers*' and complainers, that's what kicked this crazy idea of writing a book off.

I questioned my judgment at the time, but I have no regrets. Yes I could have left the match as others did before it had ended, I could have done a runner but didn't. As one recent messenger put it – 'It's all part of an intensive character building programme involving a lifetime of disappointment, thwarted ambition and continual setback.' But there are the positives - there is always the next game, next season and NEXT TIME!

For Elgin fans 'next time' could be today as their team have seldom won at Links Park. Elgin have been playing well under new manager Brian Irvine, Martin Johnston who has been cracking in the goals will be a handful for the Montrose defence. Johnston is currently the leagues top scorer having netted twenty times so far this season.

Apr 15th. ELGIN, Home - report and teams

I saw the headline during the week- 'Montrose refuses to get in a flap.' It referred to the 'Bird Flu' but could have quiet easily been applied to today's game. We dominated this match from start to finish, played some terrific football but were thwarted by an Elgin side assisted by the referee who was consistently awful throughout the match.

Wolecki played a 3-1-4-1-1 system which at times resembled 3-5-2. Wood was fronted with a back three of Kelly, Hay and Fraser with Barry Donnachie filling the hole in between the defence and midfield. Webster Davidson Henslee and Brash filled the midfield, Kerrigan assumed the role in the hole and supported front man Watson. The formation worked; there are still a few weaknesses but it looks like a system that can now be tailored for next season. For instance the back three are young and need the support of an older head. If we are going to play from midfield we will need a left-sided player who can cross first-time, as today Brash took too many touches. Who knows what players Eddie will bring in over the summer, the season is not ended but on today's showing the future looks bright and on the right track.

We didn't dent Elgin's hopes of a fourth place finish as for their fans this was 'next time' as they got out of jail free! The first goal came in 7 minutes, Wood attended to a through ball with Elgin's Johnston rushing on. The ball ricocheted off the young keeper's body before Johnston collided where upon the referee, from the edge of the centre circle, saw fit to award a penalty. Booth converted.

Elgin keeper Renton held a Webster drive in 12 minutes then Henslee and Davidson both had shots on target. In 37 minutes Montrose had a blatant penalty for hand ball turned down; only the referee who once again was not up with play, chose to ignore the claims. A minute later, Barry was booked! The equaliser however came on the 41 minute mark and for me it was the goal of the season, as Watson volleyed home in style from twenty-five yards. The goal was deserved as Montrose had worked hard to over come playing against twelve men.

There were many incidents in the first half resulting from poor refereeing decisions. Donnachie was booked for winning the ball cleanly with no contact with the other player and Kerrigan was booked for contact with the ball. There was absolutely no logic behind these decisions, except in Barry's case, maybe he has to work on his silver-tongue technique. However the second period saw both assistants wearing buzzers to enable contact with the whistler as something must have been said, but even that went against us as the damage had already been done. 56 minutes and a stonewall penalty as Watson is wrestled to the ground by his two minders. The referee pointed to the spot but awards Elgin a foul and promptly booked Watson. There were gasps of disbelief-talk about knocking a team when they are down, there is no justice! Minutes later Henslee had a golden chance to rifle home but his shot just went over. It was all Montrose but the game was soon to turn as Kaczan scored on the break completely against the run of play. Kerrigan was then red carded for a second bookable offence, the situation was not clear but it looked as if his fellow professional got him sent off as he turned tell-tale to the assistant referee.

The plot was lost, down to ten men and playing against twelve are not good odds. Elgin added a third in 85 minutes but the score didn't matter as we can take pride from today's game as I feel that it will be us *next time'*!

Highlights – Absolutely robbed! The past few weeks have shown that there is nothing between sides in this league only referees and today's was a comedian, except we weren't laughing!

Another Stenny defeat sees them out of the running for the title. Five points adrift from leaders Cowdenbeath, they now need the Miners to lose both of their remaining games. A 2-1 win, for the Spiders who scored at the death was enough to kill off Ochilview hopes. Cowdenbeath put five past the Shire to continue in pole position and Berwick dropped points in their 1-1 draw with East Fife. Arbroath's 1-0 win at Gayfield gives the Angus club a lifeline for fourth place if they win their remaining matches but need Elgin and Queen's Park to drop points. Never has there been such interest in the final two matches of this league.

Final day in the Dutch League, the trophy stays in Eindhoven with PSV, play-off positions are at stake as they decide the outcome of who joins the outright winner in the European Champions League and UEFA Cup. It's almost over, focus in the Netherlands turns to the World Cup and Group C, Van der Saar, Van Nistleroy and Van Frites as Germany prepares for a Dutch invasion and the *'Grote Markts'* prepare for celebrations.

NAC, had a season much as ourselves, a sixteenth place finish and they have not yet escaped the embarrassment of relegation play-offs. High hopes, Pierre was back, great win against table toppers AZ and that was it!

Hopes briefly raised, a new manager, changes in personnel during January, but too late as supporters looked for instant success. It's a disease that is all over, the instant manager, the merchants of *'gloom and doom'!*

It may seem meaningless but there is pride at stake and an opportunity to raise our league position as we play-out the last but one match against Albion Rovers at Cliftonhill. Eighth after all is better than ninth!

Apr 22nd. ALBION ROVERS, Away - report and teams

For twenty-three minutes we were eighth and for a second week running the opposition were awarded a penalty. We didn't win, but then again we didn't loose and can still in our last game live the dream of eighth place!

With Kerrigan and Calum Watson both suspended for today's game, Montrose were left with a void to fill. Keeping the same system we lined-up with Wood in goal, Kelly, Hay and Fraser as the back three, Donnachie sat in behind a midfield of Webster, Davidson, Henslee and Brash. James Russell was brought in for Kerrigan sitting in the link role and Middleton played the lone ranger. Prior to the match Wolecki had stated that we need to cut-out errors and stop losing goals to set pieces. As in some of the other matches the defence looked unsettled early on as Wood was forced to pull off saves from Young and Bonar. Against the run of play Montrose pounced on a Lennon defensive error and it was James Russell who drove the ball high into the net past keeper McGlynn. The 12th minute goal spurred Montrose on but it was Rovers who came closest due to a defensive mix-up. Donnelly got the break of the ball on the edge of the box but wasted the chance as he volleyed high over the bar with Wood left stranded. In 35 minutes Albion Rovers equalised from the penalty spot as Graham Hay was judged to have handled the ball. Donnelly this time made a better job as he struck the ball past Wood from the spot.

In life we all have a ticket that has our name on it. Like a coat-peg to hang our jacket on or in Barry Donnachie's case a SFA standard issue yellow card – "Donnachie, Montrose, No.2". Booked again and fast becoming the referee's best friend, Barry once more stepped out of line as he contested the penalty award. He really needs to change his chat-up line as once again he was booked for dissent by the black shadow! Post conversion Middleton joined Barry's name on the yellow peril for also speaking out of turn and this will put the striker in the cooler for the first league match of next season.

Level at half-time, the second period was a non-event spoiled by high winds and scrappy passing by both sides. However it was Montrose who came closest as Middleton turned substitute Fotheringham's cross onto the post.

Highlights – On a positive point there was a healthy crowd of eight hundred and twenty-five Coatbridge faithful. A good attendance for an end of the season encounter of the bottom but one clubs, or were they there just for the pre-match entertainment, the Geordie guitarist!

A 2-2 draw at Hampden saw Cowdenbeath drop points and an influential player (Ward) for Saturday's final match. Berwick made hard work of a 1-0 win, leaving it late to score against the Shire. An Ian Diack double was enough for Stenny to win at Elgin and Arbroath added to the woes at New Bayview by scoring three.

With one Saturday of the league campaign remaining, the Scottish League will need that helicopter after all. Today's results bring Cowdenbeath and Berwick level on points, it is even closer than we could have imagined as goal difference gives the Miners the edge. Just think, if the top two are beaten and Stenny are able to score eight then it could be Ochilview that is celebrating. Arbroath lead the hunt for fourth place on goal difference from Elgin, Queen's Park lie one point behind. It's not over till it's over!

In the end three matches will decide it all, Berwick at home to Queen's Park, Cowdenbeath entertain Elgin and Arbroath have the luxury of being at Gayfield to take on bottom markers East Stirling. To all fans I say don't count your chickens just yet!

Until today it was also tight at the bottom of the Division Two relegation zone. Goal difference gave Dumbarton the right to play in the play-offs over Alloa. At four forty-five that changed as Alloa collected all three points from a 1-0 win in what was billed as a decider between the two clubs and now look set to compete in the play-offs.

The drums of Cork City beat, Irish League football and another project challenge as I split my time between Ireland and the Netherlands. Another settlement period, travel and the joy's of supporting MONTROSE, while being drawn away from HOME! The Irish football season has just commenced as the Eircom League opts for summer football that runs from March through to early November. Past experience tells me that the word "summer" doesn't come into the equation as every day is a "soft" day in this lush green Emerald Isle.

The end of a season, well at least for Montrose, the play-offs have already been decided and today is all for nothing! There is no nail biting end to the campaign, no sitting around internet cafés waiting for screens to refresh. Respite awaits the supporter, well at least until June as we have a duty to support Trinidad and Tobago at the World Cup Finals.

Nothing at stake I head for neighbouring Tilburg home of Williem II and home of "SCOTFEST 2006"! At least I will be at home for a day, Highland Games, Pipe bands and folk music. What more can you ask for? Only that MONTROSE SCORE on the final day!

Apr 29th. EAST FIFE, Home – report and teams

Fancy dress was the order of the day for East Fife fans as they marked the end of the season with a Links Park conga. For Montrose it was one last game, and one last hope of three points. Could we mark it with a win, alas no!

The first text message told me that East Fife who had four ex-Montrose players in their line-up had scored. I knew something would come back to haunt us today and that was former player Kerr Dodds, it only took three minutes. Text two just said 'EF 2 – offside' and text three summed the day up as it stated 'Middleton penalty miss'! In a changed formation Montrose fielded Wood in goal, a back four with youngsters Kelly and Ralph, plus Fraser and Brash. Donnachie sat on the right of midfield with Davidson and McManus in the middle and Henslee on the left. Watson and Kerrigan led the attack. With Dodds forcing the ball over the line from a Bradford cross, we were behind the eight ball from the start. However Montrose rallied as Watson sent a terrific shot just wide of the post. Henslee then had his shot saved by the keeper who palmed away the strike. Montrose continued to attack and Watson had another shot blocked on the line. Kerrigan was next with an overhead kick that ended wide of the target. Minutes later Henslee's drive from a Kerrigan knock down was turned away again. In the final minute of the half McManus had his shot saved by the Fifer's keeper, then on the final whistle a shot on the turn from young McManus was saved again by John Dodds.

No half-time changes as the Mo plugged away for an equaliser. Henslee broke clear in 52 minutes but under pressure from his marker shot wide. In 60 minutes it was all over as East Fife's Bradford scored with a shot on the turn. Watson's strike against the post minutes later was cancelled out when Smart headed against the upright. In a match that was never physical, East Fife were reduced to ten-men as Campbell was sent-off for a last man challenge in the box on substitute Fotheringham. How many penalties have we missed this season? Today we added another, as Middleton shot wide of the post. What can I say!

Highlights – Today didn't matter as the team selection showed, but it would have been better to finish in eighth spot. One win in the last quarter and a few hard-luck stories are all that we have to show as we finish ninth. So much for having a deciding factor, although I think that may have been the case where Queen's Park are concerned as eyes were set on fourth place. Today after the first goal we played the Fifers off the park and in the second period we lost our shape and were absolutely woeful as East Fife ran out comfortable winners. The change in formation, playing 4-4-2 didn't work for us. We look better playing 3-1-4-1-1 where everyone is working hard for each other. Time will tell, the experimenting is now over, we need a set system and a set side. There is a lot of work to do, in both bringing players to the club and in pre-season preparation for the club to move forward. In the coming season there will be no forecasts, no anticipation of being champions but an improved league position is something we must attain!

On a final note, today Barry Donnachie kept a clean sheet and was also voted players' player of the year for his achievement!

Young player of the year went to Stephen Fraser, and Greg Henslee took the rest of the accolades, gongs and awards at the end of season dance.

An electrifying finish to the league season, down to goal-difference on the last day – the helicopter has landed north of the river Forth as Cowdenbeath some twenty goals better than Berwick are well deserved winners, lifting the Division Three championship title. What a way to celebrate their 125th anniversary by unfurling the third division flag. Mixu Paatelainen's men can now breathe a sigh of relief as promotion is guaranteed and in the bag. The facing of play-offs for them is no longer a threat! Stenny, pretenders to the throne for so long, have to make do with being one of the bridesmaids as final day results not only conclude the championship but the final play-off participants.

A 2-1 win saw the Miners finish in style in front of their home fans putting paid to Berwick's threat and Elgin hopes of fourth place. At Shielfield a second-half Haynes goal was enough for Berwick to equal the title points but it didn't matter as in the end it was goals that counted. Any hopes the Spider's fans had also died at Shielfield. At Gayfield (our neighbours), the "Smokies" took a narrow 2-1 victory over the Shire to clinch the final play-off spot!

The first meeting on the Irish job and, at times it can be like a family reunion, a home coming, as it is a small world in this industry. Like brothers in arms we will be family for the next few years. I will miss the European culture of the Netherlands as through time my visits will become less. Summer nights sitting in the Grote Markt putting the world to rights will never be repeated. I will miss the display of bright colour, the slobbering kisses on alternate cheeks as they grab you with the subtlety of a grizzly bear, but most of all I will miss the "twee wheeler". The entertainment value from this mode of transport will be parked in my mind forever!

There are times in our lives that we all experience a sense of guilt as your conscience plays havoc with your senses. It's all about how we deal with change, priorities and the constant juggling of time. From past experience it is difficult to understand why we take certain choices but we do with the wisdom that we are given. In time, eventually it will all work out – but for it to work – we have to MAKE IT WORK!

The last kick of the ball has taken place, at least for Montrose anyway. We cannot turn the clock back and we can only reflect on a season best forgotten. How true that is I cannot tell, as in the months to come we may look back on a milestone that changed the future of the Club. We can only live in hope!

The final league positions

Quarter Four

POS		P	W	L	D	F	A	GD	PTS
1	Cowdenbeath	36	24	8	4	81	34	47	76
2	Berwick	36	23	6	7	54	27	27	76
3	Stenhousemuir	36	23	9	4	78	38	40	73
4	Arbroath	36	16	13	7	57	47	10	55
5	Elgin	36	15	14	7	55	58	-3	52
6	Queen's Park	36	13	11	12	47	42	5	51
7	East Fife	36	13	19	4	48	64	-16	43
8	Albion Rovers	36	7	21	8	39	60	-21	29
9	Montrose	36	6	20	10	31	59	-28	28
10	East Stirling	36	6	25	5	28	89	-61	23

The season ends. Ninth, it is then, the dream <u>was</u> a nightmare!

Chapter 8

Play-offs

Remind me, how did, we get here!

I remember reading a post on '*Pie and Bovril*' way back in October, it read 'play-off dates, does anyone know them?'. A confident post or was it the fact that his team (Cowdenbeath) had just scored five, coming ever closer to the top of the league. It is now reality, the waiting is over, we think back on all the punishment that we have subjected ourselves too and it now hinges on the play-offs!

Written-off, supporters with short memories, reporters with sharp pencils and sceptics who thought it could never happen. It's been one hell of a season and it is not over yet, I just wish - WE WERE IN THE PLAY-OFFS!

Back in October Henry Hall played that get out of jail free card from the deck of chance or was it the Board. Hall relied on the draw at Berwick to earn a stay of execution before the axe finally fell. The Board appointed Wolecki and the rest is history. A good festive period was looked for but there were no gifts and no revival. The third quarter of fixtures, the most telling on some clubs, saw East Fife almost out of play-off contention as the club suffered disruption on and off the field. All of the teams suffered from the frosty conditions of the winter, postponed matches, growing injury lists and suspensions as they dropped points.

It was a time for clubs to take stock before the onslaught of the final quarter. Would their goals be realised?

It is now down to home and away ties, semi-final and final which take place on the 3rd, 6th, 10th and 13th respectively. The town of Montrose had hope, the manager had a job to do and possibly for some players, they would have played the biggest games of their playing career. A chance for silver and a medal, I can remember Paul Masson showing my kids his runners-up medal from the final league match in the promotion year of 1993, a proud moment.

It's been a long season but the opportunity is there to be taken by one club for a final spot and it's down to two matches. There after who knows, but for some players it could be a very short close season.

It will be interesting if crowds match the expectations of the Scottish Football League as it was one of the reasons why the play-offs were brought in, to attempt to generate much needed cash to lower league clubs.

Who is through, what points did they attain, what second division team is seeking survival. In some seasons gone by, seventy-three points was more than enough to gain promotion to a higher league but this was not the case as both Stenhousemuir and Berwick received bridesmaid status or should that be "lady in waiting". It gives a measure for next term of what points tally you need, to be in the running to win the championship and if you want to be the "flower girl" it takes a minimum of fifty-five points as Arbroath demonstrated.

Stenhousemuir led for so long but disharmony in the dressing room shot the fans expectations firmly in the foot as both barrels unloaded. One, the championship flag was lost which put the manager Des McKeown under pressure. A serious lack of professionalism by players dented team spirit but the second barrel fired when McKeown suspended top scorer Colin Cramb from Ochilview. Dressing room morale is low, Greg Denham has since left and the Warriors now face a play-off against the Borderers of Berwick. Things couldn't be worse!

Berwick manager John Coughlin is known to be a hard task master and not a good loser. His side will be determined, his defence will give little away and the strength of his forwards will be a handful to most teams. You cannot rule-out Stenhousemuir just yet as it is up to the players to make amends, but their last result against the Borderers did really take away their confidence.

With a gap of eighteen points, Arbroath took the final third division play-off place. The "Smokies" will face Second division relegation candidates Alloa who were in a sweat on the final day as Dumbarton led 2-0 at the half-time interval and things weren't looking too good at Kirkcaldy for them. A second-half turnaround for both teams saw Dumbarton slither on the snake to Division Three after losing 3-2 and a goal for Alloa was enough to put a foot on the rung of the ladder.

Arbroath and Alloa have it all to play for, but I would say the pressure is on the second division club as it is always easier to survive than to regain promotion from a lower division.

Difficult to gain promotion – you bet, as an additional test is set giving a one in four chance of success! There are winners and losers and some that will have to fight another day and another season in Division Three.

The outlook is bright for one club as they will be *'Fly-n-Hy'*!

The Dutch play-offs started long ago, for NAC Breda it was a matter of surviving the drop or 'promotie en degradatie', basically relegation, it's just sometimes the Dutch language has a nice way of putting things. Playing home and away legs against TOP Oss (don't ask, as I do not even know where they come from!), a win was essential for NAC to have half a chance of staying in the top Eredivisie league. After a 1st leg of abysmal finishing resulting in the dismissal of the coach Cees Lok, a second leg at home ended in a two all draw and fan riots, NAC finally won through at a third attempt but only by a goal scored in the ninety-fifth minute of extra time as they finally ran-out 3-1 winners. Talk about taking things to the limit!

A further double header with F.C. Volendam saw NAC survive, as they now live to fight another season with the big boys. Willem II also survive the play-offs and there is no real change, only Roosendaal suffer the humiliation of relegation.

May 3rd. – Semi-Final (1st. leg)
Ochilview was the venue with Stenhousemuir having home advantage, if you can call it an advantage, as sometimes it is better to be away for the first leg. As expected this match was a close fought dual with the Berwick defence putting up the shutters, hoping to take the game on home turf, but when you least expect it, your once loyal servant (Gareth Hutchison) reacts to sweep home from close range. 1-0 is not the end of the world but Stenny's side, minus Denham and Cramb, looked make-shift. It is like taking the spine out of the rib cage and it would fall to pieces but it is still all to play for come Saturday as Berwick hold not only home advantage but a one goal lead.

It's good to see that the play-offs increased the Ochilview attendance to 593.

In the other tie Arbroath welcomed Alloa to Gayfield Park with nothing to lose as gaining fourth place was seen as a bonus. Alloa under new manager Allan Maitland meantime have tightened things up defensively and will be difficult to breakdown. For the tie Arbroath have initiated free admission to children under 12's who are accompanied by an adult. This should bolster the attendance of home support as it takes you back to the days of 'Lift me in mister' when as lads we used our own initiative to enable us to buy a pie at half time!

With a reported crowd of 1,163, this was more like it as a cup-tie atmosphere developed. Arbroath, having gained a creditable one all draw after playing the whole of the second period with ten men are still in it. After losing Roddy Black on half-time for a second bookable offence (the referee got it right) Arbroath then had to defend a one goal lead. Reilly had scored for the "Smokies" in the first half but in fifty-three minutes Sloan equalised for Alloa as the Recreation Park side got out of jail. The tie for both clubs is very much alive and kicking. Arbroath may have been penalised as they will not have the services of Roddy Black for the return leg, maybe manager John McGlashan can fill the void that is left. This game could be won on the toss of a coin or a penalty shoot-out!

Today, May 4th liberation is remembered in the Netherlands (May 4th 20.00 hours). Liberated from German occupation, a mark of respect is paid for those who died and a delayed moment of celebration. This is a date in history remembered by all as they pay their respects in many ways. It is only now that I realise the significance of the statue in the park, of the child pulling his father. The Netherlands is a proud nation, a small country who fly-the-flag, but today it was at half-mast. We remember those who fell!

May 6th. – Semi-Final (2nd. leg)
A goal-less draw was enough to see Berwick proceed to the final as they put up the shutters for the day at Shielfield. In the end, Gareth Hutchison's first leg goal was the difference between the two teams. Stenhousemuir were always going to be up against it due to the split in team spirit, and the loss of Cramb and Denham contributed to their demise.

Alloa took the honours on home ground as the Recreation Park side won the tie on aggregate by two goals to one. After Wednesday night's draw Arbroath manager John McGlashan had held an impromptu penalty shoot-out pinning his hopes on his defence holding firm. A Jamie Stevenson goal on sixty-nine minutes put the 'Wasps' in the driving seat, a lead that they were able to protect and hold on to, till the final whistle.

A "Black and Gold" final, it's confirmed as Stenny and Arbroath are both "Marooned" (excuse the club colours pun) and drop from contention.

Gretna, are in the Scottish Cup Final this weekend, they even make the centre pages of the AD Rotterdam press with a double page spread. Peterhead and the ex-Montrose contingent are one step away from Division One status come Sunday. Season 2004/05 saw promotion to Division Two, a season later and the magic wand casts a First division spell for the pair and

UEFA Cup hopes for Gretna. One door closes and another opens, why can't it be us, why can't our dream be fulfilled!

May 10th. – The Final (1st. leg)
Two games and two teams, it could go either way and basically it is down to "who has the bottle"! Will Alloa utilise the open space that Recreation Park offers in the first-leg or will it be Berwick's tight defence that will win the day. The first leg is so crucial for both sides and will be the benchmark for Saturday's finale.

Prior to the match Alloa manager Allan Maitland had stated that his side needs to relax. How relaxed do they need to be!

A 4-0 win and the curtain call closes on Berwick. Manager Allan Maitland can now relax as his side just needs to keep their nerve at Shielfield as a four goal cushion should be enough. It's not the Wasps bite that you have to watch but the sting in the tail!

A Stevenson penalty in 42 minutes followed by a strike by McLeod on the half-time mark gave Alloa a 2-0 lead. An Ovenstone double in 79 and 89 minutes followed the rout as Alloa cruised to an unbelievable first-leg win.

From today's performance Alloa take the advantage into the final leg, for Berwick, ninety minutes of agony awaits, but it's not over till it's over!

It's May 13th, the eve of the final leg, and it will be unlucky for one! Arbroath and Stenhousemuir are already resigned to life in Division Three; all that is left now is to see who will join them. In a black and gold final it looks black for Berwick as Alloa will surely strike gold!

May 14th. – The Final Leg
Confirmed – the final curtain falls on the season and on Berwick as Alloa go Dutch!

It's all over now, one last "croak" from my mobile and Berwick are dead and buried on aggregate 5-2. Although Berwick did regain a morsel of pride, Alloa did stem the tide. A 2-1 victory for the Borderer's was not enough in a game that had almost nothing at stake as the first leg wiped out any glimmer of Berwick hope. Does it matter who scored, only Robbie Horn will reflect" I scored a double in the final" as he reminises with family members. No runners up medals, a cost saving to the Scottish League, and for Berwick, what could have been after losing out on goal difference for league promotion!

As Billy Bremner once said – "You get nout for being second!

It's been exciting, play-offs have kept the league alive right to the end despite the anti-climax, but as expected the down side is that a runners up spot does not guarantee promotion as all three clubs lose out to Division Two's relegation candidate Alloa. Stenhousemuir scored seventy eight goals in their campaign and Berwick lost out on goal difference despite having the same points as champions Cowdenbeath. The Ochilview side had also amassed seventy-three points, enough to win promotion in any league. But there is the other side of the coin, a team that has only won eight games and taken thirty-two points, scoring less than half the tally of goals fights to live again as they win the right of reprieve!

On this occasion Stenhousemuir and Berwick who were within kicking distance of the title lost out. Stung by the Wasp's!

Normal people believe that if it ain't broke, don't fix it. The Scottish League believes that if it ain't broke, IT DOESN'T HAVE ENOUGH FEATURES YET!

There must be a threshold that can be applied when a second division side does not gain "X" number of points, then if they are in the relegation position they are relegated and a "round robin" competition can then take place between the play-off teams. We could always take a leaf out of the Dutch system and have the doomed second division side play-off against 5th, 6th, and 7th with the winner destined to go through to make-up the final play-off selection. It's possibly easier if two teams go up and two come down!

Commiserations go to Stenhousemuir, Berwick and Arbroath –
SEE YOU NEXT SEASON !

Chapter 9

End of Season - Purple Rain or FLY'N'HY !

It's raining, things never go as you may think, there is always a dark horse, it was meant to be us- how wrong can you be. Another season of hope dashed! Cast your mind back to season 1990-91, Bryan Keith owner of Bon Accord Glass had bought the Club and Doug Rougvie was installed as player-manager. It was the start of a period and seasons of more lows than highs. Henry Hall was the eighth manager from this period who followed "Big Doug".

1. Jim Leishman & assistant Cammy Fraser
2. John Holt & assistant Ross Jack
3. Andy Dornan
4. Dave Smith
5. Tommy Campbell & assistant Brian McLaughlin (I remember Brian from my school days in Zetland Park,Grangemouth)
6. Kevin Drinkell
7. John Sheran & assistants Malcolm Lowe and Dave Larter
8. Henry Hall & assistant Ian Gilzean

In their day any club would have been proud for this line-up to grace their playing field. Playing is one thing but being a successful manager is another!

The Reign of Henry the VIII – Oct.2003 to Nov.2005

Statisitically, Henry Hall was the best manager the club has had since John Holt. Last season, he completely out-thought Ray Stewart in the Scottish Cup tie at Forfar with a 5-1 away win, and was also highly impressive in the second round at Keith. Continually cajoling and encouraging from the sidelines, HH helped the team through a very sticky opening half hour, and then guided them to victory. Hall's performance and his astute tactical guidance of the players, in that game at Kynoch Park, was very impressive.

Henry got the job on a non-contract basis after the resignation of John Sheran, in the wake of a genuinely catastrophic calendar year in 2003. Initially given a month's trial, HH impressed the board sufficiently by staying unbeaten in that period. On his appointment, John Paton described him as a 'coach's coach', an encouraging comment for the supporters.

For the rest of 2003/4 Henry Hall piloted the club steadily up the table, on the back of a long unbeaten run which stretched into early spring. The club, which had been floundering badly in ninth, eventually finished in sixth position, with the only blemish being a truly apocalyptic 6-0 pummelling at Stair Park, towards the end of the campaign. Fans looked forward to season 2004/5 expecting the side to be genuinely competitive in the top half of the table. With the league warped out of all proportion by the presence of big spending Gretna, and cash-rich Peterhead, no one ever expected a genuine promotion challenge, but were looking to build foundations for a real promotion push in 2005/6.

The rest is history, covered in the opening chapters of this book. With just three wins in seventeen competitive games, and only two genuinely sharp and competitive performances (Ross County away in the CIS Cup, and the home defeat of the Shire) Henry's reign as manager came to an end on November 28th, 2005. It's an ignominious end to what had been a highly promising spell in charge.

Author - Steeplejack

It's not good for a club to have had so many managers over the last few years. The Board this time opted for stability and a longer objective as this is what is needed at the club.

Eddie "The Hurricane" Wolecki – December 2005

A Links Park revolution as the new broom sweeps clean, with ten players in during January and nine out. A backroom staff that demands commitment during training and a manager who has a dream! What more do you want except success! It won't be this season or even the next, as youth development is long term and it will possibly be three years till we see the possibilities, the fruits of this harvest.

In the first few weeks of his charge Wolecki stamped his mark of authority and set a strategy plan for the future. There was no immediate success, which frustrated some fans, but his methodical approach of getting things right from the goalkeeper out is systematic. You can't win football matches unless you defend, from there you can move forward!

A new season and it will be Eddie's locally based team, and with it a real challenge ahead of them. Wolecki shows passion and obviously cares about the club. That same passion rubs off on players giving confidence as success breeds success, a bit of luck in the long term and the will to win, is what will take us forward.

In the beginning I was a little sceptical of the play-offs but the run in for fourth place had kept the league alive right to the end with Elgin, Queen's Park and Arbroath jostling for that final position. It wasn't all over at the top either as Berwick and Cowdenbeath were both capable of catching Stenhousemuir. It set up an exciting final quarter of matches, followed by a nail-biting end and a piece of history as one team finally gained promotion for the first time in Scottish Football through a play-off system but it did have it's downside. A precedent took place as a Division Two side (Alloa) facing relegation was in fact promoted to Division Two!

For Montrose the opportunity was there, teams taking points off each other, we only had to put a run together at the right time. Finishing in ninth place, time ran out at the start of the third quarter to seal our fate to another season in the Third Division!

It hasn't all been about us, as Cowdenbeath are crowned deserved champions of Division Three. After suffering an enforced early managerial change the Miners found their feet under Mixu Paatelainen who took his first steps in management. Some shrewd January signings put the Central Park side on a run which ended in the title.

Throughout the season the form-book was full of ups and downs. The first quarter saw Berwick take twenty-five points and lead the pack. Six points adrift were Stenhousemuir closely followed by Cowdenbeath. At this point Berwick were runaway leaders and only stumbled to Montrose, having to settle for a draw at home. A terrific unbeaten run by the Borderers, but the second period saw their fall from grace and a fall from top spot. Eleven points from a possible twenty-seven and Berwick dropped to third place. Stenhousemuir took over as leaders having secured twenty-two points from the second period and Cowdenbeath's consistency brought another eighteen points from eight matches and secured second place for the Fife club. The third quarter ended with Berwick fighting back into second place with Cowdenbeath dropping to the third spot but this was a false dawn as postponements dictated the placing of the two teams. Going into the fourth quarter Stenhousemuir were able to be caught but with points in the bag the pressure was on Cowdenbeath and Berwick to stake their title claim, and stake their claim they did, as they relegated Stenny to third place.

In summing up the season, Cowdenbeath showed real footballing abilities on the field of play. Berwick had their mean defence and Stenhousemuir had their strong physical presence and strike force envied by most sides, but there is a cost of having failed to achieve promotion. That may be reflected next season as budgets are trimmed.

For many clubs the pressure of success ended in managerial casualties, Elgin seem reborn under the direction of Brian Irvine and will not be the place for an expected three points next season, the appointment of John McGlashan by Arbroath was timely in gaining a play-off spot. Some sides were looking to work to the end of the season under care-taker management as was the case at Bayview but with a few matches to go a new broom was appointed.

If there were prizes for best support, then that would go to the fans of East Fife, who through a season of demonstrations against the Board, managerial change(or should I say non-appointment, as even the care-taker manager resigned) and general turmoil, they have stuck together. At this level they really are a dedicated crew who care about their Club and deserve better.

Wooden spoon specialists, East Stirling retain their trophy. As you know I have a soft spot for the 'Shire as I have been there in all weathers in better times and have a few fond memories. I wish their support well for next season as it is really hard going, being a Shire supporter!

It may seem strange considering goal difference but Elgin striker Martin Johnston takes the title of top goal-scorer. Stenhousemuir may have scored most of their goals through Colin Cramb, McGrillen and Diack but it was goals that counted at the end of the day in deciding the league title and this is where the Berwick strike force fell short. Buchanan top scorer for the Miners demonstrated this by collecting a championship medal. I remember speaking to Henner at the beginning of the season, he was looking for double figures and he just made it. In scoring ten goals, Henslee pipped Martyn Fotheringham's contribution of eight goals but goals were in short supply at Montrose as we could only muster thirty-one in the season.

The 'play-offs' showed that in the future, if you want to escape this Colditz league then you have to win it! There is no real change to next season as we get ready to do the rounds of the same grounds for yet another campaign and swap the stock-car track of Central Park for the highs of Dumbarton 'Rock' or is it the 'Rock of Dumbarton'.

Never the less we are now hardened to that fact, we live to fight another day and another season!

All that is left are P45's for those who's contracts have expired, some will be re-signed, some will line-up on an opposing side and invariably come back to haunt us during the next league campaign. Loyalty to club, manager and fans counts for nothing as players are often misguided by agents (at times it should be the agent who should be on the receiving end of fans anger) and the days of instantly re-signing are gone. Agents now tout their product around clubs for the best deal which is not always to the benefit of their client as some would flog them on E-Bay given half the chance. The middle-men are a cost most clubs cannot afford at this level as they feed off clubs who can offer little in re-signing fees and invariably they lose their prize asset for a pittance.

Small clubs with small budgets dealing with even smaller attendances to make ends meet!

Before the season ended, so that tabloids can go into hibernation, the exit door opens as Eddie Wolecki decides on those to be released by the club. Departing the Links Park scene are Euan Hall, Michael Hankinson and Frenchman Gael Corre as they are freed to find other clubs. Martyn Fotheringham and club captain Stuart Ferguson have indicated that their future lies elsewhere. Loan signings Graham Hay and Sandy Wood return to their respective clubs Dundee and Celtic.

Some players have put pen to paper as Wolecki builds for next season, Calum Watson and Barry Donnachie had both signed two year deals, Steve Kerrigan has accepted another season at Links Park and Kevin Webster is rumoured to be putting pen to paper at Forfar.

Having identified possible new signings, Wolecki will further supplement his squad of eighteen with four youngsters from the under 19 squad. By doing this every position will be covered and competition for a team place will be tense.

Over the next few weeks, new faces will arrive to pull on the blue of Montrose F.C., we wish them well. A good start is required for next season and that begins with preparation for pre-season.

For Montrose it's been a season to remember - for all the wrong reasons- but we have to remain hopeful.

As some have said, we have waited ten years, you can't turn it around in a few months, given time the sceptics will have their answer!

The Facts

Date	Pre Season		Opposition	Result	Mo Scorer's
12/7/05	Montrose	v	Aberdeen	0 - 2	
16/7/05	Montrose	v	Forfar Athletic	1 - 1	Martin, (pen) 40
19/7/05	Montrose	v	Deveronvale	4 - 2	Martin, (3) 22,28,66 Webster, 79
23/7/05	Montrose	v	Buckie Thistle	1 - 2	Henslee, 70
	Bells Cup				
30/7/05	Ross County	v	Montrose	2 - 1	Martin 33
	League				
06/8/05	Elgin	v	Montrose	0 - 0	
	Challenge Cup				
09/8/05	Montrose	v	Clyde	0 - 1	
	League				
13/8/05	Montrose	v	Albion Rovers	0 - 2	
20/8/05	East Fife	v	Montrose	3 - 2	Fotheringham 64, 78
27/8/05	Montrose	v	Arbroath	1 - 0	Martin 19
	Friendly				
06/9/05	Montrose	v	Peterhead	1 - 2	Watson 5
	League				
10/9/05	East Stirling	v	Montrose	1 - 1	Henslee 82
17/9/05	Cowdenbeath	v	Montrose	2 - 0	
24/9/05	Montrose	v	Stenhousemuir	0 - 3	
1/10/05	Berwick	v	Montrose	1 - 1	Webster 65
15/10/05	Montrose	v	Queens Park	0 - 1	
22/10/05	Montrose	v	Elgin	2 - 0	Henslee 13, Kerrigan 61

25/10/05	Albion Rovers	v	Montrose	1 - 1	Henslee 10
29/10/05	Montrose	v	East Stirling	3 - 0	Henslee 11,35,67
05/11/05	Arbroath	v	Montrose	2 - 1	Fotheringham4
12/11/05	Montrose	v	Cowdenbeath	0 - 1	
	Scottish Cup 1st. Round				
19/11/05	Bye	v		-	
	Forfarshire Cup 1st. Rd.				
22/11/05	Montrose	v	Brechin	P - P	
	League				
26/11/05	Stenhousemuir	v	Montrose	6 -2	Henslee 16, Webster 75
03/12/05	Queens Park	v	Montrose		Kerrigan 52 Fotherngham 72, 76
	Scottish Cup 2nd. Round				
10/12/05	Alloa	v	Montrose	1 - 0	
	League				
17/12/05	Montrose	v	Berwick	P - P	
	Friendly				
21/12/05	Montrose	v	Montrose Roselea	2 - 0	McLean, Fotheringham
	League				
26/12/05	Elgin	v	Montrose	1 - 0	
31/12/05	Montrose	v	East Fife	3 - 1	Henslee 65 Fotheringham 73 pen Russell 90
02/01/06	Montrose	v	Arbroath	0 - 1	
07/01/06	Montrose	v	Berwick	0 - 0	
14/01/06	East Stirling	v	Montrose	1 - 0	
21/01/06	Cowdenbeath	v	Montrose	2 - 0	

28/01/06	Montrose	v	Stenhousemuir	0 - 2	
04/02/06	Berwick	v	Montrose	1 - 1	Middleton 60
11/02/06	Montrose	v	Queens Park	0 - 0	
18/02/06	Montrose	v	Albion Rovers	2- 2	Macleod 40, Davidson 85
25/02/06	East Fife	v	Montrose	4 - 0	
	Forfarshire Cup 1st. Rd.				
28/02/06	Montrose	v	Brechin	P - P	
	League				
04/03/06	Arbroath	v	Montrose	P - P	
11/03/06	Montrose	v	East Stirling	2 - 0	Henslee 14, Middleton 19
18/03/06	Montrose	v	Cowdenbeath	0 - 3	
21/03/06	Arbroath	v	Montrose	3 - 0	
25/03/06	Stenhousemuir	v	Montrose	5 - 1	Fotheringham 11
01/04/06	Montrose	v	Berwick	1 - 2	Fotheringham 57
	Forfarshire Cup 1st. Rd.				
04/04/06	Montrose	v	Brechin	1 - 2	Russell 7
08/04/06	Queens Park	v	Montrose	2 - 2	Henslee 53, Fraser 79
15/04/06	Montrose	v	Elgin	1 - 3	Watson 41
22/04/06	Albion Rovers	v	Montrose	1 - 1	Russell 12
29/04/06	Montrose	v	East Fife	0 - 2	

Epilogue

- Enter the twelfth man – Kenny Black.

Like a game of chess, he has been there lurking in the background, a 'black knight' waiting to move L-shaped into position.

An Aberdeen businessman, Black has taken up the position of "Director of Football" at Links Park. As at Elgin, Black's position will be to look after youth development at the club but will also work with Eddie Wolecki in identifying possible signings for the Senior side. A former Celtic youth coach, Black had also gained coaching credentials in America and is well respected in the game for unearthing football talent.

Where there is youth development, there is Kenny Black. He is a believer in building from the bottom up. Youth development comes at a cost and Mr and Mrs Black's investment as shareholders is a welcome contribution to the club. In becoming a major shareholder, Kenny Black has had an immediate impact, as Montrose have made an offer for the signature of leading scorer Martin Johnson from Elgin. With Kenny Black on board and his connections, a few more experienced players may make their way to Links Park.

Future plans I am quite sure will be unveiled shortly, but in the meantime it is important that Eddie Wolecki receives support from his director of football in bringing the best players to the club as they work towards the pre-season.

As with previous ambitions at Elgin, it is hoped that Kenny Black's plans will provide an Astroturf all-weather surface (to Links Park) and a training facility for the youth of Montrose at some stage. Time will tell.

So it could be the end of the "Knoll" if plans come to fruition. The Links Park playing surface would be reshaped and an all weather surface would be laid in place. Gone will be the Links Park 'soap-box', gone will be the influence (or was it rapport?) with the linesman, and gone is the spot where I stand!

There are times we all need to change, re-build and start over. Let's not do what we did yesterday, tomorrow. This coming season is another chance – the question is, is it too early to aim high?

The answer will be available – May 2007!

- Next

Like a guardian angel he has watched my every move since arriving in Breda, as he sits perched on top of the gable end. Made to feel at home this is the view from my third storey bedroom window. He has been there all this time, a *Gable Endie!*

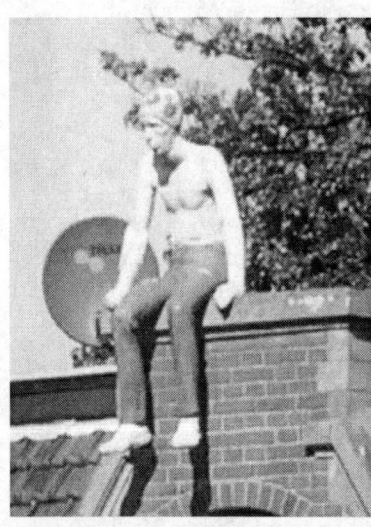

In the end it didn't work out. We can't say, Division Two here we come! But maybe next year!!!!!

Sometimes you need the roll of the dice, a double six, and a piece of luck. We didn't get it!

My inner-self say's "Oh No!" More games, another season and not knowing – What is the Montrose score?

What next? A time of reflection in Cork, a time in Breda for jazz festivals, balloon feasts and *Harley dagen*? A time for signings and a pre-season and a time to do it all again!

It's August. Already I hear the sounds of John Foggerty and the words, there's new grass on the field (well Astroturf – some hope!). A new season is born and we live in hope, in hope of a season to remember.

Will I ever learn? - I don't think so.

As I live in that hope!

- Links (Highlight's of the season)

Looking back on the season, there are some things that stick in my mind: from my infrequent visits to Links Park; text messages that I had received; and reports from the internet-press. It's a serious business, but when it's all over, and there is time to reflect in a rational manner, it is only then that you see the funnier side. Some could be classified as out-takes from a soap opera; others as just memories that will be spoken about to our grandchildren as we seek to enrol them in tradition.

Throughout the book there is one player's name that slips off the tongue, it is that of Barry Donnachie. If an autobiography is ever written then it would be titled *And Barry Was Booked!*

It's here that the controversies begin…

- That "Barry Donnachie" moment, barely two minutes on the park and in dialogue with the referee – was it something he said!

- The "Dugout" Take One - Henry's back at school moment, "Barry, Barry, Barry!" as the star pupil is too engrossed to respond.

- The "Dugout" Take Two – just how many can you get in a dugout when you have a management team of five, a physio, and substitutes!

- The Quote - "We are too attack-minded" (after a two–nil defeat at home)

- The Blog – 'Gable End Graffiti' and the twelve man team – what an arithmetical error!

- The *Montrose Review* - Same old tale of missed chances!

- The Board - the undisclosed fee for Henner!

- The Tannoy – *'Should I Stay or Should I Go'* – a real crowd puller!

- The Player – For sheer effort and professionalism it's got to be Steve Kerrigan

- The Goal – Calum Watson's strike against Elgin, it was worth waiting for!

- The Miss - too many to print but Martyn Fotheringham's miss against the Shire is close!

- The Celebration - the first Arbroath derby win (completely over the top)

- The Fans - Moan, moan, moan. *'I was Born Under a Gable End*", but there is always hope that one day they will support the team!

- The Famous Last Words - "We almost did enough to win a game!"

- The lasting 'MOment' – Division Two here we come - 2007

                              - Ever hopeful, let's wait and see!

Finally

Ecstatic that Montrose F.C. have won promotion in a hard fought Division Three battle. I would like to say, well done lads and well done Eddie Wolecki!

Unfortunately I can't! Well done anyway.

You may like this book, you may not. It may also be inaccurate and that is what happens when you are - Drawn Away From Home. Writing this book has undoubtedly been a challenge and an experience, something I have never done before, something I may never repeat. Not in this lifetime anyway!

Difficult times (going self-employed), mean difficult measures, bread snappers need to be fed, don't look back, stay positive, venture forth and keep the faith. It becomes routine. So for the time being, frequent visit's to Breda and Cork is the order of the day before I finally move on to the next challenge. The great plan can only tell where and when.

This book wouldn't have been written if it hadn't been for my son Gareth, who contributed as co-writer, researcher and reporter. Thank-you!

Also, to my colleagues who don't know it as yet, who supplied the inspiration and happy times during my quest in the Bio-pharmaceutical world of time, cost and quality.

To Jon "Steeplejack", "Gable End Graffiti", thanks for the blog, it really is the ex-pat's lifeline. Thanks for the support and ramblings.

To my wife, who can spell, correct grammar, and be there. Loved ones make many sacrifices and my going self-employed was a big one. Thank-you!

To the citizen's of the town of Montrose,

Keep the faith, come on the MO!

Season Ticket 001. Another season going through the mill or was that the washing machine!! It doesn't matter, the season is over!

A 'team' father and son, one
home, and one away!

Sandy Miller – Father, novice
writer and self employed
engineer. A dreamer - but also
a believer of better times and a
season to remember!

Gareth Bryan Miller – Son
Indoctrinated at an early age,
has a passion for the game and
underdog.
Studied History at Aberdeen
University.

Also a dreamer – Like father,
like son!